D0336472

A Sportswriter's Year

Also by Simon Barnes

Phil Edmonds: A Singular Man
Horsesweat and Tears

A SPORTSWRITER'S YEAR

Simon Barnes

HEINEMANN : LONDON

William Heinemann Ltd
Michelin House, 81 Fulham Road, London SW3 6RB
LONDON MELBOURNE AUCKLAND

First published in 1989

A CIP catalogue record for this book
is available from the British Library

ISBN 0 434 98180 X

Photoset by Rowland Phototypesetting Ltd
Bury St Edmunds, Suffolk
Printed and bound in Great Britain
by Butler and Tanner Ltd, Frome, Somerset

To the first professional writer I ever met . . . my mother

Contents

Illustrations

Acknowledgements

In any sportswriting year, but most particularly this one, I owe thanks to everyone in the *Times* sports department. From the top: Tom Clarke, Sports Editor, Simon O'Hagan, Paul Newman and David Powell. I also owe very special thanks – as does every writer who ever penned a line for a newspaper – to the great legion of down-table sub-editors, without whom there would be no newspapers and no sportswriters.

More thanks to *Times* colleagues with whom I shared assignments in 1988, especially David Miller, Rex Bellamy, John Goodbody, Pat Butcher, Michael Seely, Jenny MacArthur, John Blunsden and Sydney Friskin.

Further thanks to colleagues on rival newspapers, people who cheer you up, talk you down, give you the facts you have missed, and tease you rotten. Of these, special mention is due to Ian Wooldridge, Jim Lawton, Roy Collins, Mike Calvin, Matthew Engel, Frank Keating, Simon Kelner, Hugh McIlvanney . . . well, everybody really.

On the book side of things, my thanks to all at Heinemann, especially Margot Richardson.

To John Pawsey, thanks as ever. And for my wife, Cindy Lee Wright, thanks are not enough.

INTRODUCTION: HOW TO BECOME A SPORTSWRITER BY COMPLETE ACCIDENT

'Well, Bill,' I said. 'I have always wanted to be a sportswriter.'

I was lying through my teeth at the time.

It was this piece of transparent deception that led me, by a wild, circuitous route via Redhill, Reigate and most of Asia, to one of the most envied jobs in the history of the world. I get paid for doing what normal people gladly pay to do. Through ridiculous luck, coincidence and deception, I seem to be the holder of a kind of fantasy job. It is the curiosity and fantasy that seems to surround this bizarre and absurd way of making a living that has prompted me to write this book. Ego-gratification had nothing to do with it. (Please note that my taste for deception – at least for self-deception – is unabated.)

How do I get a job like yours? It is one of the questions I get asked, and one of the many for which I have no satisfactory answer. I made my first move into sports journalism when I was working for a group of local papers. I was a trainee news reporter on the *Surrey Mirror* in Redhill; I covered magistrates' court, pets, local residents up in arms, and occasionally major stories like Must Some One Be Killed Before Something Is Done About The Buckland Bends.

It was an uncomfortable time. It was painfully obvious to everyone that I did not have whatever it took to be a great reporter, and I was shifted from office to office in the newspaper group as if I were an unexploded bomb. Epsom, Dorking, Oxted, Sutton, Tooting: all of these are places where I failed to impress. I ended up in one particular office where I was supposed to be licked into shape. I preferred the shape I already had, and this led to tensions: fear and loathing in Surrey and South London. It was probably the most hateful six months of my life. The editor once said of me later: 'I've had an awful lot of reporters in my time, but of them all he was the one I hated the most.' This was as near to distinction as I ever got.

I decided that I would do anything in my power to get away from the horrible and depressing professional life I was leading. The next vacancy that occurred, I would go for. It happened to be on the sports desk at Redhill. Bill Woodhatch, the sports editor and an extraordinarily nice man, took me on. He also gave me enormous areas of responsibility – Redhill Football Club, the mighty Athenian Leaguers, were all mine to report. This really was a plum assignment: none of that irony stuff here. In the football season, we led on Redhill every single week. Once I started working with Bill I started enjoying work: I have enjoyed work enormously ever since.

All the same, I cannot deny that this is a weird way of making a living. People often ask me how I got like this, and what it's like buzzing about the world and getting paid for it. It is the people who ask me such things who must shoulder a great deal of blame for this book.

After joining the great Bill Woodhatch, I spent a couple of years working in sport for local papers, by which time I was doing shifts in Fleet Street and new and exciting areas of journalism were opening up for me. So I did the only sensible thing: I ran like a rabbit.

I ended up in Hong Kong, working as a news sub-editor for the *South China Morning Post*. I gambled my future on this newspaper, uprooted and went East. Within about six weeks, I was sacked. This was in 1978: that memorable November afternoon on which Robin Hutcheon told me, in tones of measured and pedantic clarity, to vacate the building at once was the last time I have held anything that might in the formal sense of the word be called a job.

The sacking was, I say without rancour or false effect, the greatest professional leap forward I have had in my life. I became a freelance writer, and still am. Freedom is addictive stuff when you have got the taste for it. I moved out to Lamma Island, one of Hong Kong's outlying islands, and wrote about anything that would make me a dollar. I wrote a lot about travel and, to do so, travelled all around Asia. I loved the place; I never thought about returning 'home'.

But I met a girl, as people do. She was planning to return to England to put herself through drama school and work as an actress, which is exactly what she did. Reader, I married her. I returned to England at the age of 32, and set up house in a bedsit. I went round Fleet Street trying to get sub-editing jobs. The first people to give me regular work were *Titbits*, and God bless them for it. After that, I got work on the *Daily Mail* features desk; I was normally asked to handle the horoscopes. Later on, I was able to get some work subbing on the *Times* sports desk.

After I had been working there two or three nights a week for a few months, I found the courage to approach the sports editor, Norman Fox.

'Norman, I was wondering if, ah, I might have a bash at, ah, writing a *feature* for you . . .'

'All right,' Norman said. 'So long as you understand it's completely on spec.'

Blessed be the name of Norman Fox for ever more. He accepted the piece (I decided to write it on Henlow dog track, for some unfathomable reason), and asked me to try another. He accepted that too (it was about Redhill Football Club, a visit back to old haunts). After that, Norman asked me to write a weekly column on exotic minor sports. It was a chance in a lifetime: the rare, unlooked-for luck of being in the right place at the right time was all mine. The column was a great brief, and impossible to fail with.

Norman subsequently converted me to a mainstream sports feature writer, and then to an out-and-out columnist, complete with that wondrous thing, the little picture of yourself at the top of the column. This is the sacred and gorgeous photo-byline. Try asking a journo about his photo-byline: 'Oh my God, why do they use that awful thing? I'm always trying to persuade them not to.' Lies, all lies: why don't they use it even bigger?

The photo-byline is not a mere sop to a writer's vanity (though it is supremely effective in that respect). It is also a blob of ink that means: this bloke has his own opinions and what follows is unlikely to be a routine match-report. The photo means even more than vanity: it means freedom.

Norman moved on to become deputy managing editor of *The Times*, and Tom Clarke took over as sports editor. His first move was to start throwing aeroplane tickets at me: I did not duck. It might seem from the pages of this book that Tom spends all his time giving me advice, encouragement and aeroplane tickets, and that I spend all of my time greedily accepting all three. This would be a fair approximation of the truth.

So here we have quite a lot of pages on a sportswriter's lot. I hope it does not come as a complete shock to the world that the job involves a spot of work here and there. Still, I have tried not to overstress such things, for fear of the dreaded response 'the lady doth protest too much'.

I do not write this book as the country's top sportswriter, nor as the most travelled, nor as the most energetic, nor as the most distinguished. My position in the scale of things was summed up for all time by my friend Frances Edmonds who, when extremely cross with me after a titanic row in Trinidad that involved all the players and the entire press corps, wrote, as I remember it: 'The trouble was caused by two people: brilliant, award-winning globe-trotting columnist Ian Wooldridge, and Simon Barnes.'

1. FEAR AND LOATHING IN ATLANTIC CITY: THE TRIUMPH OF THE RABBIT-PACK

I wasn't really sure what I was doing in Atlantic City. Still, that doesn't make Atlantic City unique by any means. True, there was a world heavyweight fight taking place, but why was I covering it? I loathe and despise boxing. I think it should be banned, and I have written as much many times. So there I was, all set to cover Mike Tyson against Larry Holmes. What the hell was going on?

I had covered one big fight before. Tom Clarke had humoured a long held ambition of mine to go to Las Vegas. I covered Tyson against Mike Tucker there. I had, in a gritty, horrified kind of way, rather enjoyed the assignment. Las Vegas is a loathsome place, but it is fascinating. It has a surreal quality; and it has pretensions to a tawdry kind of style. Atlantic City has pretensions to being a tawdry kind of Las Vegas. And worse, in January it is freezing cold.

In Las Vegas I had paid a daily fascinated and appalled visit to a place called Circus Circus. I had sat in the revolving bar, watched the casino gambling below, the circus acts (trapezes, acrobats and clowns) above, and the insane games – flip a rubber chicken carcase into a frying pan and win a toy dinosaur – and meditated on Hunter S. Thompson, prince of Gonzo journalism. In his book *Fear and Loathing in Las Vegas* he wrote that Circus Circus was 'what the whole hip world would be doing every Saturday night if the Nazis had won the war . . . no, Las Vegas is not a good town for psychedelic drugs. Reality itself is too twisted.' Atlantic City is like Las Vegas, but with slightly less innocence and charm. It is a perfect place for fear and loathing. But what the hell was I doing there?

Now Tom is a canny man, for all that his employment of me might suggest the contrary. I was on my way to San Diego to cover the Super Bowl, but I was certain I had not been asked to take in the fight as well as a mere ploy to save a transatlantic plane fare. I arrived in Atlantic City, and within about three minutes I had taken a violent dislike to the place. Was this part of Tom's great plan?

I had had a poor journey over. I spent an involuntary night in Boston, because some runway was iced over, or fogged up; I can't remember what, but winter was doing its best to make everything miserable. The airline had put us stranded passengers up for the night, but I failed to get a meal – with an entire jumbo-load of passengers fighting to get into the dining room at once, I gave up. I dined off a couple of quarts of Corona beer (with a slice of lime, naturally) and had a long discussion with fellow-strandees about life, air travel, the Washington Redskins and the Denver Broncos. Of these, probably the Redskins' defence was the toughest.

I love being in America. I adore that sense of being lost in the maw of an entire continent, of being the star of a film without a script. I acquire protective colouring, I ride in elevators, drink Bourbon, have nice days. I say, 'Can I get a beer?' to the barman, I meet *with* people, I love the way that America is different *than* England. I have eggs Benedict for breakfast, after which there is not a day that cannot be faced. I'm in good shape over there, d'you hear? I even have a secret identity. I do every time I travel anywhere. It is only in Britain that I am Barnes. Everywhere else in the world (except America) I am Barnez. But in America I am Barons. I really introduce myself like that, really hit that R. If I don't, they say, 'You mean like *James* Bond?' Yes, absolutely, but with a completely different name.

I landed in Atlantic City with a weird buzz in my ears. Well, I told myself, that's unpressurised planes for you. We globe-trotting journalists know all about that sort of thing. I checked into my hotel at lunchtime – 'Reservation for Barons' – and then set about getting my eye in and press accreditation worked out. The press centre was just a few minutes 'along the boardwalk'. Atlantic City, the famous bit, is all built on the seafront, and the boardwalk is its wooden promenade. But local colour could wait: I always feel terrifically insecure in any place until I know how I am going to get into the event I am supposed to be covering.

No problem. You're in good shape here, Mr Barons. Have a nice fight. When America is on form, it works so beautifully you start to get angry at the slightest failure in competence. That is what it must be like being an American anywhere in the world. I went to gather official press releases, such things as 'The Tale Of The Tape', with the biceps and inside leg measurements of the boxers. I ran into a bunch of colleagues from the British press. The hard men. Cynical banter. Tight togetherness. Classic ratpack journalism: no one was going to steal a march on the others. The wariest possible welcome to me: I'm the poofter from the posh paper who doesn't approve of manly things like boxing. They sloped out together almost in step, in search of some mystical appointment towards some great story they knew I wouldn't even understand. One said to me, 'First time in Atlantic City?'

'Yes.'

'Don't go off the boardwalk. This is tough town.'

'Ah . . . thank you.'

My normal policy with such tough-talking traveller's advice is to ignore it. Don't do this, don't drink that, don't take a *pak-pai*, don't go south of 44th Street, and if you touch a Thai on the head, you're dead, man. People love to tell you horror stories about travel: the point is not the advice, but the adviser's own vast reserves of experience and superiority. So I ignored what I was told – and discovered that the advice was spot on.

Atlantic City is an architectural paradigm of hypocrisy. How right, I thought, that this should be the world's second capital of boxing. This, and not by coincidence, is also America's second gambling capital. The place is in New Jersey, just along the coast from New York City, and was once a smart new seaside resort catering to New Yorkers. Then it became a terrible, scruffy old seaside town with nothing to recommend it. But in 1977 it discovered the secret of eternal youth: casino gambling was legalised.

Now enormous and ever more hideous casinos line the seafront, and police cars park everywhere along the boardwalk. Between the casinos, shops sell hot dogs and coffee in styrofoam containers. You can buy a kind of sweet (or candy) called salt water taffy, and any amount of cheap tat for souvenirs. There is a shopping mall (pronounced 'maul') in the shape of an ocean liner. The boardwalk is packed solid with perambulating holiday-folk, and I seemed to be the youngest person there by 30 years and the lightest by about 130 pounds.

But move just a block inland, and you are in Shitsville, USA. Go two blocks and you are no longer wondering if the atmosphere of edginess and resentment is your own paranoia: you know it is the real thing. I love America, and I love travelling, but I was quite prepared to make an exception for Atlantic City. It is a perfectly awful place. I was building up a serious case of the traveller's sulks. Fear and loathing were cooking up a treat.

Never mind. Come the evening. I was able to put this mood into abeyance. I bumped into a couple of colleagues, James Lawton of the *Daily Express* and Roy Collins of *Today*. Both are men of parts, neither a specialist boxing writer. They are both excellent company, and I was much cheered by them. Jim looks like Dylan Thomas, though his writing style is different. Roy is the finest Basil Fawlty impersonator in Atlantic City. A few drinks and a few jokes help keep one sane in this bizarre and silly line of work.

'Seen any one else from the English papers?' Jim asked.

'God, yes. The entire ratpack in full cry. It was terrifying, they look so *heavy*. They always look like real journalists, and I get overcome with guilt.'

'If you can't stand the pace, dear boy, you should establish a rival group to the ratpack. The Simon Barnes rabbit-pack.'

This was a tease at my vegetarianism. There are not many vegetarian boxing lovers, and I am not one of them. I am a member of loads of environmental pressure groups, and am a card-carrying Green Party member, but I try not to bore people on the subject. I bore them on other subjects instead. We all went from the bar to a Chinese restaurant: good colleagues are cheering, sustaining, and infinitely tolerant people, and their company is often a great solace. I went to bed in reasonable spirits, but I noticed I still felt odd. Something to do with my balance was it? Damn these unpressurised planes.

The following day, I had cracked the oddness. It was flu. How perfectly splendid. And my hotel turned out to be the only one in America that did not serve eggs Benedict. By the time I was writing my first piece, I was already in a foul temper. I hated the place, didn't want to be in it, didn't want to cover the hateful, horrible fight. In Las Vegas, there at my own request, I had adopted a softly-softly policy. With my fight preview pieces, I had been restrained and careful. Cover the story, duty to the readers, and all that. It was only in my final, my wrap-up piece, that I abandoned objectivity, and came out of the corner with my handbag flying, telling the world what I really thought of the event, and restating my own unequivocal view of boxing: that it should be banned. But this time, in Atlantic City, I was feeling too twisted to do anything but look for trouble.

There was plenty to find. The fight was between Larry Holmes, the former world champion, and now a grandfather aged 38, and the phenomenal young champion, Mike Tyson. Tyson is perhaps the most frightening man I have ever met. He is charming. He has a lisp, and gilded, broken teeth that make his smile oddly touching. He is polite, almost humble in demeanour: 'Yeth, I gueth that'th tho.'

He is also the greatest living example of that most fatuous of sporting clichés, the most ridiculous of justifications for boxing: that it provides 'a way out of the ghetto'. Let us leave aside the notion that there is a job as world heavyweight champion waiting for any black man prepared to get off his ass: Tyson's appalling upbringing and subsequent success stand, for all America, or all the Western world, as a justification for the fact that ghettos exist. One such fairy story makes the whole world of deprivation acceptable to the public mind. How can there be anything wrong with an upbringing that produces such a man as Mike Tyson?

The legend of his rackety past gets a little better with every retelling in the slavish, violence-worshipping press that boxing attracts. 'As a kid I carried a gun,' Tyson has been quoted as saying. 'All the gangs had guns back in Brownsville, Brooklyn. They used them on hold-ups and in gang fights. The fights only started with fists. Then the guns and knives came out. Sure, I fired mine. Thank God I never hit anybody.'

Tyson is a man of violence through and through. He smoulders with the most appalling aggression, which is channelled mostly into legitimate, or at least legal directions. There was a famous story of his beating of a car-park attendant who happened to get in his way, and various other darkly hinted rumours. This, I must stress, was before his desperate public marriage and various other disasters had beset him. At the time it was already clear that Tyson was beginning to lose his grip on things. The one thing he was certain about was his ability to destroy opponents in the ring: to take a brutal, almost – almost? – sadistic delight in his demolition of those who faced him.

He was as nice as pie to us press chaps. At least, he was most of the time: a bad question, one that hinted that his style might have limitations, or that at some time or other he might lose a boxing match, and something happened to his eyes. They became hooded, opaque, the pupils seemed to go crescent-shaped, like those of a comic-book villain, and the room crackled with barely suppressed violence. The furies possess this man, his menace is unmistakable.

Holmes was playing it like Greta Garbo, and refused to come to this pre-fight press conference. Tyson did, and the assembled ranks of the press treated him to one of the most outrageous displays of mass sycophancy I have ever seen. If Tyson said anything that could possibly be interpreted as a joke, he was greeted with roars. Every bullish statement brought bursts of applause. Applause? At a press conference? But boxing is not like the rest of sport.

'I'm glad Larry Holmeth ith not here,' Tython was thaying. 'Thometimeth he thpeakth before hith brain ith in mothion, and no one hath time to hear barroom epithetth.' Hohoho, good ol' Mike.

'But what about his ten-inch reach advantage, Mike?'

'My whole life hath been a dithadvantage. I'm the greatetht fighter on thith planet, and no one can beat me!' Hurray hurray, clapclapclap.

Big fight press conferences are made still more nauseating by the presence of Don King, the promoter. King is the man you always see in the ring before a fight, the one who looks like a negative of Beethoven, with that extraordinary, gravity-defying haircut. He believes that he is the best-read man in the world, and mixes misquotations, malapropisms, rolling phrases and the names of sponsors in a heady cocktail of garbage. Few find him an amusing figure, however. He is a man of power, and a genius at the art of the deal. Like Tyson, he has a rackety past, but he seems to have been a better shot. He shot and killed one man, the sort of thing that could happen to anyone and which was written off as 'justifiable homicide'. He was convicted for manslaughter after another man was beaten to death: it was the prison library that gave King his famous 'education'. They call him – perhaps I mean, he calls himself – 'the only-in-America man'. I have no quarrel with that designation.

The following day we had the weigh-in. By this time I was reeling with flu, and seeing the whole world of boxing through a red mist. A real mist had descended as well, a sea mist rolling in from the Atlantic and reducing visibility along the boardwalk to 20 yards. Still, the sun always shines inside the casinos. When there is a big fight in town, the take at the casino tables goes up by around $7 million. The people who love boxing the most also love to play moronic games for a grand a hand.

Holmes made his long delayed entrance in time for the weigh-in. He had decided to play the whole thing as Daddy Cool. He went through the rigmarole with a bland smile on his face, refusing to answer questions, or to pose for the massed bank of cameras. 'I'll see you all tomorrow,' was all he would say as he left, adding, 'Especially Tyson.'

Tyson had been seething under this performance of cool. After all, he was champion, was he not? He lost his temper at this last shot from Holmes, stabbed a finger at Holmes's retreating back, and shouted, 'I'll be there!'

Holmes turned his head, bestowed a last faint, unquestionably patronising smile on Tyson, and said, 'I hope so!' And he was gone.

Tyson, completely outcooled, was a man in a rage. He ripped off his T-shirt and stepped back onto the scales, flexed his football-sized biceps, and drew back his lips in a snarl of ferocity: as yesterday, with a bad question, the entire room – and a big room, too – was filled with the force of Tyson's enmity. All at once it exploded with the roar of a

Mike Tyson, the destroyer, and index of machismo in a nation obsessed with violence . . . The man who gave me so evil a night in Atlantic City.
(Mike Powell/AllSport)

hundred cameras on motor-drive. And then everyone sprinted to the telephones.

By Friday things had all become a blur for me. I had filed a piece on Tyson, and a second on Holmes. The fight was on the Friday evening, and the office had decided there was a chance of getting a live report in the paper. The fight was likely to end round about two in the morning, London time. Would I send copy after every round until we had a finish? This means making it up as you go along, 'ad libbing' as journos says, no chance to write a line with a pen or anything. Just holler the stuff over the din of the cheering from a telephone at ringside. Some journos love this kind of emergency. I hate it. I like to write in calm and peace. But sports journalism is not always the perfect medium for writing of the spontaneous overflow of powerful feelings recollected in tranquillity. I spent most of Friday afternoon harassing people to fix a telephone for me. Jim Lawton was doing the same thing – in fact, he did most of the harassing because I wasn't up to much. Journos on rival papers are not rivals in the strict sense of the term. Most people help most people. If you miss a quote that is in the public domain, or forget a fact, a colleague will give it to you. If you need to borrow a phone, or the team-sheet, or the tale of the tape, someone will help you out.

I had written a piece predicting a night of horror. The fight seemed, even to me, a boxing ignoramus, a mismatch. What was Holmes doing it for? The simple answer, $3.1 million, really would not do. Holmes had made his pile already. Larry Holmes Inc had $10 million worth of hotel, with a $10 million complex being built. Holmes had a house worth $1.5 million and a further million bucks' worth of cars, trucks and motorbikes. He certainly didn't need to get beaten up, even for three million.

It seemed that some twisted notion of pride had infected him. Well, athletes always believe they are immortal, unconquerable. Any other mental position lets in the possibility of defeat, with self-doubt forcing its way in behind. No, athletes believe they are indestructible, and this counts double for boxers. But Holmes also felt cheated. He could see that he had already been written off as the man who came between Muhammad Ali and the new godling, Mike Tyson. Holmes resented this, resented it deeply, and was overcome by the thought that he might knock the cocky kid off his pedestal. And he believed he could do it all right. Naturally he did. Tyson, said his few critics, is an unschooled brawler; Holmes has always been a neat and canny boxing man. 'To beat Tyson it would take a good left with lateral movement,' Holmes said. 'Two of the things I do best.' Or did best.

It all looked very ugly to me. My head was ringing like a bell: my little bout of flu now seemed like the result of contagion from this foul town and from the whole ghastly panoply of this revolting sport. The high rollers had moved in, the 24-hour casino floors had reached new levels of intensity. I am no man of steel. I like a bet. But when I stroll across a casino – and it is virtually impossible to reach your hotel room without passing several dozen methods of putting your money at hazard – I feel only one urge: to get out as soon as humanly possible. Oscar Wilde said that he could resist anything except temptation. A casino represents as much temptation to me as would an all-male brothel. Like Odysseus on Circe's island, I am immune. Atlantic City possessed nothing to tempt me, nothing to give me any kind of pleasure. Except the airport: oh, how I longed to be at the airport.

On, then, to the fight. That night furthered the legend of Tyson the destroyer; Tyson the merciless; Tyson the iron-fisted sadist. And, in an infinitely tiny way, it furthered the local legend among British sports-writers of Barnes as the wimp of the sporting round. Time after time throughout the year, people approached me to ask if it was really true that I had hidden under the press desk for the duration of the fight. I wish I had done: it was a horror show. Holmes was made to fight on when he was already plainly concussed. The contest was over, Holmes was reeling. But he was not destroyed, and people had paid a lot of money to see this fight. So Holmes had to suffer an assault of unbelievable savagery when no longer in any condition to defend himself, or take evasive action. Holmes, remarkably brave, did all he could to stay on his feet, to fight on. And when he was reduced to helplessness, he was battered anew. At last, he was battered into complete unconsciousness.

For a long and hideous moment I thought Holmes might be seriously hurt, perhaps even dead. He was down a very long time: there were suggestions afterwards that he was swallowing his tongue. The audience certainly got its money's worth that night. Holmes showed remarkable courage: Tyson remarkable, sadistic brutality. Ali's last fight had been against Holmes, and Holmes had backed off, reluctant to destroy the great man. Tyson showed no such squeamishness. He hurt Holmes: he liked doing it. Holmes eventually got to his feet, and made the following immortal remark to Tyson: 'Fuck you! You are a great champion.' Which seemed to sum up the occasion.

I left as soon as I could, thankful that Holmes was still alive. I had not, in the end, been required to ad lib from the ringside. The fight overran the paper's deadline. Jim, beside me, was luckier, or less lucky: he is a terrific ad libber and, raising his voice to the decibel level of a jetliner at take-off, he roared his copy with immense panache as the world went mad all around him.

I wrote a piece for Monday's paper, and did not mess about. The horror of the occasion and of the entire sport was my subject. I have never been much of a one for macho posturing: I wrote that the fight had me wondering whether or not to throw up. The place, and the fight, had goaded me into writing three pieces of sustained and reasoned invective on the nastiness, greed and horror of boxing. If that was Tom's design in having me cover the story – and from my past record on boxing he can have expected little else – then it was a triumph of man-management. And as a bonus, the bout of flu had erased any thought of temporising from my mind.

My reward was a bizarre paragraph in the *Observer* written by a man called Alan Hubbard, who was covering the fight for the Singapore newspaper the *Straits Times*. In the *Ob*'s column, 'At Large', he wrote: 'Boxer Larry Holmes was not alone in feeling sick as a pugilist after last weekend's world heavyweight title fight. At the ringside, the *Times* representative, a somewhat sensitive soul, was left ashen-faced and seemed about to throw up after witnessing the savagery inflicted by Mike Tyson. "I never want to cover another boxing match," he vowed to askance-looking colleagues. Doubtless this will interest the paper's regular boxing correspondent, whom they had decided not to send.'

Thanks, Al.

Perhaps there are two sorts of people in the world: those who get off on watching people getting beaten up, and those who do not. Those of the second category are rare at boxing matches. To send such a person to cover a big fight was an unusual journalistic exercise, not one designed to please all the world. Alan Hubbard saw it as a simple mistake. He did not realise that he was witnessing the triumph of the rabbit-pack.

Let me add as a footnote that in the course of research on boxing, I met a Harley Street neurologist called Dr Peter Harvey. He explained to me that if you suffer concussion, you *invariably* suffer permanent brain damage. The object of boxing is to concuss your opponent: that is what a knockout means. A British Medical Association report on boxing said: 'Boxing is a contest in which the winner seems often to be the one who produces more brain damage in his opponent than he himself sustains.' If any boxing writer wishes to applaud such a thing, will he please take his justification from there? And if anyone tells me boxing is a way out of the ghetto, please do not mind if I throw up.

Sport is mostly a metaphor: tennis is a mock fight, for example, football is a mock battle, any kind of race is about hunters and hunted. Young animals enjoy sport, even in the wild: fox cubs wrestle and tussle, lion cubs hunt each other. No one gets hurt.

But boxing is a form of duelling. There is no metaphor here: this is a real fight. In the *Times* house style book, the word 'fight' is not encouraged for boxing writers. I ignored that: boxing is not a 'bout' or a 'match' – it is a bloody, potentially deadly fight. No wonder boxing can be awesome, stirring, amazing; no wonder that its champions are unbelievable, remarkable men. And no wonder that writers have found such satisfaction in writing about it. This is not sport: this is the real stuff of life and death. That it should be a public spectacle is grotesque.

I was happy to leave boxing to such writers. With my head buzzing with beastly images and with the scrambling of this well-constructed bout of flu, I went to bed, setting my alarm good and early. The following day I was flying out to New York. Thank God for that. I needed a breath of quietness, good sense, sanity and civilised behaviour.

2. SURFEIT AND RAVISHMENT AT THE SUPER BOWL: *TIMES* MAN FAILS TO HANDLE THE HYPE

A free weekend in New York, and on expenses to boot. Surely, I thought, this was one of those rare occasions when life slips you a fiver. Beware such occasions: life always wants six quid back in change.

'Mr Barons, wumble bumble crumble sweet?'

'Ah . . . sorry?' Deaf as a post, you see. Another jaunt by unpressurised plane had done something peculiar to my ears. If I held my head to one side, like a man trying to look up a woman's skirt, my ears cleared for about 30 seconds. If I held my head between my knees for a while, in the manner of someone about to throw a faint, then I could hear for several minutes on end. Neither performance goes down that well in the lobby of a smart hotel, but I adopted the dirty-old-man tactic as being the less offensive. The clerk's voice cut through the static.

'Mr Barons, we don't seem to have a room for you. Would you mind if we upgraded you to a suite?'

'Oh . . . ah . . . not at all.'

'Looks like a good deal to me.'

'Absolutely.'

I was at the Mayflower as usual – you can't imagine how swanky I feel, writing that 'as usual'. How glorious it is, to have a hotel I 'always' stay at in New York. And the suite was a treat – what a pity it kept going round and round when I sat down, and me sober. This was a good, serious, hallucinating flu, no question about it.

I shall draw a veil over most of the rest of the weekend, but I must mention one adventure. I had decided, before I left on this trip, to buy a pair of walking boots. American boots are cheap, and the best. But because I was out of my head with this flu, I was overcome by a mania once I had staggered as far as the boot shop. I became possessed by a desire to own the finest boots ever made. I insisted on being shown the most expensive pair in the shop, and as soon as I was sure they were expensive *enough*, I produced the plastic and paid. Later in the trip, when I had gathered my wits, I discovered I had paid $150 for a pair of

Timberland's finest. I saw an ad for the boots on television: it showed a competitor in the Iditarod, the husky sled-dog race across Alaska. It seemed that I had chosen the boots the competitors wear. The television boomed: 'More protection . . . than you'll ever need.' I was inclined to agree.

But I was drawing a veil, was I not? Let us move on to Monday, more or less recovered (that's enough flu – Ed.), and catching a dawn flight to San Diego. San Diego is in the bottom left-hand corner of the United States, and this year it was the site of the Super Bowl.

The Super Bowl is the Cup Final, as it were, of American football. It is the culmination, justification, orgasm, apotheosis, quintessential experience and ultimate celebration, not just of the game, but of all America. And now it is part of British life: Channel 4 has made gridiron football part of the pattern of the sporting year, and I am delighted that this is so. I went to San Diego as an old hand, a veteran, for this was my second Super Bowl.

The previous Super Bowl, in Pasadena, had been what I am sure I ought to call 'a watershed experience'. It was the first serious aeroplane ticket that Tom had thrown at me, my first attempt at being brilliant and globe-trotting, and I think I can say without fear of contradiction that it had me in an abject state of panic. When I got there, I discovered that all my irrational fears were totally justified. Within five hours of arriving, I was about $200 out of pocket, the money going on three taxi rides. They were all essential. All I had *achieved* was to get accredited to the event. It was then that I worked out the time difference, and discovered that I was required to file 1,000 words by six in the morning the following day, or in eight hours' time. I did not think that my experiences of sitting in traffic jams on the Los Angeles freeway system would stretch quite that far.

However, the basic law of journalism is that you always get your copy out somehow, and always fill the space. This is an inexorable fact: the only variable is the quality. Every journo in the world has been in similar situations, and often far, far worse. The only journo who finds my achievement in writing the story at all impressive is, of course, me. I set the alarm for four, and wrote off one thousand words on a couple of the salient characters of the game, garnished with quotes lifted from the local papers. Easy-peasy, for all that I sweated in the writing of it.

This year, I had resolved to get there right at the beginning of Super Bowl Week, in the interests of avoiding panic, getting accredited good and early, and improving the quality of coverage. Sporting journalism is full of tales of people who arrive late, drunk, phoneless and without proper accreditation. They talk their way into the ground, using a tube ticket in lieu of a press pass, borrow a phone, beg the goal details from a mate, and right on the final whistle start dictating reams and reams of classically elegant and wholly ad libbed copy, with never a fact wrong or a nuance missed. The pay-off of such stories is always: 'and it fitted to the last bloody comma'. Well, I am the journo that always arrives two hours early, having checked his ticket 14 times on the journey to the ground. I am the one that always gets thrown out of places where I have a perfect right to be. There are plenty of journos with similar anxieties, I am sure, but we are supposed to keep quiet about them. Rabbit-pack journalism is not a mainstream concept.

By Monday lunchtime, I was fully accredited. I had a metal badge in my lapel – the media 'pin', which is the key to covering the Super Bowl. With that badge on your bosom you are allowed in to all the press conferences, given access to all the players, allowed into the media workroom to grab press releases and other handouts, and into the media lounge where you can drink for free. The press organisation at the Super Bowl is slick beyond all measure. It starts to warm up on the Monday, and I, cold beer (free) in my hand, was already hot to trot.

This is a colossal event. There were 2,200 media people accredited. The build-up to the event never seems to be off the television screen; every newspaper in the States carries Super Bowl pages with more words than you will find in the entire sports section of an English paper. The Super Bowl is phenomenal, ludicrous, utterly alien: no American could fail to be cynical, no Englishman fail to be enraptured. To arrive in Super Bowl Town in Super Bowl Week is to find your fingers itching for the keyboard. To have the Super Bowl as my first experience of being brilliant and globe-trotting was overwhelming, but the second time around, it was quite clear: this is the easiest story in the world.

Stories fall into your lap. You are spoon-fed information. Every player is available to you. Every time you want to go somewhere, you find a vast fleet of media buses ready to take you. The National Football League runs one of the slickest publicity juggernauts in sport. So let us zip-pan to the Jack Murphy Stadium, San Diego, on a bright Tuesday morning in January. They only ever have bright mornings in California. Simon Kelner, then of *The Independent*, and I had ridden the coach fleet to the ground and, media pins shining on our breasts, passed into the vast bowl of the stadium, the playing surface already covered with enormous and elaborate paintings in the endzones, the television-aerial goalposts pointing to the sun, and the seats, tier upon tier, reached skyscraper heights above us. 'Just like Swinton rugby league ground,' said Kelner, who had been saving that one up for a heartbreaking 12 months since we had been together in the Rose Bowl at Pasadena.

The contrast with British events is spectacular. The press is made love to, is ravished, is surfeited with every delight the NFL can imagine. This is not quite as much fun as it sounds but it certainly makes the job easier. Before, say, the Cup Final in England, no one will talk to you unless you cross his palm with silver. Even when Wimbledon tried to break the mould in 1988, their press morning was mostly remembered for a little agent running around forbidding his own clients to talk. And just about every professional athlete in Britain will tell you, with unconcealed delight, that he or she 'hates the press'. To hate the press is a great status symbol: to be in a position in which you find the press hateful proves that you have made it. To say 'I hate the press' is every bit as swanky as to say 'I always stay at the Mayflower'. It is a rule of life that everybody's vanities are ludicrous except one's own.

In America athletes do not hate the press at all. They almost *like* us. Certainly they see us as, on the whole, a good thing. If you want to be famous and make lots of money, you have to be in the newspapers and on television. Just playing sports rather well is not quite enough: if you want to make money out of the public, the public has to know who you are, and American athletes will therefore ungrudgingly make themselves available to the press. At the very worst, they will see talking to the press as part of the job, something worth doing well and certainly amiably. It really *is* part of the job: it is in every player's contract that he must make himself available for interviews at his club's request.

If you seek a big-name footballer in England, you first have to find out the name and number of his agent. Often the club won't tell you. You need to use the skill of investigative journalism just to speak to someone who will then demand, say, five hundred quid for the pleasures of speaking to his client. For the aforementioned quids, he will say things like: 'The Cup's a great leveller' and 'They've got eleven men same as us'.

At the Super Bowl, you can speak to any millionaire superstar you please, and all for free. And as a bonus, all American footballers can talk well. They have all been through the college system, they have all been used to talking to press people since high school. They have all been stars at some level or other, for years, and it sits very easily on them.

And so, at the Jack Murphy Stadium, there was nothing to do but walk about collecting stories. Once the journos are in the stadium, the players arrive, and all in their kit, which makes the photographers happy. And as they enter, it's one, two, three: harass a superstar. You

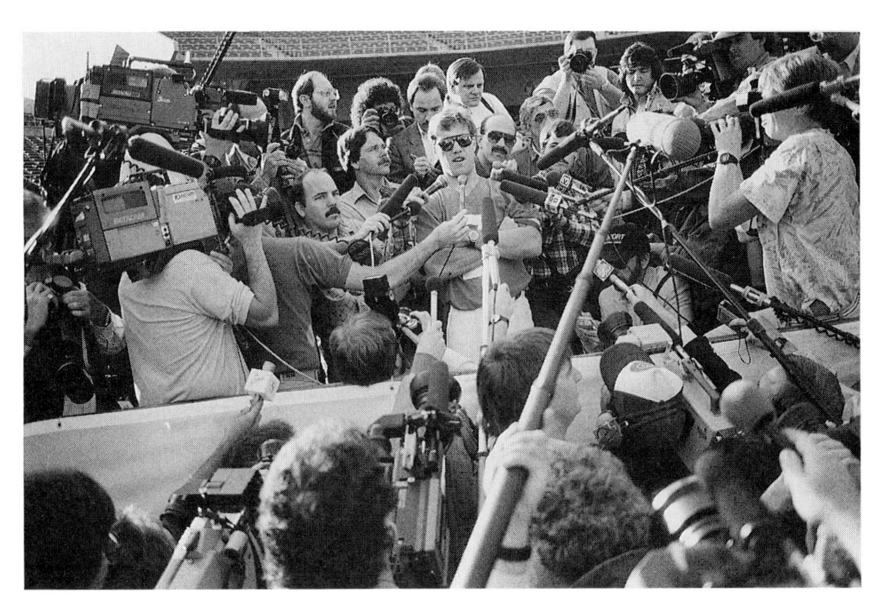

This is a normal day in Super Bowl Week. The cool guy is John Elway, quarterback of the Denver Broncos. The uncool guys are the 2,200 accredited media people, especially the author.
(Michael Steele)

could tell the exact degree of fame of each player from about a thousand feet in the air. Who is at the centre of the crowd of 300? It must be John Elway, the golden boy, quarterback of the Denver Broncos. The group of 100? They'll be gathered around the Three Amigos, the wide receivers, those who must catch Elway's bullet passes in the game. The group of 10 or 15? That must be someone like the kicker, Rich Karlis. The two players talking to each other? They are probably offensive linemen, the spear-carriers of American football, or, in the vernacular, the grunts. The ones that do all the work for none of the praise, but all of the blame when it goes wrong. Like sub-editors in newspapers, really, but more of subs in due course.

For an hour of every day, each Super Bowl team must submit itself to the media in this way. It is part of the deal, part of the Super Bowl contract. No journo ever goes hungry for a story. Every petty detail makes the paper. It is the festival of hype, and the only thing hyped more than the game is the hype itself. What about the hype? How are you handling the hype? What do you *think* of the hype? 'It's like going to the dentist every day for a week to have the same tooth filled,' one player once remarked. What is your relationship with Dexter Manley, John? How does last year's Super Bowl defeat affect you, John? How are you handling the hype, John? John, if you were a tree, what kind of tree would you be?

'That's the dumbest question I've ever been asked.'

'Stick around, John.'

Then, bang, the hour was up, and the Broncos vanished. The Washington Redskins were not due for another hour: how would we poor press men fill in the time? Not to worry, the NFL had laid on breakfast for 2,200. We had a cholesterol mountain to climb: the largest pile of scrambled egg in the history of the universe was awaiting us. Bacon? Sausage? Coffee or de-caff? Say, are you guys British? Would you mind doing an interview for TV? The Super Bowl must be the only event in sport in which a large number of the press go to report on the press coverage of the event. Kelner agreed to be interviewed; me, I was keen to preserve my mystique and to get stuck into the scrambled eggs. 'What do you think of all the Super Bowl hype, Mr Kelner?'

I adore it, myself. Breakfast done, it was time to face the Washington Redskins. *Great* story. Towards the end of the regular season, the Redskins, feeling that their challenge was fading, demoted their number one quarterback, the all-American superstar, Jay Schroeder, and promoted the understudy as the star. Not bad. But there was more: Doug Williams was black.

Team sports are competitions between groups of equals, but of course, in every team there has ever been, some players are more equal than others. The nature of American football makes one player paramount: the key to every team is its quarterback. He is the player through whom every attacking play is channelled, controlled, and directed. He can be efficient, or he can be inspired, but he must be an athlete and a natural leader, he must be tough and capable of thinking at top speed and on his feet. He needs flair and he needs intelligence. America has long believed that black men cannot play quarterback.

Williams was the mould-breaker, the first black quarterback to play in the Super Bowl. There were, at that time, two other black starting quarterbacks in the NFL, but it was at Williams that the spotlight was aimed. The Super Bowl, the hype, was all his. 'What is the significance of being the first black quarterback to play in the Super Bowl, Doug?'

'The significance is we can win it.'

Good answer. The significance was that Williams was manifestly good enough a leader to win the game: that was why he was chosen. The significance is in the sport: this was clearly the best way to play it, and Williams played it all splendidly. He refused to be drawn on questions of racial harassment and incidents of prejudice from his past. 'I'm not here to erase stereotypes. I don't have to. Enough has been done to prove that we're capable of playing quarterback. And I know that you guys are all waiting for me to say the wrong thing.'

The black quarterback business was enlivened by a spectacular American idiot called Jimmy 'The Greek' Snyder. Snyder was a television sporting pundit who, by his own account at least, had made fortunes by gambling on sporting events. He was asked on television why there were so many brilliant black athletes in America, and explained that this was the result of selective breeding by white slave masters, who habitually put their biggest men to their biggest women. He spoke with gusto about the 'thighs' of black people.

Apart from anything else, this is historically inaccurate; selective breeding was one of the few indignities black slaves did not suffer. But Snyder's remarks were odious for a further reason: they demonstrated an unconscious acceptance of the second-rate status of black people: you can say what you like about those guys, but they sure can slamdunk a basketball / catch a football / outrun them white guys. It is the modern version of 'they gotta great sense of rhythm'.

Sport happens to be a great area of opportunity for black people, in America and in Britain. This is because sport is quantifiable: most other areas of professional life are not. There is little profit in debating attitude and little room for prejudice when a man has led his side to the Super Bowl. In sport, achievements cannot be ducked. When results are all that matter, there is no room for the whims of prejudice. Williams, by playing in the Super Bowl, had been handed the chance to show all America that black people can think fast, and can lead. Who said that sport is always trivial?

And on to the game. One of the exercises when writing before any kind of big match is prediction. I don't mean the 'Barnes says Tyson to fall in four' bit, or not necessarily. Prediction is always there by implication, by story selection. At the previous Super Bowl, the New York Giants against the Denver Broncos, I had written about the flaws in John Elway, the mental frailties of the Denver kicker, Rich Karlis, and ended up by writing that the crucial quarterback was not Elway, but Phil Simms of the Giants. In the event, Elway was overwhelmed, Karlis missed a field goal from virtually under the posts, and Simms had a magnificent game and won the Most Valuable Player award. Not bad, eh?

This year, I wrote about the pressure on Williams, black quarterback of the Redskins, the rehabilitation of Karlis, and the perfection of Elway. 'Elway is that rarest of ball-players, one who re-invents the game as he plays it,' I crooned. 'Just as there was no point in telling George Best not to try and beat the third defender, because next time he would beat the fourth defender and score, so there is no legislating for Elway.'

There was a gorgeous moment when I thought I had called it all correctly, as, with his very first touch of the ball, glorious, golden Elway lifted the ball into the endzone for a touchdown. Almost immediately afterwards, Williams was injured and limped off the field. I had wanted to see a sumptuous exhibition of skill, but I feared then that it was all about to become one-way traffic: nothing less than embarrassing. And I was right, but wrong at the same time.

One of the fascinating things about sport is the way in which the Force will pass from one side or one contestant to the other. It happened then. After the first quarter, Denver were 10–0 up, and all those who admire the skill of the nonpareil were purring at Elway's contribution. But after the second quarter, Williams was not only back in the game, he had taken complete control of it as well. The Washington Redskins were 35–10 in front and it was all over. Denver collapsed, and the game became an anticlimax, a limp study in disappointment.

As a spectacle, it was sorry stuff. But for Williams, it was glory, triumph, and sweet, sweet victory. His father used to tell him: 'When people call you nigger, be so good they have to call you Mr Nigger.' Mr Williams led the Redskins to a 42–10 victory, and I could not begrudge it him, sad though I was to see organisation beat flair. Williams had handled the hype better than I had.

The following day, and 1,000 words further on down the road, it was time to go to the airport, like the other 2,199 media men. Most of the Brits were heading for home. I was off to Los Angeles to spend three days talking to horses, and I couldn't wait to ask them how they handle the hype at Santa Anita racetrack.

3. GREEN THOUGHTS IN A DC-10 AND AN ENCOUNTER WITH AN AMERICAN LEGEND

Every trip, no matter how busy you are, or how sociable you make yourself, has moments when you sit about and think things over. Jetlag will give you sleepless periods in which you go through your life and wonder what its point has been. The long waits in airport lounges have you recalling all the most embarrassing things you have ever done: the time in the restaurant when the bill was more than you could pay: the time you tried to pick up that girl in the youth club: the time you had to sing a solo at primary school: and on, and on. Aeroplanes themselves fill you with intimations of mortality: one decent patch of turbulence and it becomes impossible to suppress the question of how much it matters, in the context of the history of the universe, that you wrote quite a nice piece about Doug Williams on the morning of the crash.

Sport is trivial, even if the issues that arise from it (Doug Williams) are not. I suspect that most sportswriters are afflicted with periodic fits of gloom about spending their lives in pursuit of the trivial. I have some advice for any sportswriter thus afflicted: do not write books. To finish a book is to bring on the most terrible fit of restlessness and dissatisfaction. Finishing a book is a crushing anticlimax. I had just spent a year and more researching and writing a book about a year in the life of a racing stable. It was called *Horsesweat and Tears* (almost universally agreed to be one of the worst titles ever dreamed up) and the research, the living of it and even the writing of it had been enjoyable. I had delivered the manuscript shortly before flying out to Atlantic City.

I had been too busy and too sociable to feel the dreaded book-finisher's backlash in Atlantic City and San Diego, but on the aeroplane between San Diego and Los Angeles, it struck mercilessly. It hit, not in the form of depression, or anguish, or awareness of new problems, but as the restless, urgent discovery of a possible solution. It was the view out of the plane window that did it.

For the plane was overflying the migration route of the grey whale. I knew this, because a couple of days earlier, I had made a trip out in a boat to meet the whales. It really was the most marvellous experience: about a cricket pitch away, these great barnacly monsters cruised their leisurely way towards their breeding grounds, signalling their arrival at the surface with a heart-shaped cloud of spume and a huge sigh. Then they would dive again, with arched backs, and 40 or 50 feet of whale would slip by, till at last, with a neat little flick, the great tail-flukes would break the surface and at once disappear, and the beasts would sound once again.

I had felt my heart lift with joy to see that such lovely monsters still exist: that we haven't destroyed all the world, not quite yet. And as I flew north above the sea, above the Whale Nation, my restlessness assumed a bright green colour. A sportswriter is accustomed to writing about the things that give him, and much of the world, joy. Why should I not extend this, and write also about animals?

Animals matter; and incidentally, they are great bringers of joy and wonder to people. I like animals far too much to want to eat them, for a start. Sport is full of occasions when people all sit down for formal dinners: I never go. I shall not, either, until I have thought up a good answer to the inevitable question: 'Why are you a vegetarian?' There are plenty, but none socially acceptable to a person about get stuck into chicken chasseur. Jeremy Bentham, the nineteenth-century political philosopher ('the greatest good for the greatest number' – that chap) summed it up rather well when he wrote about the moral dividing line between man and the animals he may morally abuse: 'Is it the faculty of reason, or perhaps the faculty of discourse? But a full-grown horse or dog is beyond comparison a more rational, as well as a more conversable animal, than an infant of a day or a week or even a month old. But suppose they were otherwise, what would it avail? The question is not "Can they *reason*?" nor "*Can they talk?*" but "*Can they suffer?*"

I never say this at mealtimes, feeling it might spoil the atmosphere, and because of this I have to endure banter along the lines of 'What about cruelty to vegetables?' The number of people who find this both original and amusing is quite remarkable.

I was set to spend three days surrounded by animals, and this was a very good thought. I have a special thing for horses: under normal circumstances, I keep a horse myself, and ride it as often as I can. At that time, I was without one, my old fellow having died a few weeks previously. So all the more reason to spend some time watching the gallops, rubbing noses, pulling ears, slapping necks, and talking and smelling horse for days on end.

This trip to the Santa Anita races was an idea of my own, a little bonus to put on the end of the trip once I had convinced Tom that it was a good notion. Throughout my year with John Dunlop, I had received a lot of help from Jeremy Noseda, who was Dunlop's second assistant. He was a young, upcoming and ambitious man, who had joined Dunlop as a pupil assistant and made himself increasingly valuable. He had spent several winters in California on working holidays learning the very different ways of American racing. This time he was giving informal help to an expatriate English trainer called Chris Speckert. The idea of the trip was to write a story about the differences between English and American racing: not a tough brief. And I had another notion in my head – well, we would have to see about that.

Jeremy and Chris met me at the airport, and took me to the place where I was to stay for the next three nights, the Santa Anita Motel. They left me there, promising to pick me up in an hour to take me down to the track. 'Simon, do you have any shoes other than those trainers? It's very muddy underfoot.'

'No problem,' I said. 'I have the very thing.'

I got to my room, and unpacked. I have always had a fantasy about American motels, believing that the only reason people ever stay in them is to commit adultery. I had not been in my room five minutes before the room next door burst into life.

'Yes! Oh God, yes! My God, you're so strong, yes! *YES!*'

I put on my Timberland boots and set off for the racetrack. That would be pleasure enough to be going on with.

I had, naturally, grown used to the rhythms of the English stable yard: the noisy bantering and swearing of the lads, the rituals of morning work on the gallops, and evening stables when every horse is inspected by the trainer. I was accustomed, too, to the climate of rumour and counter-rumour: the Derby winner has gone over the top and shown nothing in his work this week; that smart two-year-old has got a leg and won't be running for a month; that thing of whatsisname's is really burning up the gallops and should win first time out. Just about everything in Santa Anita was different: only the smell, and the obsession with winning, were the same.

When the lads are about, English stables are turbulent places. The lads, male and female, racket around, clanging buckets, belabouring the floor with brooms, swapping insults with each other, yelling noisy endearments to their horses and stamping about the place. This is partly because English stables are normally so cold, partly it is just the nature of the English lad. At Santa Anita racetrack, the horses are looked after by slow-moving, gentle, sad-eyed Mexicans. They shuffle from horse to horse as if in slippers and attend their charges' needs with quiet, almost devotional attention. They tend to be clad in white, their eyes shine in the darkness of the stable-boxes, and you can never hear them coming. The hard, unyielding dirt surfaces of American racetracks are tough on the tendons: the Mexican grooms will massage a horse's legs for hours, endlessly patient. Often the horse will conclude his exercise by standing for half an hour in a bucket of ice to fight any incipient swelling: every stable block has its own ice machine. Newmarket is a long way away.

'Ah, these Mexicans, they're the boys to tame your outlaw horse,' said John Sullivan. Sullivan trains in California, and has done so for 30 years. He still sounds as if he had left Ireland the previous week. Santa Anita is full of foreigners: sometimes there seems to be hardly an American in sight: English, Irish, Mexican, anyone. Some even have work permits. But if you speak the international language of horse, that is passport enough . . . when no one is looking, anyway.

This, you see, is centralised racing. Santa Anita is the racetrack, and the training headquarters in one. The race meeting lasts, not for a few days, but for two or three months at a time, and in that time, all the horse, all the trainers, all the work riders, and all the grooms, move to Santa Anita. Everyone is here, all the time: from the topmost people like Bill Shoemaker, the legendary American jockey, to Chris Speckert's hot-walkers. A hot-walker is someone who has the job of taking a horse after it has exercised and walking round and round with it until it is cool. It is probably the world's dullest job, and sometimes I fear that if I am sufficiently wicked in this life, I will be reincarnated as a Mexican hot-walker. Still, better to be with horses than without horses, for all that the job would tax the patience of a saint, or even of a Mexican groom.

There was no banging about, no banter, and there was no rumour either. It was bizarre. English racing thrives on suspicion: everyone watches everyone and no one is sure about anyone. But in America, everyone knows everything. There was no rumour that Ferdinand, the great chestnut champion, was working extra well, or even extra badly. Every exercise gallop he has ever done has been timed, and the results published and available to all the world.

The lack of suspiciousness colours the entire atmosphere: everything is cheery and open. These are, after all, American virtues. I remember speaking to the Italian-born Newmarket trainer, Luca Cumani, and asking if he had imported any Italian training methods. 'No, I don't think so,' he replied. 'But even if I had, I wouldn't tell you.' I laughed and told him that Newmarket trainers were all paranoid, and so they are. It is Newmarket's occupational disease: it does not exist at Santa Anita. There is nowhere to hide, no illusions to foster. Everyone sees everything you do and knows everything you have achieved right up to that last gallop.

No one there has the chance to pull rank. The class system is unobtrusive here, and, as such, very American. The legendary figures of Bill Shoemaker and Charlie Whittingham walk around like ordinary people, 'Hi, Bill.' 'Hi, Charlie.' They may be the top, but they will talk to everyone. Even me. America is a wonderful place in which to be a sportswriter.

Whittingham is one of those American love-objects. You don't get a nickname like 'the bald eagle' just for having no hair. He provides a great theatrical presence. He is in his seventies, trains Ferdinand, and spends a lot of time acting the larger-than-life person. 'How do you keep going, Mr Whittingham?'

'Charlie.'

'Well, how *do* you keep going, Charlie,' I asked, suppressing a fantasy about Major Hern demanding of a writer 'Call me Dick'.

'Just my job, Simon. Besides, I got young horses, promising young horses. Nobody ever commits suicide with a young horse. It might be the next Derby winner. Anyway, if I didn't do this, I'd probably just be an old drunk.'

Hoho, Charlie, very likely: Whittingham is a man of much force. My friend and colleague Brough Scott told me a story about Whittingham. Whittingham was giving Brough a lift, and Brough happened to notice (as you would) that there was a gun on the dash in front of him. 'I went all public school, and said, Oh, I say, isn't that a gun?' The conversation continued. Whittingham admitted he had used the gun fairly recently, when he had discovered somebody trying to break into his car. 'You mean you, ah, shot him?' Brough asked.

'Naw. Pistol-whipped the sonofabitch.'

Racing is about winning, and the men who command respect at Santa Anita are the men who have won and won. At this time, I was putting together a three part series, under the less-than-complex title 'The Winners'. My notion was to collect three big interviews, with people who were associated, more than anything else, with victory. I had chosen Steve Davis as my starting point: indeed, where better to start? Davis is, I promise you, a very interesting man, one given to incessant self-analysis. He told me that his happiest moments were when things had gone wrong, and he was at the practice table, and had suddenly cracked the problem. 'You say, like, Blimey, I've got it, I've been standing wrong! And then you say, Cor! I'm looking forward to the next tournament. I've never looked back at things that were bad. I've always tried to work out why things were bad. And then do something about it.'

To my great delight, Bill Shoemaker agreed to be interviewed for this series. He is probably the finest jockey there has ever been, certainly the most successful. He stands 4ft 11in, was born in 1931, and when I met him, had ridden all but 9,000 winners. Piggott rode 5,191.

I went to his house, a nice, long, sprawling Californian bungalow, not spectacularly part of millionairesville, just a big, comfortable house full of horsey pictures. It is natural for legends to look smaller in real life: Shoemaker looked Lilliputian, especially alongside his wife, who stands an inch or two under six feet. But Shoemaker has the gift of perfect self-possession, and boundless, if unstated self-confidence, and this is something that leaves you feeling awkward and over-sized. Shoemaker does an advertising promotion with Kareem Abdul-Jabbar, the almost equally legendary basketball player. Kareem is 7 ft 2 in. The fact that they do the promotions together says a lot for the sense of humour of both of them.

It was a fascinating interview, though not an easy one. I do not mean that Shoemaker is a difficult person: far from it. He is, like Butch Cassidy, 'the affablest man I ever met'. But self-analysis is not part of his method. Davis is an intense man who needs to dissect every problem into its component molecules. Shoemaker just drawls away, and chuckles a lot. Often a sportsman will shy away from any question that invites self-analysis, from pure fear, from superstitious dread: they daren't look too hard at what they've got, in case it disappears. To the average athlete, skill is like a handful of water: grasp it too firmly and it is gone. But Shoemaker is a pure spring of natural talent; he finds it hard to imagine what it must be to live *without* such a talent. He is, simply, the most wonderful horseman. More than any Mexican groom, he will tame your outlaw horse. Put him on some rogue animal that has been scattering work riders like confetti, and the horse will turn into a lamb at once. And he does *nothing*. You see him sitting there, not moving, not doing a thing, and the wickedest horse in the world is acting good as gold. 'Aww, I just play with him, fool around, you know? He responds. He knows I'm trying to be nice. I guess, anyway. Play with the bit, give and take. Touch, I guess. That's my theory, anyway.'

And he gives a little chuckle at such a remark. He is a man with unique gifts: 'Never thought about it that way. But I knew as soon as I first got to a ranch, first started working with these horses, I knew that

Bill Shoemaker is the finest jockey in history, and one of the few men of his trade with whom a writer can have a couple of beers and a few laughs.
(AllSport)

was what I enjoyed. That was what I was going to do. Took to it like a duck to water.' And he made that cliché ring, gave it a stamp of newness.

There is not a jot of Steve-Davis-obsessiveness in his nature. 'I'm an easy-going sort of guy, and I like to do my job and to play with the other guys in the jockey's room.' Those athletes who find it so hard to live with the crackling tensions of their jobs would find it hardest of all to understand Bill Shoemaker. He is, perhaps, the most successful athlete in the history of sport, but he is the most easy-going man in the world. Perhaps only men with such a monstrous natural talent have room in their natures for affability.

I transcribed my tape from this interview in my motel room. The adulterous couple had moved on, perhaps never to return . . . or perhaps they go there every Monday (*yes!*) but never on any other day. My boots, resplendent with real dirt, had provided me with more protection than I ever needed, and had now been packed away, still smelling faintly of horseshit. I had completed three pleasant days at the races and around the stables: great time, great weather, and great, lovely horses. Now it was time to prepare for England and February. I concluded my stay by taking various racing contacts out to a thank-you meal in Beverly Hills, and running up the largest bill I have ever dared to put in for expenses. It had been a splendid interlude, with large and splendid stories coming from it: a very pleasant double to pull off. The meal, the company, and the evening were great. No one asked me why I am a vegetarian.

4. RITUAL CURSING OF THE GRUNTS: HOW TO GET THRILLED AND EXCITED IN WAPPING

The ideal length for a trip is a little under three weeks. I can hear the cricket correspondents howling as I write this, which perhaps is a kind of agreement. The first week has the excitement of novelty, the second offers the prospect, nauseating to the rest of the world, of a sportswriter at the top of his form, and by the third week, for all that your step still has a spring in it, you have begun to feel that home is the place to be.

Those addicted to travel relish the flight from the humdrum, the flight from routine, the flight from responsibility. When travel itself becomes routine, it is time to break the pattern once again. Besides, though I love travel, I also love being home. I love to get in aeroplanes and cross the world, but the first thing I do when I get to these places is telephone my wife. This is a book about professional life, not about marriage, but let me say this in passing: marriage plays as enormous a role in the life of a professional traveller as it does for the person who returns home every night: perhaps more important. Every sortie across the world in an aeroplane, every day in a foreign land is lived in the context of home . . . wherever that might be, because mine is not a very domestic marriage. My wife is an actress, and often on tour. Travelling is always a joy: returning home is part of that joy.

My journey home from Los Angeles was a good one. As chance would have it, I met Derek Wyatt, then my publisher, on the plane.

'Barnesy!'

'Del-boy!'

'Let's have some champagne, my man.'

'If you think that's wise.'

'Certainly. This is great.'

'Isn't this what famous and successful people are supposed to do?' I asked. 'I mean, meeting on aeroplanes at LA airport?'

'That's right.'

'Then why are we both in Economy?'

'Details!'

There is, however, only one drink nicer than champagne, and that is champagne that one's publisher has paid for. Later I found two adjacent seats, pulled the Irish Lone Ranger Mask over my eyes, curled up like a hamster, and slept. For any traveller, sleep is even better than free champagne.

A good sleep on the plane brings you home in decent shape. Indeed, you need to be in good shape for arriving home. A mountain of mail awaits. You resolve not to touch this, not until the following day at least, but the temptation is always too much. You say, well, I'll open one or two *nice* letters. You look for a nice sort of envelope, and slit it open, hoping it will be a cheque, or a letter with a brilliant new professional opportunity, or a letter beginning: 'Dear Mr Barnes, Thank you for that brilliant article in which . . .'. It never is. The cheque is a press release for something to do with badminton; the new professional opportunity is an invitation to some black tie dinner (at which someone would ask 'What about the agony that piece of broccoli suffered?' if I were foolish enough to accept); and the fan letter begins, 'Once again you choose to foist your ridiculous opinions . . .'.

After that you are trapped. You go on through the pile, opening letter after letter, hoping for a nice one. And of course, among all the rest we have those horrible envelopes with windows. In particular, the one labelled 'American Express'. All travelling journos, perhaps most travelling people, know what it is to suffer the Amex Double Whammy. It goes like this: 1) Get an advance on your expenses; 2) Right away, this is charged against your monthly income; 3) You go somewhere and spend all the money on living expenses, and you pay your hotel bill by credit card; 4) You have to pay credit card bill right away, or they send the boys round; 5) You don't get the money back from the firm until a month after you have done your expenses. The horror, the horror.

Stand by for the shattering of the last illusion: for most journos, doing the expenses is a nightmare. This is not the happy, carefree manipulation of the old fiddle-sheet – would that it were. For which meals can you claim your allowance? Did you pay cash to get the telephone fixed in Atlantic City? Have you got the receipt? Can you get away with calling that meal 'entertaining boxing contacts'? Don't forget the airport taxi was from Kennedy, not La Guardia, so it's forty bucks. All of life becomes a hopeless tangle of forgotten truths and recklessly optimistic half-truths, a tickertape parade of lost receipts and bar bills you really can't get away with this time. No, you *can't* claim those boots, either. Journos are wordsmen: most of us have a fit of the vapours when it comes to facing a column of figures. We would do anything rather than add things up. We talk cheerily about expenses as we tuck a bill-stub into our pocket, but ten to one the stub goes into the washing machine with the shirt. Show me a brilliant, globe-trotting journalist, and I shall show you a man grievously behind on his expenses. The fastest sleep-eradicator in existence is the thought of the backlog on your expenses. No, doing your expenses is not the easy way to pay the mortgage: it is more like running up the down escalator, and you already late for a desperately important engagement.

There must be a few people out there who really do fill in their expenses with brilliant, creative dishonesty, I don't know. I imagine them with an attaché case bulging with blank receipt books and rubber stamps that say 'Received With Thanks'. But for most of us, it is a matter of muddling through with the light of desperation in our eyes, and being driven by desperation to be more or less honest . . . in a pale grey sort of way . . .

And then there is the pile of newspapers that greets you when you return from a trip. There is nothing more disheartening than old newspapers. They make a great pile about a foot in height . . . no one in his right mind is going to *read* them. But, ignore them as you might, you know that sooner or later, and probably before you go to bed, you are going to start *looking* at them. You want to see what they have done with your pieces. Have they been displayed nicely? Have they put them at the top of the page with a nice big picture? Or have they tucked them away at the bottom right-hand corner where no one will see them?

Atlantic City: yes, good, great, they *have* done well. So they bloody well should, of course. And then you start whingeing about the Super Bowl: why only a single-column picture? And that single-column shot of Elway is ridiculous. The final piece on the game, well, that was OK. I suppose. Huh. Of course, you never look at the rest of the paper, at all the red-hot stories they had to include on the same day: you only see that your story has been given less space than you would have given it, it being, obviously, the most important thing in the paper on that or any other day in history.

Then, with the grumps already beginning to strike, you make the really fatal mistake: you start to read your own copy. In fact, most journos read their own stuff in the paper. I try not to. Partly this is a pre-emptive move against impotent fury; and partly this is because the *Times* subs rarely make changes in my copy, and when they do, they normally talk them through with me. These two qualities I value very highly in a sub-editor.

But it is one of the rules of life that if you start to skim your own pieces on returning from a trip, all you will see will be alterations and errors. Leaping from the pages of the paper was the pay-off line to my final Super Bowl piece. It had dealt with Doug Williams, the black quarterback of the Washington Redskins, who had led his side to victory and set a new Super Bowl record by passing for 340 yards. I had concluded: 'It was Williams's day, and he was the obvious, inevitable winner of the Most Valuable Player award: the first black quarterback to throw for 340 yards in a Super Bowl.' Not bad, eh? Except that the world 'black' had been removed.

I had sent the stuff by the old-fashioned method of dictation. You ring the paper, and someone at the other end – a professional copy-taker, in fact – writes it all down: 'Open quotes when people call you nigger comma be so good that they have to call you Mr cap en Nigger point close quotes.' Inevitably, errors creep in. Some copy-takers are a joy, fast and machine-accurate. Not all. Journos spend half their lives cursing ignorant deaf bastard copy-takers. Copy-takers spend all their lives cursing rude temperamental journalists.

It is the copy-taker that holds all the good cards. When you are halfway through a brilliantly written, profoundly moving piece, you will get: 'Much more of this, old boy?' When you finish – 'point close quotes ends' – it is less than cheering to hear the response: 'Thank God.' A favourite tactic is the question, asked halfway through: 'Was this ordered?' which means the copy-taker suspects you are putting the stuff over on a vague whim, so unsuitable for the newspaper does the piece seem to him. When I was first dictating copy to the national papers, as a breathless and timorous tyro working for the *Wimbledon News*, I was absolutely tyrannised by a copy-taker on the *News of the World*. I was sending legitimate copy from Wimbledon football matches, but every time, I got: 'Was this ordered?' Then a couple of minutes on, just after the best sentence you have put together all day: 'They won't want all this, you know.' And after every phrase, instead of saying 'Yes?' as most copy-takers do, he would say: 'Tchah!' He would snort with derision in mid-sentence, and say: 'Do you really mean that?' or 'That's hardly English, is it?'

But errors happen in newspapers, all the time. Newspapers have to happen quickly: it is amazing to me how much that gets in the paper is actually right. But errors drive you mad, and you never know who to blame, the copy-takers or the subs. Hedge your bets and blame both sets of bastards: that's my technique. The sub-editors are the people with the job of shifting your piece onto the printed page, a task that includes checking it through for mistakes in official *Times* style, English language, or facts. They trim it to length if necessary, rewrite if necessary, write any picture captions that may be required, and top the whole thing off with a headline. The writer *never* writes his own headline. Half the rows between the writer and his contacts occur because of headlines: the sensitivity of people is directly related to the size of print in which they are represented. But because of the nature of newspaper production, the subs write the headings.

In fact, writing the headlines is the fun part of sub-editing. It is like crossword puzzle solving, but a spot more creative. You must sum up the story, and do so, if you have any pride and/or time, with force and wit. You are given a certain number of columns across which your headline must spread: this refines down to the number of characters available. You must use all, or nearly all the characters available to you: too much white space in a headline is seen as a sin. And you must never write a headline that is too long: to send a headline that busts is a real idiot's trick. I have done a fair amount of subbing, and I used to love writing headlines. My favourite was a story about Aston Villa, who went to Tokyo to play a football match, got stuffed, but never mind, they all brought back heaps of expensive electronic equipment. I sent: 'Villa: Veni, Video, Vanquished.' To be strictly accurate, this is an awful headline, one that gave pleasure to the sub, but one that requires a subheading reading: 'Please read this story to see what this headline means.' The other trap for subs is simply to write boring headlines. 'Why write a headline like this?' I occasionally fume as I peruse the paper. 'Why not write a headline instead that says: "Please do not read this story"?' A further horrific crime the subs can commit is to find your pay-off line, and use that as the head. The joke, the concealed punch, the sting, is thereby neatly removed.

Subbing is a tough job. The hours are long and late. A sub must be precise, often under hard-pressing deadlines. A good one will show flair and sympathy as well. Intelligent suggestions from a good sub are a boon to a writer. If a smart sub finds something confusing, I know the error is mine in confusing him. If he finds something over-the-top, or obscure, I will reconsider my point, and more often than not (well, just about) make a change. And a good sub will spot your errors and get you out of trouble. I remember writing about Zola Budd on the day she announced that her new coach was to be Harry Wilson. My brain was not functioning that day: I wrote that her new coach was Harry Webb. Harry Webb is in fact the real name of Cliff Richard. Harry Webb went

Inside Fortress Wapping . . . Tom Clarke, *Times* sports editor, meritably centre stage, while Simon O'Hagan, David Powell and Paul Newman discuss cutting Simon Barnes's best line.
(Chris Cole)

through all editions, dodging the double, treble and quadruple error-catching mesh.

I make errors all right, but, praise the Lord, or praise the subs, most of them fail to reach the paper. It is the sub's function to accept blame: he is supposed to catch errors. If he catches one, it is because it is his job. If he misses one, it is his fault. And he or she is there in Wapping, staring at the green screen of the computer terminal, while I am in California making my final check call to the subs' desk ('OK, Dougie? Yes, great, it's about 75 degrees. Any queries? Great, thanks a lot, talk tomorrow.') And then I am off to have my first Corona of the day, with a slice of lime, naturally. I miss subbing sometimes, but not very often. Subs are the grunts of the newspaper industry, the poor bloody infantry, and I (and anyone who ever writes a line for newspapers) am permanently in their debt. They have the tough, often boring, and always unglamorous task: they actually bring out the newspaper.

And so, on your return from any assignment, the first thing you do is curse the lot of them, and all who work back at the office.

'The office' plays a vital role to a brilliant, globe-trotting journalist. The call to the office is an umbilical cord: it links the writer with reality.

Tom is a virtuoso performer on the telephone. Ten minutes' talk with 'the office' can restore the wanderer's distorted perspective of the world to something that is easier to manage, and the talk put a spring back in the step of anyone going through one of those lost, isolated and bewildered periods that occur to any writer of any kind on any trip. 'Super piece, Simon, we've used it very big, lovely pic, used it over four columns. I think you'll be pleased. *Very* very glad we decided on this trip, it's working *very* very well. Really *super* piece today . . .' And suddenly it becomes clear that there is a purpose in this mad life after all. I believe the technical term is ego-massage: and the bigger the ego, the more massaging it needs.

There must be some people on the desk who resent your being away. They never show it, which is wonderfully restrained of them. I have heard that such teases as 'enjoying your holiday?' are part of some offices' repartee: a remark carefully calculated to drive any travelling journo into a frenzy . . . if he is not in a frenzy already, that is. These trips are the most enormous stimulus, but they aren't paid holidays with a nice bit of sport to watch as a treat thrown in – but hush, once again the lady doth protest too much. Let us move on: the copy-takers and the subs duly and unjustly cursed, the mail opened, and me back in the rhythm of English and domestic life, remembering not to enrage my wife by saying 'can I get the check?' in the Barnet Tandoori or putting lime in my beer at the Two Brewers. I am off to Wapping to meet with, I mean meet, Tom.

I am often asked who decides what stories I write and where I should travel to pursue them. Me? Tom? Anyone else? Hard to answer. There may indeed be some journos around whose every suggestion is avidly accepted, but I suspect not. It is a journalist's nature to push his, or her luck, and to suggest, say, a trip to Australia just after the department budget has come up for review. The decision made on my writing and travel plans are all rather tediously civilised: I have ideas, Tom has a lot more ideas. Some of these we both like, some he doesn't like or can't afford, some I can't imagine writing, others have me 'thrilled and excited', to use a favourite locution of Tom's. It is all worked out in long and amiable discussion at Wapping. The relationship between sports editor and columnist must involve a lot of talking. With, say, a cricket correspondent, it is obvious: he goes to Test matches, and the rest of his year fits in around that. A columnist could go anywhere: I could spend the autumn covering, say, Rangers *v.* Celtic, or the World Series baseball . . . or the Olympic Games.

The Olympics was the place I wanted to be, and that was where I was to go. It would be my first Games: even in that far distant moment in February I felt a stab of unease.

We moved to other matters, other trips, and, of course, my fat series on The Winners. With Shoemaker and Davis already in the can, I was looking good: but I was struggling for the third subject. Who was big enough a winner, and big enough a personality, to live with those two? Tom has ideas the way writers have insecurities.

'What about Nelson Piquet?'

Motor racing bores me into a catatonic stupor. I can't even drive. You would never get me going to a grand prix. 'That's rather boring, Tom.'

'He's a winner. He's won the world championship three times, who else has done that?'

'No idea. Stirling Moss?'

'No. Hardly anybody, anyway, that's the answer. And he's an odd man, interesting man.'

'He just drives motor cars rather fast, doesn't he?'

'Give him a try. I think he'll surprise you.'

'All right, Tom. If you say so.' I know that when Tom is strong on a notion, it is likely to be a good one. But I can't say that I was thrilled and excited.

5. NELSON PIQUET: THE MAN, THE INTERVIEW AND THE WOBBLER

The most important part of any journalist's kit is the telephone. You could do the job without a typewriter, or even without a word-processor, but without a telephone you don't exist. I had to find Nelson Piquet: the first article of a journo's faith is that he wonders not whether such a thing is possible, but how many phone calls it will take.

From the moment you enter your first newsroom, in my case the *Surrey Mirror* in Redhill, the paramount importance of the telephone is made clear. You are taught to believe that there is nothing it cannot do. The first skill a journalist strives to acquire is not writing, or even doing the expenses, but creative use of the telephone.

When I walked into the newsroom that first day, the room at once exploded into a fury of telephonic energy. Everyone in the room instantly felt the urge to act the ace reporter: the room was full of people camping it up like mad. The prevailing style was a kind of dogged matiness it was fashionable to lard with sub-cockney speech patterns.

'Sergeant Selley please . . . oh 'ello Perce, all right? Got any more gen on the smash at Buckland Bends?'

'Councillor Pullen? . . . Arthur, hello, mate, about this planning application . . . that's right, the factory extension onto the allotments.'

I remember how disconcerted I was when my sister joined the same newspaper group, and started to close our telephone conversations with 'Cheers, mate'. Gambits are for use, not over-use. A new reporter finds all this telephonic byplay mightily disconcerting, as he or she is supposed to. All around you, reporters seem to be competing with each other as to who can have the most raucous conversation with the most important contact. There is a sub-competition as to who can hold the telephone in the most original way: using your hands to hold the phone is definitely *vieux jeu*: you are supposed to hold it against your ear with your shoulder – an extension of the method developed by violinists to hold the principal tool of their own profession. You take shorthand notes with one hand, and with the other you feed yourself with extra strong mints or smoke cigarettes. 'Cheers, mate.'

The idea behind all this is to make the newcomer feel doubly and trebly uncomfortable, especially when the news editor makes a brief speech stating his belief that tenacity is the most important virtue in a journalist. In translation, tenacity means ringing up lots and lots of people. You are then plonked down at a desk, and given something to do, which means ringing somebody up. 'Ah hello, this is, ah, the Surrey, ah ah, Mirror, here and, ah . . .' It is one of the most ghastly experiences of any reporter's life. Within about a week I was cocky as any of them. When the next new trainee came in, there I was, eating cheese sandwiches and guffawing down the telephone while making obscene gestures at colleagues with *both* spare hands and calling everyone in the world 'mate'. 'Certainly, mother, cheers, mate.'

Telephonic tenacity, it soon transpired, was not the moral quality it was presented as. It is no more than professional habit, professional method. You might as well say that cooking edible food is a moral virtue in a chef. If you need anything, the telephone will supply you: that is the journalist's credo. I needed Nelson Piquet. It took two phone calls.

I claim no virtue in this, no skill. Telephonic frustration is as much a part of the job as successful telephone tenacity. It helps if you have somewhere to start. I rang our motor racing man, John Blunsden. 'Hello, old boy.' I explained I was looking for Nelson Piquet.

'Not easy. He lives on a boat with no telephone.'

'Oh.'

John recommended I try the PR agency that represents Camel cigarettes sporting involvements, which included the sponsorship of the Lotus team, for which Piquet was driving. It all seemed rather a long way round to me. 'The chap you need is called Byron. Byron Young. He'll fix you up, I expect, if you give him a kick in the arse.' All my life I have yearned to give someone – anyone – called Byron a kick in the arse.

'Is Piquet co-operative, John?'

Hollow laughter down the phone. 'He's dreadful. Very temperamental chap. Hates the press. No one gets much from him. He won't talk to anyone. Still, good luck.' Cheers, mate, I thought, and rang Byron Young. He really was called Byron, it seemed. I explained my ambition to write about Piquet.

'What are you doing Sunday and Monday?'

'Nothing planned.'

'Why not come to the South of France with us, then? We're launching the new car, and Nelson is giving a press conference.'

'Well . . . I need more than a press conference. I need time with him, time alone with him. I can't do a major interview with dozens of people chipping in.'

'No problem. I'll fix you up with him after the press conference, you'll have plenty of time.'

'OK, then. Great.'

'I'll fix the tickets and the hotel for overnight. You'll be back in England Monday evening.'

'Sounds perfect.'

'Oh . . . you will say Camel, won't you? Team Lotus Camel.'

'Sure.'

'I'll see you at Heathrow, I'll have the tickets.'

Cheers, mate. This all left me rather breathless. It was time to get thrilled and excited. I rang the office, and asked them to send me some cuts on Piquet, 'cuts' being newspaper clippings. The same day they arrived, borne by a Hell's Angel, this being the office term for a motorcycle courier. Soon I was learning about Piquet, that he is Brazilian, for example, and was the current world champion. He had been in the same team as Nigel Mansell the previous year, and their relationship had been simple and uncomplicated. They hated each other. Mansell will feel forever robbed of the world championship in 1987: he reeled off a total of six victories, while Piquet won only three races. But when Mansell wasn't winning, he was generally blowing up in mid-race, and when he did win, there was Piquet, always cannily tucked in behind him, driving carefully within the car's limits, always picking up the points for second or third. You may dislike the points system by which the Formula One world championship works, and by which it rewards the non-winning drivers, you may believe it is stupid and unjust: but if you are smart enough you can make any system work to your advantage. Cleverness like this is quite unforgivable, certainly by the less clever. I was beginning to be intrigued by this man.

I went to Heathrow to meet Byron. I was on time, which for practical purposes means early. With some people, punctuality is a virtue; with me, it is a vice. I am like Uncle Matthew in Nancy Mitford: 'if he's not here in five minutes the damn fellow will be late.' Eventually I linked up with Byron, a young and cheery fellow, and with Tony Jardine, who runs the PR company. Tony, in response to my complaints that not being in extremely good time for aeroplanes was bad for my nerves, regaled me with tales of banging on the plane doors and having them reopened to admit him. 'That's the right way to treat these aeroplanes,' he said breezily.

Tony, it became apparent, is a remarkable fellow: a rally driver, a former stand-up comic, a former professional impressionist whose conversational technique often involves leaping from one persona to the next, and a former singer with bands. He is a man of tireless good humour who seems to like everybody, and whose ambition in life seems to be to have that affection returned. This makes him one of the few entirely natural PR people the world has ever seen. There is no act involved, you see. And he is quite impossible to dislike.

The motor car launch was to take place at the Paul Ricard circuit at Le Castellet in the South of France. I and a few proper motor racing journos were put up at a pleasant little hotel in an adjoining hilltop village: the Lotus team were at the same place. The evening was a long and cheery one, with a good deal of banter flying from table to table. At one stage Peter Warr, the director of Team Lotus, started to sing Byron's praise. 'You do so much, Byron, it is such a thankless job, but you really have done well today, don't think we're not grateful.' As a token of his esteem, he had *Madame la patronne* create the *specialité de la maison* for him and him alone: an enormous and beautiful pudding, a mountain range of cream studded with a hundred strawberries.

'There is something fishy about this,' Byron said at once.

'Don't be so paranoid, Byron.'

'I mean, it would be just like them to fill this up with shaving foam, or something.'

'What an unpleasant suspicious mind you have.'

Byron kept tasting it, and then offering it to others at the table to try: 'No, that's cream.'

'You're sure it doesn't taste a bit soapy?'

'Nah . . . it must be some booze she's put in it.'

About half an hour later, Byron retired in good order and dignity, and returned after about 20 minutes, having thrown his heart up, and an excellent dinner as well. Teehee – it *was* shaving foam. Practical joking is a form of sadism that in some circles is socially acceptable. It is something of a tradition in Formula One. As for Byron, he was in good company. This little jape really is a specialité de la maison, and Madame la patronne has caught Alain Prost and Ayrton Senna with the same trick. Senna ate his without turning a hair, merely commenting: '*Pas mal.*' Poor Byron; in Anthony Powell, Widmerpool is flippantly described by someone as being 'rather the sort of person people pour sugar over'. Byron is rather the sort of man to whom people serve shaving foam. I felt for Byron, but it could have been worse. It could have been me.

The following morning we went to meet the car. It was the sort of car that would stand out in a traffic jam: it was painted yellow of a searing, migraine intensity, and was plastered with logos. Everywhere you looked there was a Camel painted on something. Piquet was there, with a camel on his back, unnaturally handsome gypsy head rising from his migraine-yellow fireproofs. He leaned on the car; he sat in the car; he performed prolonged handshakes with the second driver in the team, Satoru Nakajima, in front of the car. He smiled and smiled, and all around him, the motor-drives of the assembled cameras roared.

And on to the press conference. It was here that Piquet decided to give me a clear indication of his nature. He is a nutcase. He opened the press conference by putting an unlit cigarette to his lips, and announcing: 'Since I now have the sponsorship of Camel, it is in the contract that I 'ave to smoke the cigarettes. Ha!' He sat in the chair fielding questions for about 40 minutes, and during that entire time he continued pretending to smoke the cigarette. 'Well, it is dee-ficult to say' – long drag on the cigareete – 'but I know we 'ave the potential to 'ave a very queek car.' And then he knocked imaginary ash into the real (Camel logo-ed) ashtray. A normal person might have made the joke, but would have tired of it after a couple of minutes. Something in Piquet's surreal mind found it mind-bogglingly funny that he should sit there before the world's press pretending to smoke an unlit cigarette for 40 minutes.

The mood was pre-season, which means optimistic. This was the world's number one driver, and the Honda engine was already looking like a world beater. If the rest of the car was up to this, they could sweep the board: new team, new car, new challenge. Piquet was full of enthusiasm, and could not wait to get into the car and start burning up the track. Me, I was anxious to get my interview. I was beginning to feel edgy. Tony had made the introductions: 'As soon as this is over, we do it,' Piquet had said.

'Is this going to work, Tony?' I asked. I had a clear feeling that things were about to lurch out of control.

'Look, just grab him as soon as the formal questioning is over.'

'So long as I get him on my own, as we agreed.'

'Sure, sure . . .'

I was now locked into a classic journo nightmare: I had given up two days for the sake of one conversation, and I could feel very clearly that it might not take place. Tony announced to the crowd that formal questioning was over, and, taking control, he sat me next to Piquet. As he did so, 20 or 30 other journos gathered around, eager for a less formal quote, to try a more risqué question. There were Piquet and I side by side, and there was a great shoving throng of journos, all thrusting tape recorders and notebooks at us.

'Glad to be away from Mansell, Nelson?'

'Nelson, est-que c'est vrai . . .'

'Who's your tip for the . . .'

This was not the moment for getting the full attention of a notoriously elusive character on such matters as his inner spirit and his fluctuating motivation. And so, under the influence of the Gallic atmosphere, and infected, perhaps, by Piquet's own bizarre and uncompromising nature, I threw a wobbler. Since my *Surrey Mirror* days I have lost innocence: swapped it, I fear, for arrogance.

I flung my hands in the air, and said, 'This is fucking ridiculous! *No one* can work like this! *No one* can do an interview in these conditions.' I got to my feet, planning to do a bit more yelling at a few more people, Tony or Byron for example. But I found Piquet standing beside me. 'In ten minutes. We walk to the car together. Alone. I talk to you then, long as you want.' I think this intemperate, over-the-top reaction found an answering echo in Piquet.

In any event, it all started working with consummate smoothness. Piquet shed the racing press with effortless ease, and scooped me up for a long and fascinating chat. There are people who, when interviewed, looked for the catch in the question and try to answer every question self-protectively. This can mean that everybody is wasting his time. Right from the start, Piquet – a man with a very sharp mind indeed – cottoned onto my line of thinking, and answered as fully and frankly as he was able. 'So what makes you exceptional?'

'I don't think I am exceptional.'

'Ah, come on!'

'I am consistent. It is very easy to do a good year and be world champion. Well, not easy, but not so difficult. If you are in Formula One, you have the talent already. So . . . if you have the right team and the right car, you win. To win three times, that means I am very very consistent –

'Well, in other words, I say I don't care about what I *have* done. I care about what I am going to do next season. Because I do not live with the seasons when I won the championship. This season, I live with what I do this season.'

This forward-looking approach, this ruthless pragmatism, is the difference between the sports fan and the competitor. Or between the sportsman and the sportswriter, if you prefer. If you meet Ian Botham, you would want to talk about that magic 149 of his at Headingly. Frank Keating of the *Guardian* tells a story about visiting Botham and finding a cricket bat lying in the garden in the rain. It turned out to be, yes, the bat with which Botham scored that 149. Practising sportsmen are not nostalgic: they are eager only for the next confrontation.

Sportsmen like Botham have deliberately courted fame, and have been appalled to find that the coin has a reverse side. Piquet is different. 'I don't give a shit for fame, I don't give a shit for society,' he said. 'I don't want to make friends with *anybody* who is important.'

'Do you like being famous?'

'No! I would prefer to have the same profession, and the same enjoyment – and the same money! – and nobody knows me. It is not possible, I know, but for me it would be much better. I think the most important thing, if you want to keep in motor racing, is never to read anything. If you read bad things that people write, or you think that maybe people are speaking bad things about you, you go and fight all the little details you should not fight. And then you have to stop Formula One. So first, I never read anything. Second, I am a friend of everybody. Anybody write bad things about me, next day I am talking to him, no problems. I don't make enemies.'

Well, it would be more accurate to say that he does not cultivate enemies. A couple of weeks later, Piquet managed to get himself into serious trouble with just about everyone by saying a few ludicrously indiscreet things in an interview with, of all things, *Playboy*. He had been particularly rude about Nigel Mansell's wife. Piquet is certainly not universally loved. Most racing journos find him impossible. But I had found him helpful, articulate and friendly; and what is more, he made me laugh. I found his temperament extremely sympathetic. I was ready to form a journalistic branch of the Nelson Piquet Fan Club; I was reliably informed that it would have only one member.

It has happened time and time again to me, that I interview the person that everyone finds most difficult, and find him nice as pie. I would like to claim the credit for this, claim that I have a kind of Crocodile Dundee knack of taming savage beasts, and charming confidences from the most reticent and hostile people in the world. Of course, this is not true. The fact is that if you get any person one-to-one, you see the best of him or her. Once you have got to the person, it is too late for temperament. People may be hostile in principle, but in the reality of a face-to-face meeting, civilised reactions cut in. The journo that pounds a specialist beat has the difficult time, scrambling in crowds for quotes, interrupting the moody superstar when he is in the middle of doing something else. But to come in, do a one-to-one interview, and then disappear – then it is easy to like people, easy to find them sympathetic, easy to cajole confidences from them. It is the nature of the columnist's role, rather than the nature of the columnist himself, that makes him find unlikely people a delight to deal with.

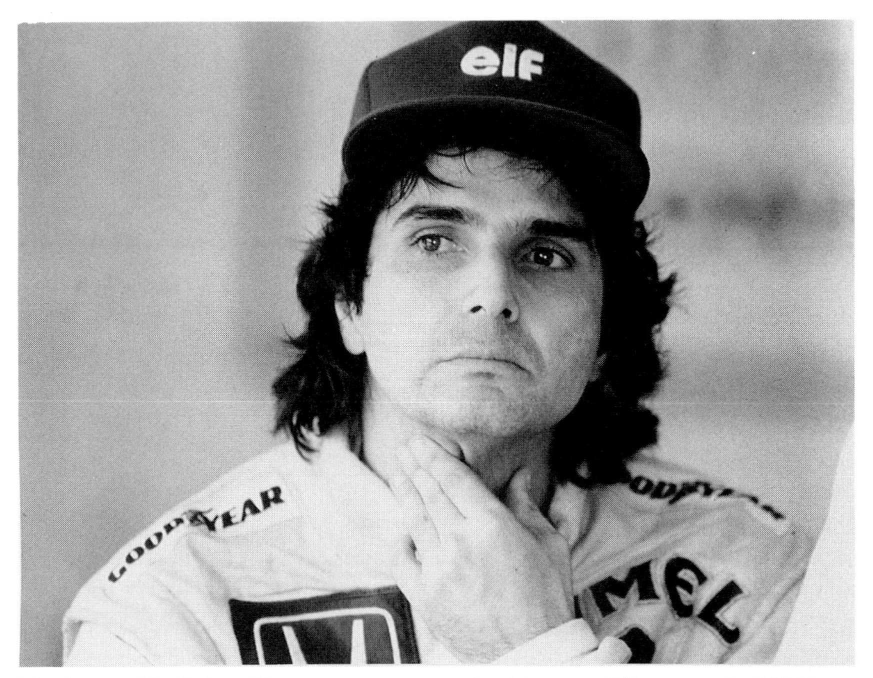

The impossible Nelson Piquet . . . a pressman's nightmare. Why on earth did I like him?
(*Mark Newcombe*)

In the afternoon, we went back to the airport, catching our plane with, oh, 20 minutes and more in hand. I made a speech of thanks to Tony and Byron at Heathrow. 'It all worked really well. Great company, great interview. Thanks a lot.'

'Pleasure to have you with us. Any time we can work together, give us a call. Or we'll call you.'

'Well, I'm always looking for stories.'

'We'll be in touch. Goodbye.'
'Goodbye.'
'Don't forget to say Camel.'

6. LUST AMONG THE GITANES BUTTS: THE QUESTION OF BIMBOS AND BIMBO-ISM

While I was writing up the Winners series, the Winter Olympics were going on without me in Calgary. I had never even thought about trying to go: it all looked like a monstrous non-event to me. *The Times* sent a small team, and some of the pop papers sent no one at all. But it is a rule of life that there cannot be a sporting event of any size without a decent story or two arising from it. This rule counts double if it is a sporting event you have not gone to.

The story of the Winter Olympics was, of course, Eddie Edwards. The Games were short on high-charisma performers, and Eddie stole the show with one ridiculous press conference – the one in which he said his glasses steamed up on the way down the ski-jump. It was the glasses that made him such a success, of course. I was sorry to miss that press conference.

This was perhaps the only occasion in history in which Tom has suffered from a complete sense of humour failure. 'Ridiculous . . . damned if I want to give him any publicity . . . incompetent idiot . . . makes Britain a laughing stock . . . *damned* if I'm going to give him any coverage.'

Faced with so uncompromising an expression of official policy on a subject, there is only one thing that a serious, sober professional with his eye to his future can do – so I did it. I wrote a piece in total contradiction to the Tom Clarke view, glorying Eddie Edwards, and throwing condemnation at all the humourless sods who found Eddie unacceptable. Are the Olympics, I asked, not for the taking part, but for the winning? Tom's sense of humour may not be up to Eddie Edwards, but it was able to take me in its stride. Certainly the piece made the paper. 'I always see you as the Eddie Edwards of sporting journalism anyway,' Tom said.

I have never met Eddie, not seen him save on the television. But I have probably written more about him than any journalist in the country. I have long believed that jokes improve with age and repetition; a long-running joke becomes not so much laboured as a form of ritual; something that stresses a link between people, something that can become almost conspiratorial in flavour. And Eddie Edwards, inevitably, became a running gag in my Diary column, a gag that runs to this day.

The Diary appears in the paper every Saturday. It appears not on the sports pages but on the page opposite the one that carries the letters and the editorials – the 'op-ed' page, in newspaper jargon. This position means everything: I am writing for the general reader, and that governs the entire approach and nature of the column, so much so that many of the Diary readers have no idea at all that I also write on the sports pages – why should they? They never turn to the sports pages. I have been writing the Diary since November 1983, and it is a perfect example of the principle that you should never wish for anything too hard, because you are likely to get it.

At that time, my wife and I were still living in our bedsit. We had, however, just arranged to buy a flat. There was only one drawback, and that was paying the mortgage. It had to be paid every month – you know how they insist on that. I was walking back to the bedsit with my wife, whinging on about the mortgage and the woes of the freelance writer and of the acting profession: 'If only there was something to rely on! If only I could, say, write a weekly column, every week without fail, that would cover the cost of the bloody mortgage.' We entered the common hallway of the house, and at once the payphone on the wall sprang into life. Though it was likely to be for the American actor living on the top floor, I answered it: it was some one at *The Times* asking if I would write a column every week without fail. How much money? Just about enough to cover the mortgage. Thus the Diary began.

It is now an irrefragable part of the week's rhythm and, I would like to think, part of the flavour of Saturday mornings for the people who read it. It is full of real stories – things that have really happened – and I wish I could think of a better word for them than 'off-beat'. Cricket matches played on frozen lakes; underarm bowling; non-league football; Italian priests excommunicating teams; sport in the Scilly Isles or Ouagadougou; all such things are grist to my mill. A loose network of informers keeps feeding me stories. A racing man gives me tips for the big races, tips often of stunning accuracy. Readers write to me with notions or stories, often at my invitation – I have run dozens of underarm bowling stories, all supplied by readers. When I asked for limericks on sporting themes, the readers supplied me with enough limericks to make a book: the book went on to make a few bob for

Christian Aid. Like ol' man river, the Diary just keeps rollin', and wherever I am in the world, I write a Diary every Friday.

Sometimes the stories in the Diary are real hard news stories that – by chance or whatever – have come my way. You may recall that there was some fuss a few years back because Zola Budd was spending all her time in South Africa. The story was first broached in the Diary – I just published, without comment, her year's time-table. The subs put up the deadline 'J'accuse Zola', which showed a certain amount of class.

But mainly the Diary is supposed to be cheering, and Eddie Edwards seemed to have been created by God in order to become a running gag in the Diary. In the week in which he first leapt into the national consciousness, I had a story about the criticism he had received from the po-faced East German press, which called him 'a self-publicising clown'. A week later, I was able to give the world the information that he had been unilaterally elected a member of the Official Monster Raving Loony Party. Then I heard of an American presidential aide who said of Eddie: 'He'd be welcome at a White House briefing. He'd fit right in here. I don't know where I'm going either.'

Before a month was up, it was clear that Eddie himself was no longer the running gag: the gag was now the column's obsession with Eddie Edwards. I kept promising that there would be no Eddie Edwards story that week, and then going back on the promise before the bottom of the column had been reached. This column, I boasted, sees itself as the Eddie Edwards of sporting journalism: this column, it will be noted, knows when (and who) to plagiarise.

As the Winter Olympics continued, it became clear that there were at least two stories I badly wanted to write. There was Eddie, and there was . . . but let us flash back to the Paul Ricard circuit, to the time just after I had finished my interview with Nelson Piquet. Piquet, doubtless inspired and rejuvenated by the experience, was howling round the track in his Camel-plastered streak-of-nicotine motor-car. There are moments that occur every now and then in the life of a sportswriter when his soul becomes possessed with the desire for a long, slow glass of beer. This was one of them. I walked about a bit without much optimism, and discovered that at the end of the pit lane, there is a wonderfully sordid little bar, full of Gitanes butts and men in overalls shrugging their shoulders. I purchased a beer, and borrowed a magazine. I borrowed it because the cover caught my eye: it showed a ravishingly pretty girl wearing tarty black leather knickers and a black leather jacket all covered in studs. The smile, on a mouth which was not so much generous as prodigal, was almost alarmingly alluring. This was a sports story, of course. The cover of the mag bore the legend, '*L'art érotique de Katarina Witt*', and my French was up to this challenge. '*Elle flirte avec les juges*,' the piece continued. It recounted a tale of how Katarina, world champion figure skater, was skating in a costume of more-than-usual skimpiness, when one of her breasts had popped out in mid-skate. '*Difficile d'être plus glasnost*,' the magazine commented lubriciously.

I may not have been in Calgary, but I was not going to let a detail like this deprive me of the pleasure of writing about Katarina. Naturally I used all the stuff from the French mag, but I was in a rather severe mood at the time, and said that no sport that gives marks for artistic impression can truly be a sport, and that if an art needs marks to make it thrilling, then it is bad art. I argued myself into a corner, because exceptional people presenting their life-work in a four-minute programme can really hardly fail to offer something worth seeing. Those who find Torvill and Dean, or Katarina, unwatchable, may not be missing high art or great sport, but they are certainly missing a treat.

There are a lot of terribly butch sportswriters who hate skating with all their hearts, and who believes it might be better sport if, say, opponents were allowed to tackle. But I could not find it in my heart to dismiss any means by which Katarina Witt is brought into my sitting-room.

By this time it was March, and the Cheltenham Festival was looming. Everybody with the remotest affection for horse racing loves the Festival; any one with half a chance goes down to watch the best jump-racing of the season at Cheltenham. I had more than half a chance, but I didn't go. I have never really got the hang of Cheltenham. I don't know why this is. I adore horses, and I enjoy racing. But Cheltenham, the dizzy height of the jumping season, the Super Bowl of National Hunt, if you like – no, I have never really got on with it. It is my loss, I know, and I rather resent that. In 1987 I had gone down for the duration of the Festival, all three days, and had written every day. The thing never really caught light, so far as I was concerned, and I was very sad that this was the case. Easily the best piece was my first, or at least, I thought it was pretty neat when I was writing it. But with my inevitable Cheltenham luck, 300 words of it got eaten by the computer system at *The Times*, the first and (touch wood) only time this has happened. 'We thought it was a bit short.'

In 1988 I wrote a series of three pre-Cheltenham pieces instead of trying to go there. I interviewed Nicky Henderson, the trainer; Tim Thompson-Jones, the amateur jockey; and Gee Armytage, a professional jockey who happens to be, well, female. Henderson, a classic neurotic/obsessive, was good value: his restless energy was disconcerting and commanded the attention. He must be wonderful company after a victory, and rather like a nuclear reactor at meltdown when crossed. I found him, in his mad way, very agreeable and stimulating company. Thompson-Jones was, as befits an amateur jockey, far more affable and easy-going. We closed the interview, and then went to have a glass or two of lunch for mere companionability. He was much easier to deal with than Henderson . . . and the piece I wrote on him wasn't nearly as good.

Gee Armytage was a difficult interview. This was because she has not quite worked out the best way to present her own considerable assets to the world. She can ride, you see, really ride. And also, she is pretty, in a conventional sort of a way. Well, God help the sportswoman who is not conventionally attractive, because the media won't. But the combination of a couple of winners at the Festival the previous season and a good camera-worthy smile made her an instant media darling. She is not a bimbo, no one who can ride like that can be a bimbo . . . and yet there is a little streak of bimbo-ism there too. After all, who could fail to find it flattering when so many people want your picture, so many journos want to interview you? Who could, every time, resist the temptation to play up to it?

The thing is that she hasn't really got her public face organised. Is she a bubbly 'personality'? Or is she a ruthless, out-and-out professional? 'I think the thing with fame, as you call it, is all out of proportion. It's because I'm a girl, and a bit of a novelty. There's a friend of mine who has ridden one more winner than me: well, how many people outside racing have heard of Martin Bosely? I enjoy the attention a lot – but I get fed up with it as well, sometimes.' But as Ian Botham will tell you, you can never have fame on your own terms.

Armytage has a lot to contend with. There is the old-fashioned prejudice of chauvinism, and all the new-fangled pressures of media-hyping. Even while debunking the hype-the-bimbo side of the publicity she has attracted, I am still a part of that very thing myself. True, I can write in realistic terms of her achievements in the context of her publicity . . . but then I was still choosing to write about her, rather than Martin Boseley, was I not? She is more interesting than Martin Boseley, because of her sex and because of the publicity she has attracted.

The series wasn't bad, but it reflected my usual Cheltenham luck. Neither Nicky Henderson nor Tim Thompson-Jones nor Gee

The author interviews Gee Armytage, the jockey, on the subject of bimbo-ism. Note who is doing the talking.
(*Tony Edenden*)

Armytage had a winner at the Festival. I carried a few tips for the big races in the Diary . . . and no, not a single one of them came in. Most of them were non-runners, so far as I remember.

But I was not downcast, no, not at all. A new and beautiful aeroplane ticket had zoomed through the letter-box. I was to go to Hong Kong, which happens to be one of my favourite cities in the world, and to cover the Hong Kong Sevens, which is a wonderful event. Two weeks in Asia: despite all those Cheltenham losers, my luck was in with a vengeance.

7. MADE IN HONG KONG: THE PRIDE AND GLORY OF THIS LABEL OF SHAME

'Made in Hong Kong' . . . it still carries a sting, does it not? It means cheap, shoddy, sub-standard, liable to fall apart at the least provocation, a reasonably good imitation that is not, when you come down to it, anything like the real thing. I was Made in Hong Kong myself, as it happens.

Well, not physically. But certainly professionally. I spent four years in the place. It was a base from which I made lunges and forays across the rest of Asia; it was, as mentioned before, the last place in which I ever had a proper job. I met my wife there, I first owned horses there. The place has left its mark on me: I have lost my taste for hot, flat beer, and am a fully paid up member of the Campaign for Real Gassy Stuff. Cold weather brings a touch of despair: whenever I get anywhere hot and horrible my spirits rise. The addiction to travel, to collecting bizarre stamps in my passport, seems to be incurable.

I shall bear the stamp of Hong Kong for ever. In Hong Kong you never think about 'having a job'. That is a poor, passive approach to the question of earning a living. You go out there and deal. You go out into the market-place and *hustle* for your money. Money is not sordid in Hong Kong: it is romantic and beautiful. Businessmen are heroes and superstars, and even the freelance writer is coloured by the optimism and the cocky self-reliance of such people.

The place is a hothouse of romantic money-hunger. Jan Morris compared the sight of office boys and secretaries flocking around the latest stock market prices when they are displayed in the street to the knots of people that gather around television shops when there is a Test Match being played . . . she has the feel of Hong Kong all right. To arrive in Hong Kong is to plug yourself into the electric main: there is a buzz to Hong Kong I have only experienced elsewhere in New York.

Naturally, horse racing is the number one sport in Hong Kong. The love of hazard is part of the texture of the place: gambling is not a matter of greed, it is a kind of sacred duty to put a few dollars at risk. But there is also a strange and lovely annual event called the Hong Kong Sevens, or, more pedantically, the Cathay Pacific/Hong Kong Bank Invitation Sevens. This was the event I was flying out to cover. It has some of the best and the worst of Hong Kong.

It is a festival of international rugby, with teams from 24 rugby-playing nations. There is a tendency to see rugby as the game played by the Five Nations and the old colonies, plus a couple of oddballs like Japan. But this is a global game: Argentina, the United States, Canada, Fiji, Western Samoa, Thailand, Singapore . . . all these nations send teams to Hong Kong for the Sevens. Such a wide-sweeping, unconventional, wholly international view, such a complete lack of parochialism: these are Hong Kong strengths . . . and yet, and yet . . .

At the event itself you will find it impossible to believe you are in China, on land that will return to China, on an island where the vast and overwhelming majority of people are Chinese. This is a great *gwailo* shindig, *gwailo* meaning literally ghost people, and it is the Chinese name for the pale-skinned foreigners. The Sevens is a great, loud, jolly, boozy festival . . . and the only male Chinese you will find in the stadium are those selling beer. It is only recently that any effort at all has been made to encourage the Chinese to play rugby, or any other *gwailo* sport. The Sevens is just another example of the contradictory nature of Hong Kong life.

Football is a different matter. When I was based in Hong Kong I lived out on Lamma, on one of the outlying islands. When I moved there I became the seventeenth non-Chinese to do so. Within a couple of years the *gwailo* population was approaching the three-figure mark, and there were occasional bursts of bad vibes between the village corner-boys and the apparently 'affluent' foreigners.

Things changed radically when we formed a football team; at least, they did for the players. It started as a brave notion in the bar – by the end of the evening every male under 50 seemed to have had trials with a first division club, and a good half had been schoolboy internationals. By the time we came to play, things had fined down a little. We got stuffed out of sight. We played under the name of Gwai-Loong, which means ghost dragons or, to be less literal, 'Superwogs'. It was a pun on *gwailo*, obviously enough, and the Chinese love puns, so we had a good start. We played matches of varying seriousness twice a week. We got better, and were linked with the corner-boys and the rest by the freemasonry of football. We played on a concrete pitch and my goalkeeping style – a mixture of Peter Bonetti acrobatics and Bruce

Grobbelaar charges (without the latter's quality of reliability) proved to the Chinese, if proof were needed, that all *gwailo* are insane.

I had arranged to stay out on Lamma on this trip, borrowing a house from an old friend, so this was already doomed to be a trip packed with nostalgia. I am a great devotee of nostalgia, though I am not a sentimentalist on that score. The point is not to return to the past, but to taste change in action – and nowhere do things change more violently than they do in Hong Kong, and nor is Lamma Island immune.

The event itself, the Hong Kong Sevens, has a good few memories, mostly of unalloyed sporting pleasure. Andy Ripley, the former British Lion and lapsed hippy, has called the Sevens the finest rugby tournament in the world, and, being a lapsed hippy myself, I cannot but agree with him. For a start, I adhere to the heresy that Sevens is a better game than the crowded 15-man stuff, especially when it becomes a contest between coaches determined only to grind the opposition down. But, more importantly, the exotic internationalism of the Sevens is what makes it: the draw pitted Kwang-Hua Taipei against the All Blacks for starters. It was the Hong Kong Sevens that first recognised that rugby is a truly international game. In short, the rugby World Cup, generally considered the best thing to happen to the game since William Webb-Ellis picked the ball up and ran with it, was Made in Hong Kong.

And in Hong Kong, the favourites are not Hong Kong, nor any of the sides that turn up from Britain every now and then (Scottish Borderers, Barbarians, Penguins, Public School Wanderers) but Fiji. Fiji line up with seven men, all of whom can run like deer and shove like bulls. The greatest rugby I have ever seen was the final of the Hong Kong Sevens in 1984, when Fiji took on the All Blacks. Just before the kick-off, a band of drunken Kiwis in the crowd invaded the pitch and performed a rather poor Haka. What followed was electric. The Fijians glared and, just a fraction of a second before the referee would have whistled the start of play, they dropped into a pugnacious crouch, eyes blazing, and performed their own war-dance, a dance of uncompromising and spectacular ferocity. Their very moustaches bristled. And then with a roar they were off into a torrent of overflowing, overwhelming rugby. They played rugby as the Brazilians play football. They flung the ball across the pitch like a bullet, they plucked it out of the air with hands like butterfly nets. They ran the All Blacks ragged. They won 28–0.

This was the moment when the All Blacks decided to take seven-a-side rugby seriously. They went back to the drawing board, and emerged with a new kind of sevens: not the festival, have-a-good-time-never-mind-if-we-lose-'cos-we're-only-messing-about kind of a game;

they decided that if sevens was to be played as serious rugby, they were not going to be left behind. So they re-invented sevens, and in doing so, they brutalised it. Well, they would, wouldn't they?

I am not disapproving here, or not exactly. Rugby is supposed to be a brutal game. The All Blacks now play sevens as if it were fifteens, and the result is, as you would expect, pretty impressive. They line up with massive-jawed, straddle-legged All Black types, who win the ball and run through people, instead of round. They have a couple of speedsters out on the flanks to do the finishing. Simple. And why disapprove? The more disciplined and brutal a side, the more flair and beauty it takes to defeat them. As a lapsed Hong Kong-er, I was looking for Fiji to provide that sort of flair.

I wrote a couple of preview pieces for Friday's and Saturday's paper, and put together a Diary. It was all easy-going stuff: the Sevens is not a high-pressure event, not the sort of thing on which to lead a paper or even a page. It comes in the nice-little-bonus category as far as sports editors are concerned. The change of pace was very pleasing for the writer; there was plenty of time for old friends and old haunts.

The Sevens is played over both days of the weekend, and Saturday never looked like being a tough day. For a start there was nothing to write. I got up unhurriedly, and drank coffee watching the Crested and the Chinese Bulbuls chasing each other about in the bamboo thicket in the garden. I had the faintest of headaches – one of those bottles of Tsingtao I had consumed with old friends the previous night must have been off – but that was soon gone. I walked down the hill to the ferry with my copy of the *South China Morning Post* in my hand, and chugged across the South China Sea in the best possible spirits. Lamma Island retreated; Hong Kong Island advanced. The ferry swung between Green Island and Western Point, and we were in Hong Kong harbour, the hills of the Kowloon peninsula on my left, the ludicrous sky-scrapered skyline on my right. In one 200-yard stretch there were eight towers that weren't there when I lived in Hong Kong – the pace of change is that rapid. I had breakfast at the Mandarin Hotel: things were tough that day, but I was up to it. I made my way to the stadium.

The first day of the Sevens is always quiet. The competition is divided into eight groups of three teams, shaking down on the second day to three knock-out competitions, a Cup for group winners, a Plate for the second-placers, and the Bowl for the losers. By the end of the day, the Bowl competitors had been decided: Thailand, Kwang-Hua Taipei, Netherlands, Papua New Guinea, Brunei, Singapore, Dubai and Sri Lanka. The competition has grown up, but it has not become a snob in the process. The minnows are as much a part of the flavour of the competition as the Australians in their green and gold, and the All Blacks.

The best bit of the day came when Jou Tian-sing of Kwang-Hua Taipei scored a try against the All Blacks, to their deep and lasting embarrassment. 'I suppose I'll be quite famous when I get home,' said Jou. To a Hong Kong Chinese, the All Blacks must be a complete caricature of the traditional *gwailo*: huge, brutal, unstylish, direct, lacking all subtlety; in a crude way, effective enough on his own terms, but really not the sort of person you would choose to marry your daughter.

I returned to Lamma in good spirits, determined to get my own back on the Tsingtao. The following day was more like business, and a strident, cheery occasion of serious sport. In 1987 I had been out for the Sevens, and the day had become rather hysterical. There were, I think, four streakers altogether. The event was teetering on the edge of going out of control: it was a beltingly sunny day, and the beer slipped down thousands of throats with the ease of long practice. I must not be priggish; I have seldom been wholly sober at the Sevens myself, until the days came when I had to write pieces about the event. By the end of the day, I always feel rather like a Bateman cartoon: The Man Who Was Sober at the Hong Kong Sevens.

This time the occasion was blessed with typical Hong Kong spring weather: chilly, with a cloud ceiling at about ten feet. That took the edge off the potential hysteria, and in fact, the occasion seemed to rumble along all day without ever really taking off. This is a competition famous for upsets, but apart from the try against the All Blacks the previous day, everything went to form, and there was not a surprise nor a shock to be had. The All Blacks steam-rollered everything in their path; Australia, playing with more imagination and with the incomparable David Campese as well, always looked the team that would meet the Kiwis in the final.

The Oz were booed every time they took the field throughout the competition. This is a tradition. Years and years ago, an Australian committed a nasty foul on one of the beloved Fijians, and this has never been forgotten. The final was between Australia and the All Blacks, a very clear example of a Satan *v.* Beelzebub situation. And Australia suddenly found themselves, bewilderingly, being cheered.

Well, no one had gone to the stadium planning to cheer the Oz, but at the Sevens the rule is, when in doubt, you shout for the side that runs. For Australia had David Campese, and Campo was the difference

This is probably my favourite city . . . and the Hong Kong rugby Sevens is one of my favourite events of the year.
(Russell Cheyne/AllSport)

between the two sides, in their natures and in their achievements, that day. He switched on the after-burners to make the decisive strike, and Australia won a cracking final 13–12. Oh, and the Taiwanese won the Bowl, and I decided that this was the thing to write about, and a very jolly, charming piece it made. Soberly enough, I sat rattling out the piece as the ground emptied in beery, shouting, singing, staggering hordes, and I telephoned it over from one of the phones provided at the ground. That's the way to work: all very slick and comfortable. Before long, I was chugging back across the South China Sea, back home as I would once have written, and this alien place will always have the tang of home about it for me. But even when I lived there, I always tried to make sure that I had an aeroplane ticket for somewhere or other. This was still true.

The following day I flew – sad to recall, at my own expense, which in my Lamma days I would have considered a real admission of failure – to Singapore. The main reason was to take a week off and spend some time with old friends, former Lamma Island neighbours, now Singapore dwellers. Though in fact there was a moment when I thought I was going to be sent straight back to Hong Kong. 'Your hair is radda long for Singapore standards,' the immigration man said in the immortal fashion of Singapore immigration officials.

'Oh, for Christ's sake don't be such a fool,' I told him. 'If there is one thing more *vieux jeu* than having long hair, it is discrimination against such a person. Besides, do you know who I am? I am incredibly important person. One step out of line, little man, and Rupert Murdoch will be down on your country like a ton of bricks, Singapore will be vilified in five continents, and it will all be *your fault*.' As a matter of fact, I didn't say anything of the kind. Barnes's first law of travel is that if the man is wearing epaulettes, you must act as if he were in the right. It is odd, I have been to Singapore hundreds of times without such a reception. Was this a reflowering of the 60s zeal that made Singapore the subject of so many international jokes? 'You must wash your hair very carefully, and brush it very well, before you go into the centre of our city.' Stuff it up, insolent bastard. 'Yes,' I said obediently. He stamped my passport. I went to seek my friends.

I spent a very pleasant week there, and did not overburden myself with work. I read the proofs of my book and put together a Diary. As a bonus I found one Diary story of considerable force. It concerned our old friend Zola Budd. She had just publicly renounced all her connections with South Africa; shortly afterwards, she had turned up in London to negotiate a shoe contract (yes, I know she runs barefoot, but nothing about the Zola story has ever been quite straightforward) and guess who her adviser was? It was Fanie van Zijl, mayor of Randfontein, and famous as Zola's most politically conscious adviser. In short, Zola had been caught out in a deception.

On my last evening in Singapore I had naturally devoted a good deal of time to my friends. We had dined not wisely but too well, and we were sitting about on the terrace drinking Anchor beer. At midnight we opted, ill-advisedly, for one more. The phone rang. It was teatime in England, and a blurred voice (blurred to me) spoke out.

'Simon?'

'Yurrs?'

'That Zola story. I'm going to have to pull it. It can't go in the paper as it is.'

'Let me . . . ah . . . explain . . .'

'What's the matter, Simon?'

'Strongest possible terms.'

'What?'

'I would like to p'test inna strongest . . . ah . . .'

'What are you saying, Simon?'

I made a heroic effort, 'Look. I'm afraid it's midnight here and I'm tot'ly pissed.' A triumph of incisive articulation, not to mention understatement.

'Yes?'

'Can we disgust, ah, discuss this tomorrow?'

'Oh . . . very well.'

It was time to go to bed, so naturally, we had another beer before doing so. The next day was destined to be a long one. I had to fly Singapore–Manila, Manila–Hong Kong, and then spend seven hours in Hong Kong before catching a plane to London. It worked quite beautifully. I phoned *The Times* from Singapore airport, and discussed Zola Budd. I had a slight headache: no doubt one of the cans of Anchor was off. Zola made the paper, after I had made her case in all sobriety, so that was all right.

With my seven hours to kill in Hong Kong, I left the airport, got a cab to town, and had a meal with a couple of friends. Back at the airport, to my indescribable pleasure, I discovered that I had been upgraded to first class. On Cathay Pacific, this is a very serious level of bliss. I boarded the plane and graciously accepted a large Bourbon. We took off. Pausing only to ask the stewardess to ignore me for the duration, I slipped the Irish Lone Ranger Mask over my eyes and slept. The thought crossed my mind that the next time I would be in Asia, it would be the Olympic Games. If only that would be as easy as this trip had been, I thought.

I landed in London cheery and refreshed, the wicked pick-me-upping Bloody Mary still tasting in my mouth. English affairs surrounded me, as they always do, the instant I was on the ground. The Grand National next weekend – I hoped the journey to Liverpool would be as pleasant as this one.

8. DOING IT THE FIRST TIME: THE HORROR OF AINTREE

Who decides what you write about? This is one of the questions I get asked every now and then, and it is a hard one. Tom and I do so much in discussion: Tom has ideas, I have ideas, and it is a fact of life that if you come up with an ace idea, Tom will give his all to trump it. Yes, go, and why don't you fly to the other coast and see so-and-so as well?

I never get *told* what to do: Tom always asks if such an idea 'appeals'. More often than not it does, though quite often it doesn't. We seem to take these things in our stride, and if there is one thing you can be certain of in a shifting world of journalistic pressures, it is that Tom Clarke will always come up with another idea. In 1987 I was bitterly disappointed to get a knockback when I asked if I could cover the cricket World Cup in India. There were sensible reasons for this, no doubt, not one of which I would have agreed with at the time. 'Do you know anything about baseball?'

'Not a thing, Tom.'

'Well, then, how about covering the World Series?'

And so, instead of worrying about Gatting and the reverse sweep, I was involved with the Minnesota Twins and St Louis Cardinals, the pitching arm of Frankie 'Sweet Music' Viola and the slugging form of Kent 'Getta Vowel' Hrbek. It turned out to be one of my favourite trips.

Tom is a restless give-it-a-go ideas-man, which is a bonus. I occasionally – well, rather often, in fact – find myself without an idea in the world: no idea what to write about, who to talk to, where to go. I think about the week's sport, and my mind goes a complete blank. It is very pathetic of me, though for a columnist, these things are not always obvious. The number one football writer goes to Liverpool *v.* Manchester United. But where does the columnist, the luxury player, go?

In some newspapers, the system is simple and brutal: if the chief sportswriter wants to go to an event, the specialist is 'jocked off', abandoned. They might have a boxing man who covers all the

Commonwealth middleweight title bouts at Alexandra Palace and then, come a big fight in Las Vegas, the boxing writer stays at home and the number one does the job. This is not how we do it at *The Times*. That trip to Atlantic City was a complete departure from normal practice: in normal circumstances all the fights are covered by our boxing man, Srikumar Sen (an Oxford boxing blue, naturally) who does the job with great style, and is heartily welcome to it. When I go to an event, I generally go alongside the specialist, not instead of him.

The question then is simple: what the bloody hell do you write about? There is one very tedious answer to this: to go perverse, and interview the bloke who came last, or, on Grand National Day to go to the meeting at Lingfield. This sort of thing has its place, no doubt, but it doesn't feel right to me. It is a sort of 'ideas journalism', it is trying too hard, it is, most importantly, not what anyone wants to read about. When a big occasion comes around, you want to be there: it is part of your vanity as a sports columnist; it is part of your *function* as a sports columnist.

I was to go to the Grand National: so was Michael Seely, the racing writer. He would write the big-race analysis and all that. The onus was on me to find something else worth writing about. Sometimes this is devastatingly easy. I can go to football, or cricket, or tennis, sit alongside the specialist, and come up with half-a-dozen notions for a piece. But racing is different. There are very few variables. Horses run, and win. In a very obvious sense, every Grand National is the same. It looks the same, it feels the same: the cheers, the tumbles, the terrible tangles of flailing legs, the same tired, triumphant, desperate slog to the line. So you tend to look for a notion.

The previous year I had come up with a real dandy: I would watch the race from Becher's, and write about the toll that the fence extracts from the race every year. Wouldn't you know it? Only one horse fell there. The rest of the day was a scurrying salvage job. I resolved that if I were to go to the National again, it would be with a pre-planned, pre-packaged scheme. In short, I needed a Notion. I came up with one all by myself and I thought it was a real beauty. I would find a jockey who had never ridden in the race before, interview him before the race, and then again afterwards. Hopes and Fears on Saturday morning: What It Was Really Like on Monday. I was rather impressed by myself. Surely, I thought, this was what real journalists do. As it happened, this was a lousy, appalling, dreadful and embarrassing idea, as feeble as all those interview-the-bloke-who-came-last ideas I hate so much, but there was no telling me that at the time.

I had no trouble finding the lucky jock. Chris Goulding, a friend on the *Times* racing desk, suggested Clive Cox, who, he said, had a pretty fair chance on a horse called Sacred Path. It is the easiest thing in the world to find a jockey: his home telephone number is listed in the *Directory of the Turf*: all you have to do is dial it. No professional athlete is as exposed as a jockey. You can ring them up at four in the morning and slag them off for ballsing up your 10p Yankee if you wish. So I rang up Cox, though not at four in the morning, and fixed an interview. I went down to Lambourn to talk.

Cox was 23, and had ridden 30 winners as a hot apprentice. Now he was a grown-up jockey, and he was finding life tougher. In racing, you have to climb the mountain twice. As an apprentice, you have a weight allowance of half a stone, and because of the advantages of taking weight off a horse's back, owners are quite often prepared to give apprentices a chance. Then as you progress, your weight allowance diminishes and finally vanishes, and you have to face the racing world as an inexperienced and callow optimist with no advantages other than such skills as you possess. The transition from good apprentice to regular pro is often a painful one. Cox was retained as second jockey by the trainer Oliver Sherwood, which was a very great deal better than being out on your own. All the same, life had not been all that easy for him: the Grand National comes when the racing season is more or less on its last knockings, and Sherwood had ridden seven winners thus far. On to the National, then, and a chance of making it eight. On, then, to talk about the First Time.

The First Time is a pretty universal human experience. The sexual comparison was obvious enough, but much of life, and practically all of young life, is about trying to act cocky and experienced when you are trying to bluff your way through a host of different kinds of First Time. As Cox talked about his ambitions when he would join the big boys in the Grand National, I was reminded of a first time of my own: the first time I had worked in The Street. Ah, to work in The Street, that dizzy, unattainable goal, light years distant from the *Surrey Mirror*: would I ever be up to working in The Street? Most people didn't think I was up to working for the *Surrey Mirror*. There was a man called Charles Laurence who embodied all the ambition a newsroom of tyro journalists could muster: he was news editor on the *Dorking Advertiser*, another title in the *Surrey Mirror* group, he rode a motorbike, and on Friday afternoons he would roar off to London to do a shift on the *Daily Mail*. He did shifts in The Street: oh, the glamour of the man! (He now works for the *Telegraph*, based in America and so is a rare example of early promise being fulfilled.)

Clive Cox (above) and the Grand National. Is the first time the best time or the worst time? Well, if you fall off before you start, it can't be too good.
(R. H. Wright)

Below, another two attack the brushwood.
(ASP/George Herringshaw)

My first attempt at being Charlie Laurence took me to the *Evening News* at eight in the morning. The *Evening News* – that dates me, for a start. Skittering with nerves, I set off to work in The Street: it is a fact of life that everyone who works in local papers thinks, or thought, that real journos refer to Fleet Street as The Street. So when a local paper journo refers to The Street, he is claiming for himself the lure and lore of the true professionals. In fact, I have never in my life heard anyone on any national paper refer to the place as The Street. It would be a terrible faux pas.

Off, then, to The Street. I should have been at work for the *Surrey Mirror* people, naturally, but I had claimed a sickie for the day. I sat at a long desk, hideously uncomfortable in my horrible suit and was bored out of my mind. In eight hours I was given two paragraphs to sub. That was it. I doodled with maniacal intensity. I read newspapers 'studiously'. I didn't dare read a book, for fear of looking insolent. (It is a fact of life that reading a book is always considered cheeky, but for some reason reading newspapers is perfectly acceptable.) The day was enlivened by a telephone call: someone had told my boss that I was not ill at all, but was working for the *Evening News*. There are some lovely people about, are there not?

So that was The Street: an eight-hour agony of boredom and worry. I went back to the *News* two or three times, but I was not greatly encouraged. The path to my dreams did not lie that way. Thank God, I can write now in all complacency, but I took it pretty hard at the time. It was about a year before I finally found regular work in what I by then no longer called The Street, subbing every Saturday at the *Sunday Telegraph*. The distance between the First Time and comfortable performance at the act is often immense. I felt for Clive Cox, so cheerful and so confident three or four days before the race . . .

'The first time I saw the fences at Aintree, I was amazed,' he said. 'I had always imagined they were so much bigger . . . still, I know they're going to look big enough on Saturday afternoon.'

I was writing about doubt and fear, but I knew before I went that Cox would not talk about such things. Athletes don't, or very seldom. These are taboo subjects. No athlete will talk about fear: he is afraid to. People often think that athletes are very one-dimensional people: well, that is exactly what they are trying to be. They strive to weed out all the fascinating doubts and insecurities from their personalities, and to become straightforward, uncompromising, up-and-down winners. But the truth of the matter is that all professional athletes lead lives surrounded by disappointment and defeat: there are always more losers in a race than there are winners. An athlete is kept afloat by his own unsinkable and unsnubbable belief in his own qualities.

'If you talk to winners, you will get a very positive attitude to life,' Steve Davis had said, when I was talking to him for the Winners series. Optimism is, in fact, the occupational disease of the professional athlete: he daren't not be optimistic. Self-doubt is part of everybody's life, but for a professional athlete it is not an affordable luxury. That is why they so often seem such an odd breed. 'I'm not at all nervous for Saturday,' Cox said, 'but I'm very, very excited.' Most sportsmen daren't be introspective . . . it takes a very odd, and very introspective fellow like Steve Davis to point this out.

But Cox came across as a nice fellow, and I wished him nothing but luck. 'Fences feel small with him. And he'll get every inch of the trip. He likes to be up there, so I will jump him out smartly and keep him up with the pace. He's got a wonderful temperament – the horse is a Christian.'

Others agreed with this assessment. By the day of the race, Sacred Path had been backed down to 17–2 favourite. I was feeling very smug indeed about this little scoopette I seemed to have pulled off. My piece looked good in the paper on Saturday, I thought, as the train rattled towards Liverpool.

I know the idea of getting paid to go to the Grand National sounds like a pretty good deal. Well, I hate to whinge. There are plenty of days when a sportswriter's life does seem, even to the sportswriter, to be a pretty good one. Grand National day is not one of these. The train is crowded and uncomfortable. Liverpool racetrack is a dump. The press room is gloomy and there are always too many people in it. You have hours to kill before the race, and when it starts, you can hardly see it at all. The 'atmosphere' on Grand National day is not something I enjoy. It has the kind of rowdy, self-conscious booziness of people enjoying themselves by numbers. The Grand National is a great event and a great story, there is no question about that. There is a professional pleasure in getting it right. But the day itself is one to be endured rather than enjoyed.

You get a better view of the race on television, but having gone all that way, I feel in duty bound to watch the race in reality. So I got up to the laughably small press viewing balcony good and early to bag a front row place. There I watched the parade, watched the interminable milling about and triple checking of the girths before the start. I raked my binoculars through the field looking for Cox: there he was, standing Sacred Path quite still, a little way apart from the others. Just like

Lester: nice touch. *The Sporting Life* had told the world to put the mortgage on Sacred Path that morning: the responsibility seemed to sit easily enough on Cox's shoulders. 'Standing apart. Like Lester,' I wrote in my notebook. If ever a young jockey had a chance to make his mark, this was it.

Then with a bang and a roar, the tapes were up and the race was off, and Cox stood up in the stirrups and set off for fame and fortune. There were 30 stiff and unforgiving fences ahead: Cox followed the plans he had revealed to me to the letter. He set off smartly and was in the first two or three as they jumped the first. The Tannoy boomed out: 'And as they come to the first . . . there's a faller . . . the horse is all right . . . they move on towards the second, the jockey is still down . . . it's Sacred Path the faller at the first and they take the second, it's . . .'

On went the horses, the great multi-coloured carpet of colours across the course, billowing up and down again at every fence, leaving a horse or two behind here and there. Through the glasses, I saw Cox get to his feet, try his leg rather gingerly, and walk away. Did I have the best story of the day, or the worst, I wondered numbly. Poor old Cox. Gee Armytage, however, seemed to be having the day of her life, leading the field around the second circuit. There was an awful moment when I thought I had missed the story of the year by writing about her before Cheltenham, when I might have done so before the National. But then she disappeared from sight: she hurt her back in mid-race and pulled up. Very peculiar. The race ended, and I set out to see Cox.

I hate to intrude on private grief. Many a time I have been too soft-hearted to seek out the latest British disappointment. After all, I don't have to ask him how he feels: I can work that out for myself. But I did need to have a word with poor Cox: he was my reason for being in Liverpool, he was my *story*. And so I joined the horrible mad scramble around the weighing room, as everybody else in the world tried to get his own story. Chris Goulding from *The Times* had the little task of trying to get a word with every single jockey in the race. I had just one to find . . . and it was not easy.

At first I thought he had managed to sneak away. In a way, I couldn't have blamed him, though I would have done anyway. After all, he had promised to speak to me afterwards. Then I thought he was probably hiding in the weighing room; well, I wouldn't blame him for that, either. Meanwhile, I stood there, shifting about to keep my place in the rugby scrum outside the door as everyone who has ever lifted a pen in newspapers struggled to get a quote. In this mad, impossible situation, there is only one thing the doorman can do – make a beeline for me and try and throw me out. My technique on these occasions is simple: I behave with great calmness and politeness. This always has the same effect: the doorman redoubles his attempt to throw me out. 'Look, you'll have to go.'

All around me my colleagues were behaving with unrestrained obstreperousness. I was standing quietly minding my own business. 'I've told you, I'm waiting for Clive Cox.'

'He's not here.'

'I'm aware of that. That is why I am waiting.' Foolish move, that, trying logic on a doorman.

'Look, you'll have to go.'

It is ever my fate to be thrown out of places. A couple of days previously, I had been thrown out of the Café Royal when attempting to have a drink with Adrian Metcalfe, then Channel 4's head of sport. The Café Royal prides itself on being the *rendezvous d'élite sportive*; I was wearing a pair of new, expensive and sparkling white sporty shoes: 'We don't serve people with trainers,' said the waiter, for whom a job in the Singapore immigration department surely awaits. Or he could work on the gates at Wimbledon. At Liverpool, the doorman was a disappointed man: Cox finally appeared.

I heaped sympathy on him; he didn't want a drop of it. No. Not him. 'That's racing,' he said, and was content – eager – to leave it at that. He told me that Sacred Path had simply hit the top of the fence. The thing about National fences is that they are hypocrites. They look nice and soft with all those jolly-looking spruce boughs covering them so snugly. But underneath, they are harder than any other fences in the country: tight bundles of thorn branches. You can skim through the top of fences at every racecourse in Britain, but not at Aintree. 'He's not normally a horse that takes liberties, but he took a liberty today. You can't take a liberty at the National.'

Cox was putting a Brave Face on it, which, of course, you have to do if you are to survive as a professional athlete. You can't afford to act like Lear on the heath every time things go a little amiss. Disaster is part of sport's daily fare – this is especially true in National Hunt racing, this is especially true on Grand National day. The Grand National has all the woes and triumph of National Hunt racing magnified to an absurd degree. The Grand National equals racing squared, or cubed. The disasters taste more horrible, the falls are more painful, the luck more capricious, the triumphs sweeter. 'Well, there's always next year,' said Cox, with sportsmanly optimism. 'As for this – well, it's such an anticlimax, isn't it? But that's racing for you. That's the Grand National for you.'

For of course, it could have been worse. He could have been badly hurt. He got a kick on the knee when he fell, but nothing that would stop him riding on Monday, if he could get a ride. A jockey called Brendan Powell had ridden in his own first Grand National the previous year, fallen at the third, and broken his arm. This year, he won.

9. A STRANGE CASE OF HEROINE WORSHIP: ARE WE NOTHING MORE THAN ANIMALS?

If you write for a newspaper, and especially if you are a writer of the pontificating, head-above-the-parapet kind, you tend to get a fair bit of post. Mostly, when readers write in, it is fairly agreeable – well, at least it shows they have read the piece.

But there are some topics that always bring in a nasty postbag. 'Once again you choose to berate this innocent girl, whose only joy . . .' Zola Budd has never failed to bring me a wagonload of angry, often bizarre and insulting letters. I had a couple of truly vicious letters after I had written on the Mike Gatting / Shakoor Rana incident, after which I had written that the basis of the great umpiring row was racism. The most polite of the anti letters called me an anti-white racist. One began: 'Dear Mr Barnes, I don't know how you got your job, but after reading your piece on Mike Gatting I can only assume it was sodomy.' What extraordinary people there are in the world. Still, at least he read the piece.

The nicest letter I have ever received came from Ginny Leng, the three day eventer. After the Burghley championships one year, I wrote about her heart-lifting performance, and gave it everything I had. The response was quite extraordinary: no athlete has ever done it before or since. She wrote to thank me for it. 'Your piece was so beautiful it made me cry,' she said. The more usual response after an interview is: 'You'll hear from me again if there's anything wrong with what you write.' Athletes are impervious to praise, yet as morbidly sensitive as Marcel Proust when it comes to anything that can possibly be interpreted as criticism. So Ginny's letter was a surprise and a delight.

That was in 1986. The following year I had a Notion – Badminton with Giny Leng, to be with her every day of the competition and to talk about the preparation and performance at each phase of the three day event. I rang Ginny: she agreed. Then came disaster. I was stuck in a horrific traffic jam between Gatwick and home when the radio smugly announced that Badminton was cancelled. Waterlogged. I had curtailed my trip in Hong Kong for this?

I resolved to try again the following year. And before I had even started to lobby for the event, Tom contacted me and asked me to go down to Badminton for the entire week. I rang Ginny, and she was happy to try for Leng's Badminton again. All in all, it looked perilously like being the sort of week that people imagine sportswriters spend all the time: actually being paid for something you would willingly pay to do. Was this my reward for surviving Atlantic City?

'Is this the ultimate ghosted column?' Tom asked.

'No, the ultimate spirited column,' I replied.

Badminton, being a three day event, lasts for four days, Thursday until Sunday, the first two days being dressage. I arrived on the Tuesday, all set to write preview pieces for Wednesday's and Thursday's papers before getting stuck into the competition proper. On the first day I had an appointment at eleven-thirty with Colonel Frank Weldon, then the event director. He is a man renowned for his military gruffness, his peppery temperament and his love of precision. What a pity, then, that I was 15 minutes late. A double pity that he was under the impression that our appointment was for eleven o'clock. His warm, friendly greeting to me was: 'You're three-quarters of an hour late!' I could see that he was itching to tell me the interview was off, dismiss, fall out, get back to barracks and getcha bloody hair cut on the way. Only way to deal with dilatory jumped-up little journalists.

However, the power of the sponsor can move mountains, can even soften Colonel Weldon. The appointment had been set up by the sponsor's fixer, Jolyon Armstrong, who was there to meet me. I have a feeling that this helped Weldon swallow his desire to have me dragged out and shot. Besides, Jolyon is 6 ft 8 in, which gives him a certain moral force. I got my interview. I asked questions, and Weldon made his replies, in a voice reminiscent in both volume and timbre of one of the larger kinds of terrier. But to my surprise, for all that he never for a moment ceased barking, he became downright agreeable within about five minutes. Like many people reluctant to be interviewed, he loves to talk. 'I always tell you chaps who want a good quote that my aim in building a course is to frighten the wits out of the riders without harming the horses.'

It was towards the end of this interview that I got to the truth of the matter: Weldon was one of the great ham actors of all time. He was really revelling in his peppery-old-sod role. He was camping it up with complete abandon. And he really is rather a remarkable man: prisoner-of-war for five years, finishing up in Colditz and escaping twice. He was commanding officer of the Royal Horse Artillery, the fellows in fancy uniforms who fire ceremonial salutes in Hyde Park.

'There seems no limit to the capacity of the human being to improve,' he pronounced. He cited the example of Emil Zatopek, the Flying Czech who won two gold medals at the 1952 Olympics; his winning times would not even qualify him for the Olympics these days. 'And in terms of the ability of human beings to train their horses, there has been the most enormous improvement. But all the same, the horses are not galloping any faster or jumping any higher than they were 80 or 90 years ago.' Weldon must design his fences within the same limits as the course builder for the 1912 Olympics: to a maximum of 3 ft 11 in high, and 5 ft 11 in spread. It is his talent, amounting almost to genius, to make his fences look at least twice as wide and five times as high as they really are.

After the interview, I checked into a rather classy little country house hotel which the office had obviously decided was appropriate for the mission. I unpacked my bag, set my Timberland boots on the floor, wrote my Colonel Weldon piece, and then had a good session at the telephone. I made contact with Ginny, and arranged to meet her at the competitors' briefing the following morning. It took several more phone calls to get permission to attend the briefing myself, but the Colonel was finally persuaded to consent. It was rather like being allowed backstage: with Ginny to meet, I felt like an old-fashioned stage door Johnny.

The following morning was grey and filthy. I found the competitors gathered around outside Badminton village hall, all gassing away and talking horse for all they were worth. Ginny was not hard to spot, dressed in an Akubra hat in vivid eye-matching blue.

When you get a bunch of athletes together, the atmosphere tends to be a bit fraught. Competitors are, well, extremely competitive people, and they are always, consciously or not, seeking for some kind of edge. But here the vibes were quite different. The place was a hotbed of camaraderie: we're all in this together. I had a flashback to my own eventing days: the same atmosphere of vast, if slightly nervous jolliness. I had thought this was because of the immense matiness of small-time competitors, but the matiness was as evident at this elevated level as it was at the level at which I had performed. Eventers are not rivals, but partners in adversity: the enemies not of the fellow-competitors, but the fences.

We all trooped into the hall, and Weldon barked at us for half an hour or so. Don't ride here, don't canter there, don't gallop at all. He explained some of the more complicated fences he had dreamed up: 'So you see it is quite possible to jump this fence clear and still incur 80 penalty points if you bugger it up sufficiently.'

Once we were well and truly briefed, it was time to inspect the course. The competitors all set off in a great convoy of countrified motors: Landrovers, Range Rovers, Jeeps, and various Japanese equivalents, bouncing and bucking their way across Badminton Park. I thumbed a lift from a man from Ireland who had recently been robbed by the IRA. They had made off with a fortune. With a delivery like that of a camp actor (of more traditional mould than Colonel Weldon) he said: 'And when they went, they told us we were the nicest people they had ever robbed.'

The first mass halt was to inspect the steeplechase course. A three day event is in three sections. The first part is dressage, the complex equestrian ballet. The third is the show-jumping. And the middle section is the 'endurance test', and it is a great deal more than the spectacular cross-country section you see on the television. It comprises 45 minutes' hack along 'roads and tracks', followed by a four-minute gallop over the steeplechase course. These are the conventional, inviting obstacles you find in National Hunt racing. You then go through another 20 minutes of roads and tracks before taking on the cross-country course and the worst that Weldon can throw at you.

We marched around the steeplechase course at a good, brisk pace: there was nothing complicated to slow you down here. Just get a good look at it, that's all. Everyone was still frightfully jolly: 'Of course you *could* make a mistake here,' Ginny said. 'You're going faster than you will be over the cross-country. But, well, it would be the ultimate embarrassment.'

Then we were back into the convoy, along more roads and tracks, until we reached the start of the cross-country course, and a four-and-a-half-mile walk to see what the Colonel had in store for us. On foot, it was to take about three hours. On horseback, it had to be done in less than 12½ minutes.

Ginny set off with her ever-present adviser, the splendid Dot Willis, and I joined them, swishing gracefully through the wet grass in my Timberlands. Ginny was relaxed and chatty as we set off, giving the first fence the briefest of glances, and passing on to the second with a light laugh. 'You don't really notice the crowd,' she said. 'You just notice that you can't see that far in front. One of the reasons for walking the course is to work out how you will ride the optimum line when your view is blocked.' This was exactly the sort of thing I had come on this walk to hear, and I was pleased that things were going so easily. But at fence three we had the first 'bloody'. It was a nice, inviting-looking fence, but with a drop on the landing side. A bold jump would make nothing of this, but a hint of hesitation from rider or horse would be disaster. Each has to trust the other to make the jump easy. In one jump, the essence of the sport is made plain: disaster is always hard upon you, and it's always a bloody long way down.

The riders were competing against the course in the same way that golfers do. At Badminton this takes on a strangely personal flavour. Weldon so dominated Badminton that, by some twisted process in the riders' minds, the enemy became not the faceless course, but Weldon himself: the Implacable He, the Grand Inquisitor of Badminton.

'How the bloody *hell* does he expect us to find a line here?' Ginny snapped out these words in my general direction, and in a seething fury. What had happened to the pleasant, smiling lady I had set out with? I had lost her to Colonel Weldon at jump three. She was locked in some mental struggle with the Colonel, whose arcane trickery had produced so devious, so evil a course that no horse and no rider would ever be able to jump it properly. 'Oh Jesus, look at this!'

It was at the Ski Jump fence that the flow of quotes dried up altogether. The jump involved a climb, a slither down a precipitous slope, and a horrid trappy little fence at the bottom. With a clever little pony, you would have found it a mildly amusing little fence: for a great big, 'scopey' horse – like the two Ginny would be riding – there seemed to be nothing but traps and potential disaster. Ginny, blazing with anger, jack-booted her way round the fence, tried one line, tried another. Finally, she produced her judgement.

'Fuck!'

Thank you, England's darling, and thank you again, lady of the Camay soap commercial. She caught my eye and smiled with her lips only. ''Scuse my French.' It was more or less the last thing she said for two hours. I walked the rest of the course with her. She walked one side of the course, I walked the other, and Dot Willis walked half a dozen paces behind. Ginny, the charming, gushing, laughing television person, had vanished. Her face was clenched shut like a trap. I could see that some strange alchemical process was going on behind those pinched features: her blazing fury was being transformed into diamond-hard competitive will. Every fence received the same long, hard assessment, all in deadly silence. She was surrounded by a cloud of cold, blue anger. Oh yes, Ginny is a delightful person, but don't let that fool you: she is also a competitor through and through, and athletes, successful athletes, have a strength of will that is almost tangible. Bill

Shoemaker, when I interviewed him for The Winners, was the affablest man in the world, but Charlie Whittingham had told me not to be fooled. He can switch competitiveness on and off at will. With Ginny during this walk, the competitiveness was turned on full. The forcefield that surrounded her was startling, almost fearsome. To oppose such a will would be like trying to carve up a diamond with a bread knife.

Competition began the following day: two days of solid dressage. Dressage is not to everybody's taste. In fact, it is probably the most boring sport ever devised. I happen to love it, myself. No other discipline tests horse and rider so thoroughly. Of course, at this level, it is hardly spectacular. Dressage is not just part of the three day event, it is also a sport in its own right, and at Grand Prix level it is more complex than you would believe possible. Three day eventers are no better than competent when it comes to dressage. The idea of the dressage test, performed when the horse is fully primed and oated up for the rigours of the cross-country test on Saturday, is to test the horse's – and the rider's – all-round ability. An event horse, and an event rider, must be jack of all trades and master of one, as the Colonel puts it. The scoring reflects this: the marks are mixed in the following proportions: dressage: endurance: show-jumping – 3:12:1.

This all goes to make the three day event the complete equestrian sport, and the top event riders are, I would say, the finest riders in the world. With the sun bursting through and bringing the temperature up to the 70s, and the heady prospect of the competition ahead, Badminton seemed to me a pretty good place to be. And as a bonus, even the press tent was a pleasant place. This is always so at equestrian events, and the reason for it is simple: many of the writers are female. The stale Y-fronts atmosphere you get in such places as football press boxes is quite absent. My friend and colleague from *The Times*, Jenny MacArthur, was showing me pictures of her new baby.

'If this was golf,' said Dudley Doust of the *Sunday Times*, 'people would be showing you pictures of their new mistress.'

'Well,' I replied, 'I never go to golf, I just don't understand it.'

'Since when have you found that factor inhibiting, Simon?'

Cheap shot, Dudley, cheap shot. And just for once, not even accurate: the one sport I can claim to know a tiny bit about is three day eventing: true Badminton as far surpasses my own efforts as greatest doth least, but I have been there. I know what it is like when your horse (or his rider) is too fired up to concentrate on his dressage. I know what it is like to suffer the agonies of imagined peritonitis before the start of the cross-country. I know, above all, what it is like to feel that pure-souled, wonderful mixture of exhilaration, relief and glory when it is all over: 'Oh, didn't he do well? Didn't he try hard? I'm so pleased for him, he gave me *everything* today.'

Non-riders may request the sick-bag at this point, but I am convinced that three day eventing is, in fact, the ultimate team sport. I am not talking about the slightly artificial international competitions, when our team of four riders tries to win Olympic Gold for Britain. I am talking about the highest, truest team of all – the team of horse and rider.

Most people think that eventing is an individual sport: Ginny against Lucinda, Ian Stark coming up on the blind side. But this is not an individual sport at all. I know – I have never been much cop at individual sports. I have a mental block that ensures that I always set my playing level just a couple of points below that of my opponent. With a vastly superior opponent I raise my game to stratospheric heights and fail to beat him by inches. With an inferior opponent, I allow my game to fall apart, so that he can steal an improbable victory. No mental strength, no character: that is probably the reason.

But when I play team sports I labour not to win the approval of my opponent, but that of my colleagues. In football and cricket, I can unstintingly give my poor all to the cause of victory. And to my surprise, when I first started competing on horseback, I discovered that the same was true. Individual terrors and foibles would vanish under the spell of team spirit. Me and my horse: it was us and them.

In racing, the relationship of horse and rider is at best fleeting. But eventers train their own horses, and ride them every day; the relationship is necessarily profound. At Badminton, it is the work of years that is on trial: the fruit of a real and lively two-way relationship between the horse and his rider. It is not a question of dominance and submission: it is co-operation, it is mutual sympathy. In eventing, you cannot get by with anything less.

I wrote something of this for the paper, and as I did so, I could almost hear the sound of scoffing readers. For some reason, the horsey sports provoke nothing less than hostility from some people. There is a kind of townee that thinks anything to do with horses is at best ludicrous: at worst, quite perverted. The football types you find on the sports desks of most newspapers always fall into this category.

People are derisive about what they believe is 'damned anthropomorphism', and think the whole business is dangerous and unhealthy. But I have a lot of time for anthropomorphism.

I think that those who most resent 'anthropomorphism', and those that most often invoke the term, are those that most dislike the essential truth of the business: that man is an animal. He is perfectly capable of having a two-way relationship with an animal of a different species. And of all the animals that get on with us, it is the horse that is the greatest. The nature of such a team, such a partnership, is the most profound.

That is why eventing is the greatest team sport of them all. It celebrates a partnership that crosses not just the barriers of individuality, or social background, or creed or colour or nation: it crosses the very boundaries of species.

The essential part of this relationship is, of course, trust. If two-way trust does not exist between horse and rider, than neither would ever dare face so much as the first obstacle at Badminton. Cross-country riding represents the highest exhibition of trust between two species ever witnessed.

On this thought, on into Saturday. Ginny's first horse, Master Craftsman, known as Crafty, had done well in the dressage. Her second horse, Murphy Himself, a bold, beautiful and slightly bastardly grey, had disgraced himself with a circus act right at the end of his test.

Cross-country day at Badminton is reckoned to be the third biggest single-day event in the world. The first is the Indianapolis 500; the second is the Indianapolis 500 practice day. Badminton pulls in getting on for a quarter-million people, yet the nature of the event is such that it disposes of them easily. They stroll about the park, they gather at the cunningly scattered jumps, they cruise the shops for Barbours and Hunter wellingtons. The event really works well, and on Saturday I abandoned the press tent – never much of a wrench – and strolled about the place like a normal person.

And a splendid, dramatic day it was. Ian Stark was in magnificent form, and it began to look as if he might do something quite unprecedented: take first and second place on his two horses. It looked as if only Ginny could trouble him: she had a splendid clear round on Crafty, and looked in great shape. She took Murphy Himself out for her second ride of the day, and then came disaster. It happened at the Ski Jump: the dreaded, horrible, ''scuse-my-French' Ski Jump. Murphy overdid it. No clever little pony, he scrambled down the slope to the trappy fence, and, in defiance of his rider's instructions, took off a stride too early, and to make up for this, made it a perfectly enormous leap. Murphy is a wonderful animal, and his motto is, if in doubt, jump it out. But his little difference of opinion with his rider saw Ginny exit sideways with remarkable velocity. She landed all wrong, turning her ankle agonisingly as she hit the ground. It was a sprain at the very least, and there was no way she could complete her round with Murphy. By

A week with Ginny Leng at Badminton sounded like an assignment made in heaven . . . but in that week I got to see her in triumph and disaster, and in sharper focus than she appears in her Camay soap commercial.
(*Kit Houghton*)

the end of the day, she was in third place with Crafty. Ian Stark was filling first and second. The only doubt was whether Ginny would be fit enough to ride the following day.

The last day, the Sunday, starts late, which gave Ginny further time to try and recover, and me hours in which to breakfast and read the papers. Dudley Doust had written an enormous piece on Ian Stark, so he would be gloating about the way the results stood. It was the Cup Final the following weekend, which would match Liverpool against Wimbledon. It was a classic confrontation: the elegant aristocrats against the turbulent, violent plebs of Wimbledon. Someone, I can't remember who, wrote, 'It is the traditional David and Goliath story, but no one is sure which one is Goliath.' I remember thinking at the time, I wish I had written that. Now I have. There was much talk of the Wimbledon hate-object, an uncompromisingly violent player called Vinny Jones. He had cultivated his over-zealousness to the point at which he boasted in a tabloid paper that when he met Kenny Dalglish he would 'tear his ear off and spit in the hole'. No Camay toilet soap contracts for Vinny Jones.

When I got to Badminton, there was no announcement about Ginny's riding plans. All I knew was that she had been pretty badly smashed up. All the same, I reckoned that she would ride. Preparing to compete is an agony, the few minutes before the off, with the knife of imaginary peritonitis in your guts, are unspeakable, but as Lorna Clarke, another eventer, said: 'You dread it, but if someone was to come up to you just before the start and say, "Oh, by the way, the cross country's been cancelled" – God, you'd be so disappointed.' Like stage fright, you dread to start, and when you get to the end, you want to start all over again. Ginny would ride.

I found Dot Willis at the collecting ring, and she said, 'Ginny will take one practice fence. She'll compete if that goes all right.' Ginny had spent the night with her ankle in ice: frozen peas are ever the athlete's friend in times of hurt.

Ice keeps a swelling down, but this time, not enough. Ginny, always so immaculately turned out, was wearing her usual beautifully polished boot on one leg, and a woefully scruffy ankle boot and a horse bandage on the other. She swung aboard Crafty with a wince, one she cunningly disguised as a smile (the one for which she uses her lips only) and set about the business of warming the horse up. Something about the lines of her body made two things absolutely clear: one, it bloody well hurt, and two, if you wanted her to stop competing you would have to drag her off by main force.

The practice fence presented itself, and she jumped it clean, gave a pleased smile, a genuine one this time, and told me as she trotted by: 'That's one jump out of the way, anyway.' And then into the ring; she jumped the lot, jumped a clear round. But then she would, wouldn't she? She dismounted; Ian Stark rode his two horses for first and second, a heroic achievement, and Ginny was so pleased for him she jumped up and down on her bad ankle before rushing off to cover him with kisses of congratulation. Ginny and Crafty were third.

There is no point in making too much of a thing about Our Brave Girl. Ginny jumped clear after spraining her ankle and damaging the odd ligament: well, there is not a competitor at Badminton, or any other sport for that matter, who would not do the same thing. All athletes would sooner face the death of a thousand cuts than miss a competition. It is the breath of life to them. It is what they dread, and what they love. When they get to the end, they want to start all over again. 'Oh he tried, didn't he try?' Ginny said, giving Crafty his fifteen thousandth pat of the day. 'He looked after me so nicely – I wasn't much help, was I?' You owe it to yourself to compete, above all you owe it to the team, to the horse. A sore ankle with mangled ligaments? That is nothing when weighed against the competitor's competitive will.

It is the same in every sport. All the Cup Final players would be prepared to play through red mists of pain just to be there at Wembley on Saturday. That is sport for you. In some respects, Vinny Jones ('I'll tear his ear off and spit in the hole') and Ginny Leng are brother and sister in competitiveness.

10. THE FIERCE AND TERRIBLE BATTLE FOR THE GOOD NAME OF BRITISH FOOTBALL

The Cup Final is, I suppose, the first thing people think of when they consider a sportswriter's lot. Imagine going to the Cup Final free. Imagine going there as a matter of course. Such excitement, such glamour!

Inevitably, a sportswriter sees it all rather differently. Unless he is even newer at the job than I am, he is unlikely to wake up on the day of the match trembling with eagerness. He won't be yawning and blasé, not if he is any good: this is the one football match of the year that everyone with the slightest vestige of interest in football will want to know about. Your views, your predictions, your expert analysis all reach a bigger audience than usual, and are read with greater attention. This is a day on which to get it right; this is a day to show what you can do. Accordingly, you don't go looking for a great match, you go looking for a great piece. If the game is deathly dull, and you come out with a searing analysis of modern coaching styles, then you have had a good Cup Final. You might have such a piece in your head when you arrive at Wembley, and be praying for a dull game.

I am in danger of overstating my case here – and a very familiar sensation that is, too – but the point is that sportswriters do not go to the Cup Final, or anything else, in the same state of mind as normal people. They might be fidgeting with nerves because they must get the goal-scorers' quotes in time for some ridiculously tough deadline; they might be writing for a Sunday paper, and at the Cup Final striving to do that impossible thing of being spontaneously profound. Or like the *Times* team, they might be writing for Monday's paper, and looking for something that will live beyond the discarding of the Sunday papers. Each journo will have his own tensions, and at the Cup Final, everyone wants to do a better-than-average piece. We don't march in singing 'ere we go, or considering how lucky and privileged we are to be there and let's hope it's a good game. We say instead, though we say it secretly, let's hope it's a good story, and that I get it . . . or at least, that I don't miss it.

The Times went into the match with a team of four. Stuart Jones, the football correspondent, was to write the match report, and Clive White, the football number two, was to gather the peripheral stories and the nannies – yes, even *The Times* collects the nannies, these being nanny-goats or quotes. David Miller, the chief sports correspondent was to go in and be David Miller, likely enough to be an analytical piece, for he has a rare eye for the course and balance of a football match. And me, I was to go which way the wind blew. In theory, David and I were in overlapping roles. I once asked David, when we were covering the same event, if we should liaise to avoid duplication. He gave the faintest Mona Lisa smile, and said, 'Would there be any point?' Well, I suppose not – the chances of David and I agreeing on anything are about one in infinity squared, at a rough calculation. David knows everything and everybody. He is rather like the brother of Sherlock Holmes, Mycroft, in that his speciality is omniscience. Expertise, political and tactical inside knowledge, and the poshest contacts in sport – all this is David's stock-in-trade.

I see my own speciality as ignorance. No clash.

In theory, the potential for a clash between David and myself is always there. We both cover a wide range of sports, we both like to write, and at length, on all issues, sporting, political and moral. This is not how it works in practice. We are not in opposition: we are temperamental opposites, but in a journalistic sense we are complementary. David is sober, serious, and awesomely knowledgeable. I play a looser, flakier role. I would not be able to do so without David as counterweight. He plays as centre-forward, head on, straight down the middle: I play in the hole behind him. David is a man of stature and ability, and working with him, even when in stark disagreement and mutual incomprehension, has always been good.

But there was one thing that David and I could hardly disagree on that day: this was a perfect writer's match. Liverpool *v.* Wimbledon: it was a classic contrast in styles and, as such, quite irresistible. Liverpool have been the subject of the most sycophantic media coverage in history. Their style, their class, their elegance, the gentlemanliness of their dynasty of managers, the legend of the sacred Boot Room, the charm and good-natured humour of their supporters. Liverpool have been made to stand for everything great and wise and noble in British football – or in the British character, come to that. This is something I find deeply suspicious.

Wimbledon, however, have become Great British hate-objects. They are depicted as men of brutal, illegal violence, and what is even worse, they don't play football in the Right Way. Now football writers like to see themselves as a pretty tough bunch. They wouldn't be seen dead at places like Badminton; they would consider my writing for the abolition of boxing as generally girlish as did Alan Hubbard. The idea of going to watch ice-skating would appal them. But they hate Wimbledon with all their hearts because Wimbledon don't win their matches the Pretty Way. They find the Wimbledon long-ball tactic aesthetically abhorrent. In short, when they come to write about Wimbledon, they all turn into a bunch of ballet critics. I find this quite hilarious.

They believe that there exists within the rules a morally right and a morally wrong way of winning a football match. This is a nonsense: you can play how you like within the rules, it is up to the exponents of the Beautiful Game to make their point in the result. Or no – maybe the answer is to introduce marks for artistic impression? When women's rowing first became a sport, they used to include marks for style as well as for the mundane business of rowing quickly. Oh, and Wimbledon get only 5.1 from the Russian judge!

In short, we had mighty, perfect, cherished Liverpool, against 'orrible ugly little Wimbledon. Trust Jim Lawton, my friend from the *Express*, to go just a little further than anyone else. 'Liverpool are fighting for the good name of British football,' he thundered. That, I thought, would do nicely when it came to teasing him in the bar before the match.

The classic Wimbledon story concerns their first trip to Anfield, home of Liverpool, to play a first division match. As the world knows, when visiting players step into the tunnel, they are confronted by a pompous notice that reads: 'THIS IS ANFIELD.' Dave Bassett, then their manager, led his team in the act of spitting, wetly, copiously and derisively, onto the notice before striding cockily onto the pitch. Wimbledon and Liverpool have always been miles apart in style and attitude and history . . . and in recent years, Wimbledon have had a slight edge.

I had, as I said earlier, spent a couple of seasons with Wimbledon when I was with the *Wimbledon News*, yet another title in the *Surrey Mirror* group. I was with them in their last season in the Southern league, when they had strutted over their rivals like aristocrats. In those days, they truly saw themselves as the Liverpool of non-League football, and they would have been mortified beyond belief if anyone had called them coarse and unsubtle. They were the standard-setters, and they were going to show those grubby fourth division boys a thing or two when they were elected to the League.

The following season, they were in League football, and I was still with the *Wimbledon News*. Mean old reality set in early. Wimbledon lost game after game. Allen Batsford, their manager, so tough and aloof the previous season, saw all his confidence evaporate. It was my task that season to send 200 words to the *Sunday Mirror* every home game, complete with nannies. At one game, poor old Batsford was more or less in tears after yet another defeat. As he saw me lurking about in a shifty way with my notebook, he made one awkward gesture, and said in a voice unlike his own: 'Just weren't good enough, were we?'

There was no answer to that then. But on Cup Final day, the consensus was that if Wimbledon didn't win, it would be because they weren't bad enough.

I got to Wembley good and early, had a beer or two, and chatted with friends. This becomes one of the pleasures of the big occasion: friends in the business are always there. I teased Jim about the good name of British football, and managed to dodge an argument with Patrick Barclay of the *Independent* about ballet criticism and the aesthetics of the long-ball game. Then out to watch the football. The press box at Wembley was at that time high over the pitch, remote from any 'atmosphere'. Very Olympian: you feel as if you are sitting there raising or lowering your thumb over an arena of bleeding gladiators, something that must suit my friend and colleague from the *Sunday Times*, Brian Glanville; Glanville, the Italophile, the polymath, the obsessive, the perennially spiky. He greeted me: 'Simon? How are you? How is that bastard — ? As they always say in Rome, *e pericoloso sporgersi*, don't you agree?' Or something along those lines anyway: the sound of trilling 'R's and rolling Italianate vowels always means you are in the Tottenham press box for a midweek game which Glanville, complaining bitterly about the inconvenience he has been put to, had been unable to resist.

Glanville was supplying copy for the *Sunday Times*; it would be stretching truth too far to say he was writing it. He has his own unique method for filing live from a match: he brings a piece of paper completely covered in 'X's. There are so many to the line. When he hears how many words are required of him, he marks off the requisite number of 'X's. Then, when he goes to the copy-taker, he has nothing before him but 'X's. He then produces his entire piece extempore (howling and cursing at the copy-takers as he goes) and as he speaks, he crosses out an 'X' for every word. It is an extraordinary method of working, but then, no one would expect an ordinary method of anything from Glanville.

Most writers had predicted an enormous victory to Liverpool. One or two had added to this prediction the hope that it didn't get too embarrassing a one-way match. Some went for such scorelines as 4–0. As you may recall, it didn't quite go like that. Wimbledon won 1–0, with Lawrie Sanchez scoring the goal, and the Wimbledon goalie, Dave Beasant, playing out of his skin, and saving a penalty as a bonus. Poor old Liverpool; poor old footy writers. The press box was filled with the sound of men wiping egg from their faces. The good name of British football, indeed: it was hard not to laugh, and I didn't try.

The silliest thing about the Wimbledon controversy was the sacred reputation of Liverpool. Deep in the psyche of every footballing person in the land is the legend that Liverpool Don't Kick. People, that is. Wimbledon brutal – Liverpool nice: this is seen as one of football's eternal verities. It is a transparent lie. McMahon kicked resolutely for Liverpool at the Cup Final; Souness kicked for Liverpool for years. But we have a need for heroes and for villains, that is part of sport's appeal, and so we have the irrational, downright false belief in Liverpool's sanctity. As a contrast, we have Wimbledon, and, cast as rough tough villains, they have played up to their cliché for all they are worth. Their mere reputation for ferocity has brought them more victories than anything any individual player could achieve.

I can't condone the genuinely dirty side of Wimbledon, of course not. But I have some sympathy for them. The League was finished as a competitive spectacle in 1983 when legislation was introducted by which the home clubs kept the gate receipts of every game. In one fell swoop, it was made certain that the rich would get richer, and the poor poorer. These days, only the vast clubs with enormous squads of players can afford to win the league. There are teams whose reserves would finish higher in the league than the first team of the little guys. Such teams as Charlton are playing in a different competition to Liverpool: Charlton aim not to win, but to finish the season round about mid-table. Their main target is to avoid relegation. To finish in the top ten is a triumph. League football has lost much of its point as a spectacle.

Cup games are different. Football, almost unique among team games, can produce an upset on almost any occasion. The freakish nature of a single 90-minute encounter, with the magic of team spirit, can make giants of the most hopeless team and incompetent bumblers of the mightiest men in the game. Wimbledon's miracle was to play Cup

The creation of a legend. Vinnie Jones, the symbol of Wimbledon's defiant awfulness, defies the caption writer's art alongside Paul Gascoigne, then with Newcastle United.
(Syndication International)

football every week of their season, surfing a wave of perversity and anti-snobbery to finish seventh in the League, and to win the Cup. This is the nearest any small club can get to the double. The greater miracle was not the Cup win, but the League position. It was a triumph and, just as importantly for the Wimbledon ethic, it was two fingers and a gob in the eye to all those who think that football is a form of ballet dancing, and those who think that the good name of football is something to do with the sanctified reputation of a single, favoured, 'non-kicking' football club.

The miracle of Wimbledon was accompanied by a result still more bizarre, though it did not get quite as much publicity. For some quite incomprehensible reason, the National Federation of Football Supporters' Clubs ended their season by voting me their Football Writer of the Year. This was as generous of them as it was bewildering. You might as well call Jim Lawton a boxing writer . . . something I did once, by accident and to his considerable amusement, a matter he still teases me about.

'What happened to your prediction for the Cup Final, Jim?'

'Well, dear boy, you can't expect a boxing writer to get it right every time.'

But me a football writer? That was stretching things even further. Jim does know a bit about boxing. I had to try and look like a football writer, so I even wore a suit when I went to collect my plaque. Members of football supporters' clubs are football nuts to begin with. Members of the National Federation of Football Supporters' Clubs are mad beyond all possible hope of redemption. They are the nutcases' nutcases, and a delightful bunch they turned out to be, as well. Proof of their basic lunacy, if proof were needed, came in the form of their award to me. I am the world's worst public speaker: on the extremely rare occasions when I get up and speak in public, I achieve a brevity that has long been absent from my writings. In a speech remarkable only for its laconic qualities, I wished them joy of their madness, and made my thanks as prettily as I could. These were nice people, who believe and trust in football: Jack-the-lads slipping out to the bar, men and women debating the future of the game as we know it with enormous seriousness and love. Wouldn't it be nice, I thought, as I went home staggering under the weight of my giant-sized plaque, if all football supporters were like that. It was a nice, sad thought with which to move into the cricket season.

11. STRANGE RUMBLINGS IN TRINIDAD: HOW CRICKET CORRESPONDENTS LIVE ON THE FAR EDGE OF SANITY

Yes, people say, but what sport do you like *best*? I still haven't found a complete answer to this one. I have discovered three ways of enjoying a sport: playing it, watching it, and writing about it. Each is completely different and to a large extent unrelated to the others. Let us leave the actual playing of it to one side for a moment; I will return to it in a later chapter (so there's something to look forward to). Let us move on to watching. Now, anyone who believes he is a sensible connoisseur of sport, a picker and chooser of the best things that sport has to offer, should try the ESPN test. It is one I fail every single time.

ESPN is a cable television channel in America. It brings sport 24 hours a day. In the morning you have aerobics, with glossy ladies performing unnatural acts; in the evening you can get four successive games of college basketball at the right time of year. True connoisseurs of sport do not find this a temptation. I do. But it gets worse. It is when you find yourself watching tenpin bowling, or tree-felling and log-rolling competitions that you must come clean and admit that you have an addictive personality. I have bizarre and unconquerable phases of being a television sports junkie. Competition is endlessly fascinating, no matter what form it takes. All sport requires is two people who believe that some kind of footling activity is serious enough, and you have a dramatic, and potentially explosive situation. That is sport for you. I love to see myself as a renaissance man. I would never, by any stretch of the imagination, call myself a sports nut. Oh yes, I have much wider horizons than that . . . why, then, do I find it almost physically impossible to switch off ESPN?

Imagine what it is like, then, when you work from home, and know that you have plenty to do, and that the deadline is pressing . . . and yet there is sport on the television. This would be a temptation for any normal person with an affection for sport, but a sportswriter has the most marvellous sop to his conscience. He can say to himself, well, watching sport is work too, isn't it? And the awful thing is that he is quite right – up to a point, anyway, I can avert my eyes in the sternest way from most sport on television during working hours. Wood-chopping and tenpin bowling would be no temptation to me. Bowls and snooker are things I can, with a revolting sanctimonious smirk, turn away from. But with the summer comes cricket: long, hypnotic, agonising, fluctuating days of it, and work can then become a very difficult thing. Of all sports, perhaps cricket is the most seductive.

It is a marvellous sport to write about. Cricket has more variables than any other. The complexity of the game, and the leisurely pace at which it unfolds combine to make it an almost perfect sport for the newspaper writer. The cricket correspondent must be the most envied journalistic figure ever created: imagine seeing all five days of every Test Match, imagine going to all those legendary places like the Gabba and Port of Spain, imagine rubbing shoulders with cricketers and cricket people every day of your life . . .

If you look at the job in purely journalistic terms, you still have an enormous amount to envy. Say you cover ten Test Matches in a year; that gives you 50 days in which your story will be guaranteed one of the most prominent places in the paper, where you will be one of the first things people turn to. You have the most glamorous and extensive exposure and you tackle wonderfully complex sporting, political and moral issues, for cricket has long been the most controversy-ridden game in the history of the world.

Yes, specialist cricket writers have an enviable job. There is only one drawback: the job is virtually guaranteed to send you off your chump. A long tour will have everyone, players and writers and all, barking mad.

Perhaps if you are single, and that by choice, and you are only truly happy in all-male company, the job is for you. I find that a trip of two-and-a-half weeks is about perfect; three months away from home every single year would send me, within three months – within six weeks – as batty as any cricket correspondent that ever lived. You see more of your fellow cricket writers than you do anyone else in the world. You spend every night eating and drinking with them. Why don't you lock yourself in your room with a decent book and get away from them once in a while, I asked one of them. 'I've tried that,' I was told. 'First of all, you think they've all got some great story, and you're the only one who's failed to get it. And then you think, they're all having a fantastic time somewhere and you're the only one missing out. And then you go down to see what's happening, as usual nothing is, and so you end up getting pissed in the bar as you do every night.'

For all its compensations, then, the job of a full-time cricket correspondent is one of the most mentally wearying in journalism. You have wonderful opportunities to write superb copy, and even more opportunities to go batty. The comparative sanity of many of the cricket correspondents represents to me a triumph of the human spirit.

I learned these essential truths when I spent a mere fortnight on a cricket tour, and that was quite enough for me. I had, as luck would have it, chosen a time when controversies of a sporting, personal and political nature had all assailed the tour simultaneously. This was in 1986, and I was flown out to Trinidad by my publishers in order to write the final chapter of my first book, *Phil Edmonds: A Singular Man. The Times* would play my living expenses and take some copy from me, but would not pay accommodation. They could not justify a second writer in Trinidad on any other terms. I put myself up at a delightful guest house in the hills of Maraval, just outside Port of Spain, and communicated with the office via a coin-in-the-slot telephone in the garden.

I made several forays around the island, and dropped into Port of Spain to watch the cricket, and to work with Phil. Ah, Edmonds – the cantankerous left-arm spinner, with his gift for controversy and the only man in history with whom Mike Brearley, the captain of legends, was unable to form a working relationship. Phil has always been a uniquely difficult man, never wholly trusted by his team-mates. 'I should have been a golfer,' he whinges every now and then. Phil is a weird as well as a singular man; I have always liked him. Working with him was never dull. Frances Edmonds, his wife, was in the throes of making her prodigious reputation at the time I was in Trinidad: she was writing a book that was to become the runaway bestseller *Another Bloody Tour*. Frances is one of the funniest ladies you could wish to meet, and, like myself, is an addict of the game of conversational ping-pong. She is gifted with a backhand kill-shot of epigrammatic violence.

There was the usual contingent of pressmen out there in Trinidad; all the regular cricket writers were doing their stuff. There was John Jackson, the charming and ruthless scandalmonger of the *Daily Mirror*, there was also the celebrated Ian Wooldridge of the *Daily Mail*, a man of great style and unbelievable consistency. The man never writes a duff piece, attacks every issue with verve and freshness, can use language like a flail when he gets across in print, which is fairly often, or can write with unabashed and still utterly readable sentimentality when it comes to such heroes as Denis Compton. He is a journalistic craftsman of the front rank. He is also a generous-spirited man: I was there in Trinidad, very much a tyro, and he went out of his way to greet me and say that he enjoyed my pieces in *The Times*. At that time, I had even less of a reputation than I have now, so I took this very kindly.

So, the English press contingent was large and impressive, and as we all gathered, so the tour fell apart in front of us. I sometimes wonder if cricket has yet recovered from that traumatic fortnight. England had beaten Australia out of sight over the summer of 1985, and they had gone to the West Indies to play for what was billed as 'the championship of the world'. Within a week, England had changed from cocky blokes who fancied their chances to a whimpering band of losers. They had just completed a Test match with the West Indies, and, on a frightening pitch at Sabina Park in Jamaica, the confidence of the entire batting side had been surgically removed. Gatting had gone home with his face caved in by a bouncer. A piece of bone was found embedded in the ball after it had struck him on the nose. Edmonds was proudly flashing the most enormous bruise in the world on his chest at the swimming-pool at the Port of Spain Hilton, and declaring that had he not been wearing a protective waistcoat, he would be dead.

Meanwhile, all of Trinidad was caught up in the politics of the tour and the morality of the members of the England team who had been part of the notorious rebels of the South African Breweries XI. The team coach was regularly bombarded by missiles, and pursued by catcalls and slogans. The team themselves shouted 'Rebs by the windows' whenever they got into the coach. Cricketers were advised not to go out alone. The corridor in the hotel was given a 24-hour armed guard; more guards stood around the swimming-pool and the lobby. This was an atmosphere conducive to paranoia and it spread like a stubble-fire. Scarcely a soul ever left the horrible Port of Spain Hilton, save to play cricket, and that was pretty horrible too. The siege mentality had taken over everyone in that cursed hotel: every day, as I took the local transport up into the hills again, I thanked the Lord for the peace of my little room in Maraval.

The journalists had problems enough of their own. The first two pressmen to arrive in Trinidad were arrested and locked up. Their gaol was a room in the Holiday Inn, but that didn't make it fun. The journalists were Matthew Engel, and a promising young writer called Geoffrey Boycott. Who was whose punishment, I asked Matthew later. Every journalist was obliged to purchase a work permit, something quite unprecedented in the history of cricket tours. This cost something like £100. I was lucky; arriving from London rather than on the team plane from Jamaica, I didn't have to pay, which was as well, because it would have taken most of my cash – all my own cash – for the trip.

The final drop of bat's blood in this witch's brew of trouble was Ian Botham. He was in desperate form at the time. The drugs scandal was still hanging over him, and he was obsessed with the idea of becoming a film star, which was the dream of his then agent, Tim Hudson. Botham was paranoid about absolutely everything, and was spending his days playing cricket very badly, and his evenings sulking in his room. He was in a poor way, and his great seething discontent hung over the team like a cloud. His vast personality added that little touch of resentment that the tour needed to slide off into disaster.

Botham's frustrations finally got the better of him in the Test match in Port of Spain. He apparently hijacked the bowling, and then went off into a fit of mad histrionics, shouting, waving his arms about, kicking the ball yards when an appeal was turned down. His first five overs went for 39, he bowled nine overs for no wicket and 64 runs. Nor was he the remotest bit unlucky. He just couldn't do it, he couldn't play cricket, and it was driving him mad.

I have written my share of hagiographies of Botham. He is the most talented cricketer I have ever seen. But this time, I wrote a piece that went the other way: for this was a woeful occasion. Botham made an idiot of himself that day, and just about all of us in the press box wrote as much, in our various ways.

The row that greeted this was cataclysmic. On a still day, you can stand at the top of the Port of Spain Hilton and still hear the bang. At last, the poor, beaten, frightened players had an enemy. The bastard press – yes, it was all their fault! No wonder everything had gone wrong!

For it happened that Reuter's news agency, reading the consensus of criticism against the superstarring Botham, decided there was something for them. They wrote a short piece on the 'fierce criticism' that Botham had received in the English press, and sent it round the world. Naturally, they quoted some of this criticism. Equally inevitably, it was to the columnists they turned: columnists are supposed to write quotable lines, after all. 'For much of the gruelling Test Match here, Ian Botham has worn the disgruntled scowl of the street bully who has met his match,' Wooldridge wrote. I was quoted too: 'He must take a healthy slice of blame for the parlous state England are now in in this Test Match,' – which is a hideous phrase, with those two 'ins', but never mind. Wooldridge and I both wrote that players had confided in us that the previous tour, in India, had been much happier because Botham had not been there.

Oh, the rage of that day. The players decided that Phil Edmonds had primed me to write this, which was not true, but none of the players has ever really trusted Edmonds – not because he is untrustworthy, but because he has never found it easy to be a comfortable part of any team he has been in. However, Phil was given a hard time because of what I had written, which was rough on him. Phil was another person the players could blame, and they seized the chance avidly; still, Phil has always been capable of looking after himself. And as a point of information, it was not Phil, but another player, a rank-and-file member of the squad, that had bent my ear most strongly on the 'happy tour of India' theme, and even now I might as well keep his name hidden. He was hardly the only person in the squad to hold such a view. Phil and I had a titanic row about it, which we settled over rather a lot of drink. This is an unaccustomed indulgence for Phil, but these were exceptional times.

The specialist cricket writers also felt betrayed by the columnists, and particularly by me, as the tyro. How dare I foist my opinions, when I was just a jumped-up, wet-behind-the-ears, etc. Needless to say, both Wooldridge and I were judged on quotes taken out of context, which for a journalist is about as comprehensive an example of being hoist with your own petard as you can get.

To make things worse, there was an official meeting between press and players, and tempers were comprehensively lost on both sides. Fortunately, I missed that; no one sent word to me up at Maraval, and just as well. Wooldridge and I were blamed for the breakdown in relationships between press and players, but an accord of a kind was reached: we were only rotten columnists, moral degenerates who did not have the best interests of the game at heart. Better still, we were both catching planes to London.

I am happy to say that despite all this excitement, I remain on the best of terms with Phil and Frances, and also with David Gower, the beleaguered captain on the tour. It was all years ago, and I can go into cricket press boxes without being hissed. And, in a bizarre way, it was the most fascinating of experiences, and it taught me that neither the lot of an England cricketer nor that of a cricket correspondent, is altogther enviable. The glory of either position can be considerable, but both earn it desperately hard.

After I had finished *A Singular Man*, I stopped going to the cricket as much as I had been. I had been covering cricket more than any other sport for about 12 months, and a break was therapeutic; no doubt cricket was pleased to have a break from me. But in 1988, with the West Indians back, I found the same tangled web of politics, personalities and sport ensnaring me once again. As the cricket season got into its stride, so I found myself again and again in front of the television, promising that at the end of the over . . . at the end of the next over . . . well, at tea certainly, I would go back to the keyboard and process some more words.

I started going to the cricket again. I went to one of the one-dayers – you may remember that England won all three, which gave the summer a false dawn of uncanny brightness. Were England about to take on the West Indians for the championship of the world? Hm.

The cricket writers get very fed up with all the endless one-dayers, which is a classic example of writers and spectators having different perspectives. One-dayers are great entertainment, but you can have too much of them, and every cricket writer has long ago reached the stage when he cannot tell one match from another in his memories. And the cricket writers see them all, get mesmerised by them, find them impossible to take with due seriousness. This is one of the occupational hazards of every kind of sportswriting: you end up hating what you started out loving.

I caught a fair bit of the cricket that summer, without writing any major pieces. On one journey, I think to Nottingham, I found myself in a train compartment with Phil Edmonds and Mike Brearley, which in theory was a highly combustible mixture. Edmonds had claimed in the book that he and Brearley were always polite to each other these days, and that all their terrible rows were part of the deeply buried past. Both behaved admirably on the journey; indeed, with flashes of amiability, for they used to be good friends before becoming so fiercely opposed. Phil is difficult, but Brearley is not the world's easiest man himself; certainly he can be charming and affable, but, like any athlete who has made his mark, he has a ruthlessly tough streak in him. It comes across as emotional coldness, a chilly determination to defy and to win. He is very civilised, very pleasant, very urbane: but that atavistic, antagonistic streak in him is a part of his nature. He is a fascinating fellow, and it was fascinating to watch him and Phil make their subtle no-hostilities pact in the train carriage, and talk, mostly on cricket, for the duration. I wonder, had I not known the tensions of their relationship – and I know about them better than most, since Phil has given me chapter and verse, and Mike has talked about the relationship to me with all the considerable objectivity he can muster – if I would have guessed anything of their troubled history, their carful, tense accord of the present day. Not for the first time, I enjoyed the privileged insights the profession of sportswriter can bring – and, not for the first time, this did not come in a straightforward way.

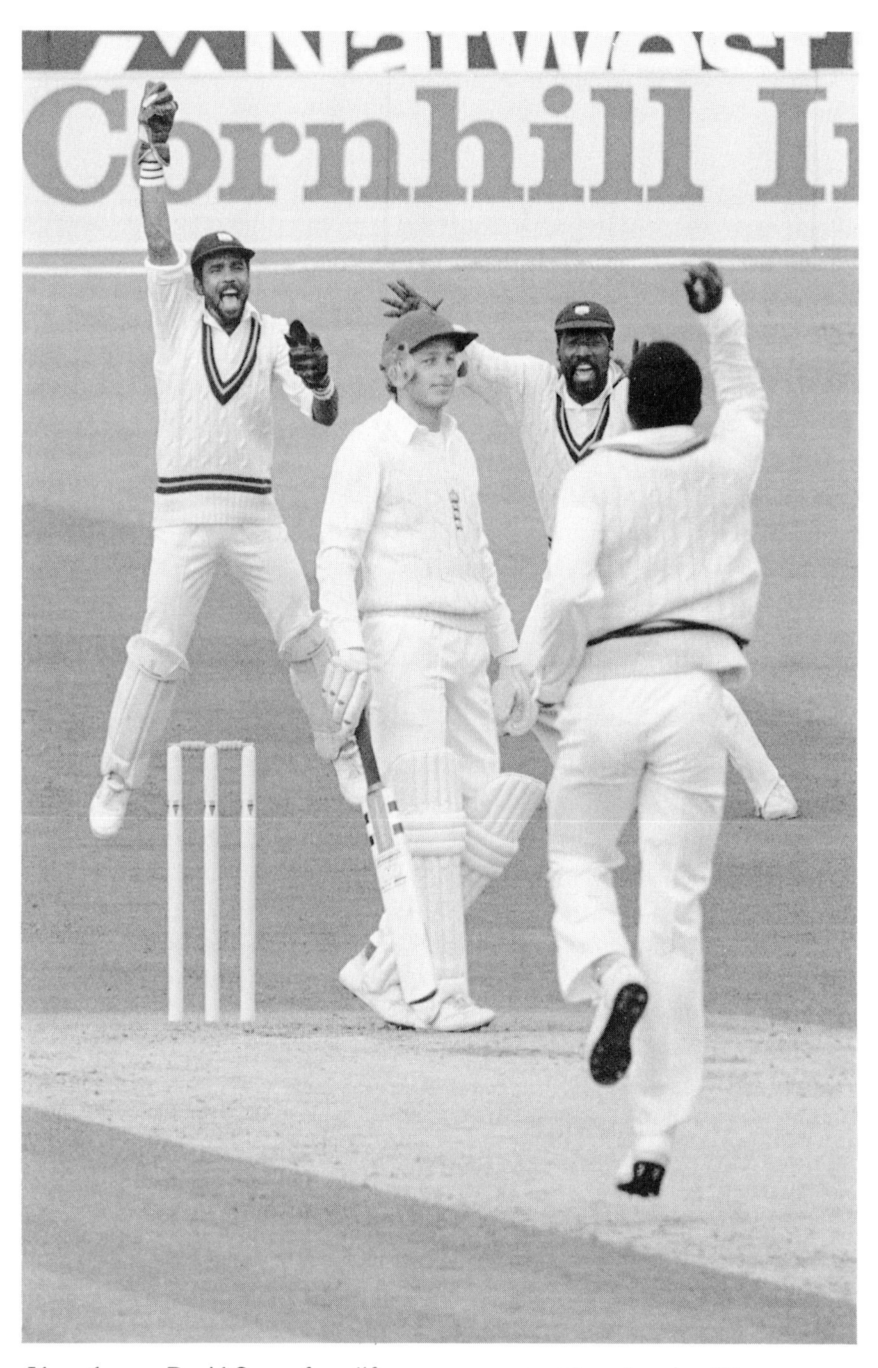

I love the way David Gower faces life as an unrepentant flawed genius. His every dismissal spoils my day. Here he goes again.
(Patrick Eagar)

The first Test was drawn, under the captaincy of Mike Gatting. I watched practically all of it: I went one day, and the rest I saw on the television. It is not just the fascination of the game that keeps a sportswriter engaged; there is also the odd matter of personal loyalty. I find this most strongly with David Gower. Now I do not for a minute claim to be an intimate friend of his, merely that we have got on reasonably well on the dozen or so times we have met. He is an amiable fellow and besides, I find his notion of attacking life as an unrepentant flawed genius rather appealing. I always want him to do well, and his failures are painful to me.

George Plimpton, the American writer, once wrote: 'One thing that Ernest Hemingway had always told me was that it was a bad idea to get to know an active fighter and become involved in his career. Sooner or later he was going to get hurt in the ring, and beaten, and it would be an almost unbearable thing to see if he were a friend.' To watch a batsman suffer the little death of dismissal has a touch of the same thing.

Sport is a precarious business; it is supposed to be. In some ways, precariousness and uncertainty are the *point* of sport. Sport is even more precarious than real life; sport is life exaggerated. A sportswriter tends to spend quite a lot of his time watching people he knows and likes performing tasks fraught with difficulty and precariousness in front of a brutally critical public. They face opponents whose lives and careers depend on their seizing the chance to do your friend down: the human dimension of these epic confrontations of sport is something that always overwhelms me when I have the smallest personal stake in what is going on. The notion of human frailty, the fragility of the great, the worries of the mighty, the uncertainty and insecurity that make up the day-to-day life of every athlete; it is these things that become the daily concern of the sportswriter, these things that create and make incurable the sportswriter's addiction to sport.

There is a special kind of pleasure when people whom you know do well, a pleasure that is made greater every time by earlier fears for their failure. The pleasures of such vicarious success are great. Worry and insecurity are an athlete's life; to worry about an athlete as an acquaintance is to get just a glimmer of what it must be like to do their job. And it is then that I know that I am the one whose job is enviable. For me, worry is a self-indulgence. For them, it is a way of life.

It was after the first Test match that the cricket season exploded into nonsense. Gatting was sacked after he made the tabloid press for alleged nocturnal romping with a barmaid. John Emburey got the job in his stead, and led England out for the second Test at Lord's. I greeted this with the most barbed piece I had written on cricket since Ian Botham in Trinidad. Actually, I like Embers, and his dogged, foul-mouthed way of approaching life, his grinding, attritional bowling and his eccentric batting. But I could not understand why he was captain of England.

For a start, sacking Gatting at the behest of the tabloid press for the crime of being found out, seemed to be profoundly hypocritical. But Emburey? Sharpening my clauses, I attacked him for his involvement in that web of lies and deception that brought about the South African Breweries tour, a tour that was a complete betrayal of English and of international cricket. The lavish sponsorship was made possible by huge tax concessions to the sponsors; this, it was quite plain, was not sport but politics, a piece of international public relations designed to show that apartheid is really all right. Emburey and the rest had served their three year ban from international cricket before being reinstated as players, but to make him captain was a different matter, I thought. I have nailed my liberal colours to the mast enough times in the paper on the South African issue, so I will not continue here. My last paragraph was: 'It was true that Gatting's late night damaged the *image* of the game. But the actions of Emburey and Gooch damaged the heart and soul of international cricket. They were appointed as captain and vice-captain on Nelson Mandela's birthday.'

The last line was asking for it rather, and of course, the letters from the right-wingers came in with the usual hectoring obstreperousness. As ever, there were some letters of support as well, something I find very cheering indeed. The piece went in on the first day of the Lord's test, which, as luck would have it, was the day I had planned to make my first visit to the Lord's press box since the excitements of Trinidad. Many of the cricket reporters take the opposite view to me on the South African issue: I went into the press box above the Warner Stand feeling, once again, like a character in a Bateman cartoon: The Man Who Mentioned Nelson Mandela In The Lord's Press Box. I sat next to Matthew Engel from the *Guardian*, a manoeuvre of shameless cowardliness. 'I may as well congratulate you on your piece, because no one else will,' he said welcomingly.

But in fact, journalists are not a vindictive bunch. We have to be pretty tolerant to put up with each other. Naturally, the odd jibe was thrown at me, but on reasonably good-tempered, bantering terms. It was a pleasure to be back in the press box.

As luck would have it, Tom also turned up to watch a little cricket. We left the ground together in a taxi, and discussed Projects and

Notions on the way. Wimbledon tennis was looming alarmingly, and yes, of course I would be involved there. And before that, I was to go to Germany, to do a piece on what was universally reckoned to be the most powerful body in world sport: Adidas.

12. THE CASH-LORDS OF SPORT: POWER, MONEY, INFLUENCE AND A NARROWLY MISSED SLAUGHTER

This is a tale of the day I rubbed shoulders with some of the mightiest men in sport, and how, in sober truth, I came within a hair's breadth of killing one. This little event I tossed off with a mild curse: that is the way we globe-trotting journalists are trained to react.

It is a tale about Adidas. Let me employ the flashback technique once again, and dissolve to 1986 and the Commonwealth Games. This horrible boycott-soured event was held in Edinburgh, and it all got so depressing that, despite being accredited to the event, I ended up boycotting it myself. But because I was on the list, I received a lucky bag through the post. It contained two different sorts of bag, a T-shirt and a woolly, both with 'UK Press' and a Union Jack embroidered on the left tit, a waterproof top with the same thing in the same embarrassing place and, the *pièce de résistance*, a pair of sparkling training shoes, the kind you get chucked out of the Café Royal for wearing. They were good shoes: I climbed up a mountain in Bali in them. I mention this for the simple pleasure of showing off.

The lucky bag was a present from Adidas. I still have absolutely no idea why I was sent all this stuff, but every single British press person accredited to the event got the same little postal surprise. Even today, you still see people wearing the shoes in the press box at some events. Well, my motto here is simple and strong: I can never be bought – but please don't let that stop anyone trying.

Adidas have a high profile in sport, rather as Everest has a high profile in mountains, or Papa Doc Duvalier had a high profile in Haiti. Adidas: *die Marke mit den drei Streifen*. Pick a sport, ladies and gentlemen, any sport, and what do you see? You see contestants wearing triple-striped shoes, triple-striped shirts, triple-striped shorts. Every contestant will, on the left tit, display the trefoil, the Adidas logo. You might see the athlete strip off his triple-striped track-top to reveal his triple-striped vest beneath. And of course his shoes: whether he is running at the speed of light, booting footballs into next week or clattering tennis balls, his shoes will bear three stripes. Even Nelson Piquet wears triple-striped boots – fireproof Adidas boots. Adidas themselves look pretty well fireproof.

And they are not simply a boots and shoes company. Adidas has a subsidiary called International Sport and Leisure, or ISL, which acts as the sole agent for the Olympic Games – not a bad little contract, that – and, as a small extra, controls sponsorship and advertising for the football World Cup. For a long while, Adidas was run and dominated by one man, the late Horst Dassler, who had acquired the journalistic cliché 'the most powerful man in sport'. This description did not overstate the truth one iota.

So I was not a little intrigued when Adidas invited me to Germany to visit their headquarters. They would fly me out, and hope I would write a piece about how lovely Adidas was. In such cases, there is no deal, no insistence that I write something, nor to vet any piece I might write. Just an invitation, in apparent benevolence. For the journos who spend most of their time in the office, such trips can be a welcome relief.

I spend almost every day of my life away from Wapping, so that was no incentive. The incentive I needed was a decent story. I told Adidas I would be happy to come along, if they could fix me up an interview with John Boulter, a Brit who is promotions director worldwide for Adidas, and a former Olympic miler, a 'nearly top runner' as he described himself. Adidas went into a huddle, decided this was a good idea, fixed the interview and so, frantically doing last-minute research about Adidas, I flew out to Germany.

I was met at Nuremberg airport, and whizzed off to the Adidas headquarters, in a place called Herzogenaurach. The first little delight they had for me was a trip to their Shoe Museum, a prospect that had my heart sinking to the level of my own unstriped boots. The shoes themselves were less than enthralling, but the reverence with which they were displayed said a great deal about what Adidas think of themselves. The firm was started by Adolf Dassler, the father of the late Horst. He was known as 'the victor's cobbler', I was told; he was also called Adi – Adi Dassler – hence Adidas. One of the most holy objects in this temple of boots is the pair in which Jesse Owen won his four gold medals. They only had two stripes; Adi introduced the stripes of stiff leather to strengthen his creations, and only subsequently decided that the look was also groovy, especially when you put a third stripe in.

I was shown around the shrine by a charming German lad, built like a wall, wearing shining new triple-striped shoes and carrying a trefoil on his shirt in the only possible place. He showed me a picture of Adi with the West German football team at the World Cup final in 1954. Adi changed their studs at half-time, and the Germans went out and won. They even had some archive footage of the game.

'Do you, ah, have any film of the 1966 World Cup final?'

'No – and it voz never a goal!'

'Ask the Russian linesman, mate.'

After this pleasantly infantile exchange, I was taken to a hotel. They were very sorry, but it was not the Adidas Hotel. The Adidas Hotel was full, this was another hotel, but it was quite near the Adidas Hotel, and we would all go there for an Adidas meal in the evening. The hotel was full of Adidas people, swimming in the Adidas pool, playing tennis on the Adidas court (guess what they wear when they do it), eating Adidas food, drinking lots of Adidas drinks, and, if they wished, throwing up on the Adidas floor.

We gathered together, a handful of journos and a couple of PR women. This had all the makings of a sticky evening. I normally find it impossible to deal with PR women. They always seem so interested in everything you say, but all the time you can tell that you are boring them to death. PR ladies like men who look comfortable in suits, and people who don't feel self-conscious about holding long, one-sided conversations on mobile telephones in public places . . . or long one-sided conversations with PR ladies, for that matter. My own lack of any redeeming social graces registers instant despair on the face of the average PR girl. Knowing that I won't know how much my house is worth now, can't talk about my car because I haven't got one and couldn't drive it if I did, and have no idea of how the correct amount of social flirtatiousness is delivered, they are reduced to talking to me about sport. With the meal comes relief, they can now talk about vegetarianism: 'And I'm almost a vegetarian myself, but I do love an enormous rare steak, and I don't think I could ever . . .'

But this was a very jolly evening. Jenny Cropper turned out to be a human being disguised as a PR lady, and she led a merry party through all the Adidas food and drink. For that relief, much thanks.

The following day, I was in another aeroplane, this time heading for Frankfurt, in order to meet John Boulter for this famous Adidas interview. At this time, the European Football Championship was just starting, which meant that, along with the odd footballer, the power-brokers of world sport were gathering. I had arranged to meet Boulter at a hotel that was right at the centre of the dealing. Drop a bomb on the place, I thought, and you would alter the balance of power in world sport for ever . . . I thought this little realising how close I was to come to causing mayhem and death myself that day.

I was early, and waited in the lobby bar, sipping a beer and getting my eye in. All around me people were greeting each other with that particular combination of effusiveness and wariness that characterises all dealings of businessmen. This was a great financial cosy-up; there was a giant cocktail party already in full swing, and a vast lunch to follow. One company was paying for one, another for the other: it didn't really matter which, for no one would be paying for a thing with his own personal lolly. This was a chance to feed oneself, true, but more important than that, it was one of the great opportunities to feed one's self-esteem. The only reason for being here was that you were important. You shook hands, you talked, you talked business. The football was starting – that is what made all this lovely business possible. This was sport in the 80s: men in suits holding drinks and talking millions. I was as much an outsider here as any footballer would have been.

Right at the centre, at the still point of the turning wheel, was Adidas. Adidas shoes are sold in 160 countries. Perhaps 30 per cent of the shoes are used for playing sport. The rest go in what the Americans call the leezhure market, and English people call leisure. In short, these are the shoes in which you walk to the fridge to collect your beer when the big match is on telly. Was this why the European Championship was being played, I wondered – so that when you needed a new pair of shoes to walk to the fridge in, you chose a pair *mit den drei Streifen*?

And then Boulter arrived. He stood out from the crowd with effortless ease. Everyone was wearing a suit (including me – how about that, wearing a suit twice in three chapters?) but he was wearing a sports jacket. Everyone looked effusive: Boulter looked vague. He looked like a schoolteacher who had forgotten where he put the board-duster. It needed only a pipe to complete the picture. I introduced myself.

Boulter smiled benignly and said, 'Oh – ah – hello.'

The impression of vagueness is probably one of the most bogus fronts in the history of sport. But the schoolmasterly presentation is wholly genuine: Boulter was a very ordinary schoolteacher before he was asked to join the power-brokers. His affability was also perfectly genuine. He took me to one of the cocktail parties, and, as power was broked and millions were flung about the conversational airwaves all around us, he spoke into my tape recorder with unruffled benignity, despite the hostility of my questions.

Normally, I am reasonably friendly in my interview technique,

John Boulter (right), in 1969 a nearly-top runner for Britain; in 1988 one of the most powerful men in world sport.
(*AllSport*)

hoping to elicit response by asking sufficiently challenging questions. Here, I thought I would do better by adopting a more adversarial position. 'Horst Dassler said the company is simply in the business of selling boots and shoes. How false-naïve is that?'

'Well, it's the bottom line for us. We have other lines of equipment and clothing . . . but yes, we're in the business to sell. If you've read Denis Howell's report, you'll know that they were very critical of our wider involvement.'

'Yes – so we wonder if the Olympics are being run for the benefit of a bootmaker.'

'But they are not. The Olympics are not being run by us, the European Football Championship is not being run by us. We started ISL because sports leaders were always coming to *us*, coming to Horst in particular, to ask for advice, assistance, particularly on the financial side. They'd say we want to do this, we'll make money once we are going, we'll need to rent an office, though, but when the world championships actually start, we'll get the money back . . . a lot of people wanted practical assistance. And because Horst was very clever – he'd grown up in sport, seen the way things had developed – they'd come and discuss it with him. They'd come to us for money and ideas.'

As ever, one seeks the conspiracy theory in vain. No one ever seems to get organised enough to run a global conspiracy. Don't bother to look for conspirators; look for the opportunists, and after that, for the survivors. The Dasslers, both Adi and Horst, were certainly opportunists. 'It seems extraordinary,' I said, 'that the Olympic Games and the World Cup, the two biggest shows on earth, have been turned into a cosy family business.'

'If you work with somebody for a long time, you end up being friends,' Boulter countered unemphatically. 'Horst was very influential. I worked with him for 20 years, so I don't find it extraordinary at all.'

As Boulter explains it, the diversification from boots and shoes into the unabashed money- and power-broking of ISL was a logical extension of Horst Dassler's personality. He was a man long on both ideas and money, and naturally people came to him for either or both. ISL was simply the formalisation of all this.

Throughout the interview, I had the constant feeling that I was missing something. I had plenty of good, well-aimed questions, but I scarcely laid a glove on Boulter. I had read a number of hostile pieces about Adidas, with great attention, and they all seemed to me to be rather half-cocked. Adidas were criticised for having such enormous influence . . . well, there is no doubt about it, their influence is vast and reaches everywhere in sport. But no one managed to go a step on and prove that their influence is used for ill. Obviously, the scope for harm at Adidas is immense. But there is a difference between potential and actual harm.

'I think we are one hundred per cent benign,' Boulter said, to my rising eyebrows. 'We try to help ourselves, and what we do has to have some meaning behind it. We have to link the company and its logo with sport. It's not pure charity. But having said that, I really do believe that we are bringing something to sport.' Up-and-coming athletes, great and small sports teams all over the world, get help from Adidas. Mostly this comes in the form of kit. In the Soviet Union, the stuff became so fashionable that the Jack-the-lads coined a word meaning fab and generally groovy: *adidovsky*.

The rise of Adidas is part of the ascent of sport as a panglobal political and commercial monster. It all comes down to television. Sport (with the possible exceptions of tenpin bowling and lumberjacking) is, perhaps, what television does best; television brings to millions what Boulter described rather neatly as 'that unique top-of-the-moment thing that sport alone offers'. Television has revolutionised sport and changed the nature of the athletes. The wages of stardom can be enormous; the amateurs of track and field are now giants, and a gold medal in the right hands can be worth a fortune: a fortune for the athlete – and a fortune for the companies that ride on his back, or on his left tit.

Sports arenas have become the greatest billboards in the world. If you get MacDonalds, or Camel cigarettes behind the goal at the World Cup final, you will get exposure to millions upon millions. But it costs you. Adidas do better than that: they have their advertisement worn by all 22 players, and all it costs them is time, trouble, and lashings of free kit. A trifle. It is the simple brilliance of that notion that has allowed Adidas to achieve the highest profile anyone has had in the history of sport. You can't get more *adidovksy* than that.

The interview ended, and Boulter, very civilly, invited me to lunch, and some non-adversarial conversation. We went to the official lunch: I wasn't supposed to be there, but with Boulter alongside, even I failed to get thrown out, something that says a great deal about Boulter. The room was packed with power people, the head of the German Football Association, Hermann Neuberger, or 'Hermann the German' dominating one table, and men of power and stature everywhere you looked. The floor was packed, and Boulter's party was accommodated on a small balcony above the main dining area. The balcony was surrounded by very pretty lamps, all decorated with a trio of glass globes, each one of these the size of a football. They were about four feet from the ground if you were standing on the balcony, or 20 feet above your head if you were scoffing your food with Hermann the German below.

I was given the corner seat – awkward to get to. I shuffled my way between the chair-backs and the edge of the balcony, a passage about nine inches wide. I nudged something as I passed, but thought nothing of it. One second later, there was the most heart-stopping explosion of glass, followed by a long moment of perfect silence. I had dislodged one of the glass globes. It had plummeted 20 feet down and shattered. Fortunately, it shattered on the floor, not on the head of Hermann the German. Death had been averted; a personal disaster had not. I had a moment of perfectly genuine anger. Without even looking back, I snarled, 'What a bloody *stupid* place to put a lamp.' I sat down with a furious, aggrieved expression on my face.

I consider this a minor triumph. I wish I could use this principle more often: never apologise. Always blame someone else. Perhaps I have a place in corporate business after all.

Lunch was pleasant. I chatted with Boulter, a most amiable man, and his wife Sally. She was a horse person, and particularly fond of dressage, so we swopped dressage stories with great glee.

'You thought that was embarrassing?' I said. 'I remember when one horse I had was doing his first dressage test before an audience, and was in a right state. Then he caught sight of the judge in her mirror-shades, and was so startled he leapt straight out of the ring. Then he tried to get back, and broke one of the dressage boards by tripping over it.'

Lunch ended, I made my farewells and left for the airport and home. I left the world of the power-brokers with some relief, and with a great deal of unsatisfied curiosity. Wealth and power fascinate me: I could sit and look at them for hours. And Adidas is in a uniquely powerful position. It is, I suppose, far better that such power should be concentrated in the hands of a bootmaker, rather than with people selling booze, or cigarettes, or, God help us, ideology. But all the same, a company with such power, such potential for good or for mischief, needs watching all the time, watching like a hawk. We all know what power does, and we know what absolute power does as well.

13. *DALLAS* WITH BALLS: A FORTNIGHT WITH THE GREAT JAZZ-MAN OF WIMBLEDON

When Wimbledon comes *The Times* is represented not in single spies, but in batallions. It is very much our kind of event. The pop papers will send maybe as many as two people to cover the tennis, plus a couple more for the naughty vicars and other classic Wimbledon stories. But we go there mob-handed. Rex Bellamy, our tennis correspondent, leads us into action (perhaps I mean leads us over the top), and another tennis writer, Richard Evans, adds to the fire-power. David Powell adds still more; he is our sports news editor, and also a tennis nut, and it is physically impossible to keep him away from Wimbledon, so we may as well profit from it. He tends to cover the British players – he is Losing Brit Correspondent. Plus there is David Miller and me, each of us trying to get to the best match on any given day, and to tell the world what is *really* going on.

A few years ago, I hated Wimbledon. The prissiness of the event used to get right up my nose. I used to come home wailing about the queues, the people who keep saying 'sorry' when you tread on their feet, and the self-satisfied way in which people ate their strawberries. At the same time, I used to feel a certain desperation when it came to finding the right match, or the right story. But these days I find it extremely pleasant. I have got it in perspective now, largely thanks to the fact that I cover a fair few big international events abroad. It is now blindingly obvious to me that Wimbledon is an international event. It is not a local event at all, but there is the disorientating fact that you don't arrive there in an aeroplane or live in a hotel. You go home on the tube. It is all very throwing until you have got it worked out.

But it is a good event to cover. For a fortnight, Wimbledon is in the forefront of everybody's mind. People want to read about it: what, for a writer, could be better than that? And these days, I know most of the British journos and a good few of the foreigners, which is a pleasant bonus. It is in some ways a very easy event to cover on a brief like mine. You find a match – try and make it an early match, in order to establish a comfortable relationship with the deadline – write your piece at leisure in the press room, put it over in the nice, quiet telephone room. We have our own phone, so I am not expected to fight for the right to dial.

It is all very slick and very organised there, and, as a further bonus, there is Rex Bellamy. At Wimbledon in 1988, he was pushing 60 with some force, which makes one wonder how hideous that picture in the attic must be looking. He looks like an unusually spry 40-year-old. He is also what America would call 'the dean of tennis writers'. He always dresses for Wimbledon with immense care. My own favourite is an outfit which he favours at least once during the fortnight: a green shirt that he bought from C & A. The shirt bears the images of various musicians, plus the word 'Jazz' repeated here and there in *Sun*-headline size. Mr Bellamy is a discreet and tasteful man, and wears the shirt with scarlet trousers.

A few years ago, the Association of Tennis Professionals (the players' union) decided it would be a good idea to have a Tennis Writer of the Year Award. It lasted for five years, and Rex won it every single year. After that, they scrapped the idea: it was quite obvious that no one else was ever going to win it. Chris Evert calls him 'Sexy Rexy'. You simply cannot argue with facts like that.

Rex also happens to be the world's easiest man to work with. When it comes to sharing out the stories, he is generous almost to a fault: 'No, no, no, *you* do McEnroe.' Wimbledon is a long fortnight of pretty hard work, but Rex makes it a pleasure. The first week is particularly mad: there are big matches in all kinds of odd places, seeds crash and tumble on unreachable courts, deadlines occur in the middle of vital matches; and once you have written, you have the hideous task of writing a completely new and, God willing, fresh piece for the second edition. Such things would panic a tyro, but Rex is way beyond panic. With his pipe going nicely and a bottle of Sainsbury's Chilean Riesling ('£1.79, not bad, eh?') at his side, he writes, makes jokes and answers my questions ('How many times did McEnroe win the . . . ?') all without missing a beat or suffering from any suggestion of the possibility of the failure of his sense of humour.

For us at *The Times* Wimbledon is the biggest tennis tournament. For the pops, it is more or less the only one. Britain suffers for a fortnight every year from the illusion that it is a nation of tennis lovers. This is because, for reasons of history, the most prestigious tennis tournament in the world is played in Britain. But it is not tennis but Wimbledon that is so well loved. It is loved not because of the drop-shots and the see-saw tactical affrays, but because of the personalities on view; the sudden rises, the dramatic falls, the rows, the impossible victories, the hideous defeats. Wimbledon is loved not because of the sport but because of the soap opera side of things that only Wimbledon can activate in tennis.

Barry Hearn, the snooker entrepreneur, said that snooker was '*Dallas* with balls'. Wimbledon is also *Dallas* with balls, and it is also that impossible thing, *Dallas* with scarcity value. Once a year, Wimbledon is a feast of shifting relationships, changing patterns of power and the passing of eras. Naturally, this is all meat and drink to a columnist. The basic pattern of work is that Rex takes the main stories and issues, Richard Evans takes a match, I take a personality, and David Powell sweeps up the Losing Brits. He would be the busiest. We make that joke every year.

This year, Tom had decided that in principle, David Miller and I would go to Wimbledon on alternate days. This prevented the paper having what one might vaingloriously call too much of a good thing. As luck would have it, I was there for the first day of Wimbledon fortnight, which is always a good writing day. The first match on the Centre Court is by tradition (or, as we say at Wimbledon, Tradition) the defending men's singles champion against some no-hoper or other. The match itself is nothing, and Rex knows that, come the quarter-final stage, he is likely to be writing about the defending champion just about every day. He wants to keep his powder dry, so it is natural for me to take the match instead. I write about the personality, the soap opera side of the match. In 1988 the defending champion was loathsome Pat Cash: Cash of the chequered headband, the protocol-busting climb after he had won the men's single the previous year, Cash who told us that women's tennis is a waste of time. Cash of Australia.

That evening I was having a couple of beers with some friends from the Australian papers. 'I'm going to enjoy this beer while I can,' I said, 'because tomorrow you'll none of you be talking to me. I have just filed 700 words on why Pat Cash is an arsehole.'

'Simon, mate, we'll be *buying* the bloody beers tomorrow if that's right. Pat Cash is not just an arsehole, he's the biggest bloody arsehole in the universe.'

Wimbledon seems to encourage capricious likings and loathings, and I had taken a dislike to Cash. The idiot remarks about women's tennis were a start, but that headband was too much. 'He wears that notice-box chequered headband with the air of a teenager smoking a black Russian cigarette – trying too hard to establish too easy a claim to individuality,' I wrote. And I know all about trying too hard to establish too easy a claim to individuality. He threw four headbands into the crowd afterwards and I had the unworthy thought that his agent had told him to do it. I tend to get unworthy thoughts.

After Cash's routine victory, I had gone to the routine post-match press conference. This is another part of Wimbledon ritual. It is part of the rules of professional tennis: if a quorum of journos wants words with a player after a match, then that player shows up in the interview room or faces a fine. The players are practically all helpful, and as articulate as American footballers, but the interviews are not always that useful. There is always at least one American nutcase in the front row who will ask questions like: 'Jaahn,' – this is how you address McEnroe in a press conference – 'Jaahn, in the first set you were getting 47 per cent of your first serves in, but in the second set the percentage was 62. Could I have your comments on that please, Jaahn?'

Or you will have: 'Ee-vahn, could you explain why you lost the second set?'

And to this, Lendl will reply: 'He woss playing bedder than me.'

'So can you explain why you won the last two sets so comfortably?'

'Ah, yes. Then I woss playing bedder than him.'

To be fair, Lendl is usually pretty good value in these set pieces. Those elaborate teases are more a part of his past, though still part of his sense of humour. His Transylvanian accent still colours vowels and the odd dark consonant, but his English is rapid and idiomatic and often very funny. He is probably the smartest player on the circuit.

The communications at Wimbledon really could not be much better. There is a big television room in the press area, which contains about 20 or more televisions. These cover about eight matches simultaneously, and the interviews are also broadcast on a closed circuit link. You could spend the entire fortnight in the television room, and see more of the players than anyone else in the world. You would also go completely insane (and end up asking people about first serve percentages). I tend to collect the interview quotes from the television room. The interview room itself is crowded . . . and was once the scene of a famous punch-up between the journalists.

Legend makes the scene a classic Wild West affray, with fists swinging everywhere, and bodies flying through the air. Indeed, there were several people on the floor at the end of it. It occurred before I ever went to Wimbledon, while McEnroe was in his prime. The details are a little hazy. The affair was sparked by a culture clash between American journalists asking about such things as first serve percentages, and people from the British papers trying to get some stuff about McEnroe's 'private' life. Amid a hail of 'Aw, for Chrissake geddof the guy's back' and 'We've got faaarkin' job to do an' all' – the first blow was struck. Ah Wimbledon, centre of sporting elegance. You cannot be serious.

Indeed, the beloved tabloid phrase 'bonking' came from a pre-Wimbledon tennis story. This was a famous piece in one or other of the pops, that began: 'Mats Wilander has a message for Boris Becker: stop bonking!' There was a headline like 'And Now It's Bonking Boris'. The idea of Wilander, a mild-mannered person even by Swedish standards, saying such a thing as 'I think Bawris should stawp bawnking' boggles the imagination.

Cash was tedium itself in his interview. 'Yeah, well, it's sort of different,' was about the most interesting of his remarks. Everybody has favourites and unfavourites at Wimbledon. My own capricious dislikes sometimes get read by the players: many of them take *The Times* when in London, partly for the legend of the name, and partly for the love they bear Mr Bellamy. One year, I received a public telling-off from Martina Navratilova: 'Who's this guy who writes these awful things about Ivan?' Thank God that was one of the interviews I didn't go to; I would have had to put up my hand and said, 'Please, Miss, it was me, Miss.' Or I could have adopted Atlantic City tactics and hidden under the table, I suppose.

Lendl has teased Rex about my various anti-Lendl pieces. He was annoyed when one year, after criticising his metronomic style, and his gloomy, machine-tooled approach to the game, I had blamed him for causing the bad weather. 'The kind of face that brings rain,' I wrote. Lendl felt that criticising play was fair enough, but criticising personal appearance was not. Well, no matter: Cash is the sort of person that makes you warm to Lendl. There is something haunting and noble about Lendl's grim, consistent failure at Wimbledon. He was world number one for years, but still unable to win the number one tournament. Lesser players won it, players more suited to the speed and oddities of grass courts.

Every year, I seem to warm more towards Lendl. He is a renaissance man; he collects Mucha and Lautrec, and he has seven or eight dogs, which argues for a certain quirkiness of temperament. He makes jokes, has the fastest mind in tennis, but he cannot express these pieces of himself on court. His ambition is to turn himself into a machine, with 100 per cent of his first serves in, 100 per cent of his volleys put away. He cannot do this in pumped-up exuberance, like Becker, or with the featherlight touch and transparent emotions of McEnroe. Like Steve Davis, he becomes the man in the iron mask: grim and joyless. His repeated failure at Wimbledon, the biggest tournament of all, is now oddly affecting. I write this before the 1989 tournament: perhaps he will win it, perhaps I will be a Lendl fan this time around. I can feel it coming on even now.

The second day of Wimbledon is, by Tradition, Ladies' Day. So inevitably, the star turn was McEnroe, thrust out of turn by a freak of scheduling. He was my match of the day: this was good news. I have always found McEnroe quite irresistible, at least, as a subject to write about. More obviously than anyone else in sport, he appears to be a victim rather than a master of his own talent. McEnroe seems to be a perfectly ordinary man, but one who suffers from intermittent possession by the devil. I am sure his tantrums are followed by horrible fits of remorse and/or self-justification.

McEnroe is always box office, and always grist for the sportswriter. Even those who consistently write against him find life more interesting when he is about. This was supposed to be the year of McEnroe's reform: he was coming back to Wimbledon in his new role as a grown-up. He was a married man, a father, a calmer and better McEnroe. The devil had been exorcised.

But of course, the thing about McEnroe is that the devil and the genius seem to be the same person. The devil that made him scream at linesmen, abuse rackets and forehand slam the barley water across the court, is the same thing that made him play those impossible touch shots at the moments of the highest tension that the game could manufacture.

He is ill-equipped to become an ageing player, like awful old Jimmy Connors. Connors, forever plucking at his crotch and making disgusting noises, has nevertheless made himself a rather sympathetic figure. But McEnroe's game is not based on technique: it is based on quickness of hand and eye. His entire forehand swing is iffy from a technical point of view, tennis experts (Rex Bellamy) tell me.

He won his match, and the crowd seemed very warm towards him: there is no surer sign of impending doom at Wimbledon. When the crowd starts to like a player after many years of dislike, it always means that the player's best years are over. Billie Jean was not loved until she started losing matches. Martina's recent vulnerability has won her more friends at Wimbledon than all her years of steely perfection. Connors, once despised, is now a lovable old rascal. Chris Evert, one of the darlings of Wimbledon, was, hard to imagine, utterly loathed when she first won the tournament, a time when, since she was engaged to Jimmy Connors, you'd have thought she had earned the right to all the sympathy she could get.

I was back at Wimbledon on the next Friday, and this time I wrote about Lendl. I quoted a remark of Rex's – perhaps stealing is the word I am looking for here – that his idea of hell was watching Lendl serve lets throughout all eternity. That never changing routine of ball-bouncing and shoulder shrugging (only one shoulder) drives me to distraction. 'I'd like to have dinner with Lendl,' Rex said, 'but I'd hate to share a flat with him. He'd have a special place to put the socks, and a special place for the bread knife.' Rex is a jazz-man, and loves the improvisational and the inspirational. Lendl is a player who needs the sheet-music in front of him.

I went down the following day, which was Saturday, and faced the usual Saturday problem. When it comes to straightforward reporting on a Saturday event for Monday's paper, there is little that the Sunday men haven't said. You have to second guess them or, more amusingly, whip off at a tangent. It is a moment for the inspirational and improvisational. I walked about Wimbledon fretting. And then the piece came clear with a sudden memory of New York. I was having a conversation with that almost fictional personage, the New York taxi driver, one of the few that speaks English. We discussed the World Series baseball, and then he asked me if I was going back to London – not a foolish question, since he was taking me to the airport.

'No. I'm going to the Wightman Cup.'

'Whassat? Never heard of it.'

'Tennis. United States against Britain.'

'Oh, I know. Bimbo's tennis, right?'

And so, picking up from where I left Gee Armytage, I wrote about the image-makers' love of bimbo-ism. I had been talking to Chris Cole, the photographer, in the bar. He had been asked by three separate newspapers for his Gabriela Sabatini file. He sent them the complete range. He had a picture on the front of two Sunday colour supplements, and as the centre spread in a daily. And they all used exactly the same photograph. Because it showed her forehead to its best advantage? No. Because you could see her knickers. The photograph possessed just a suggestion of Marilyn Monroe over the grating. Chris was accused of being a sexist photographer, and was very disgruntled: blame the bloody picture editors, he kept saying. I did, and at some length. I concluded by saying that the image-makers: media people, ad-men, journalists: they did not want women's sport at all. They wanted bimbo's sport. They did not want to see strong-willed women in victory: they wanted bimbos' tennis, the bimbos' marathon, the bimbos' javelin. The column was already in clear outline in my mind by the time I got to the bar, which was early. The joys of a Saturday are the joys of freedom and irresponsibility: nothing to write that day, and, to make things even merrier, you can watch the Sunday boys charging about the place and twitching.

On, then, into the second week. Rain fell on Monday, wiping out virtually all the play. This normally means straining every sinew in order not to write a story about the feasibility of putting a sliding roof over the Centre Court. I managed to escape this fate. When rain forces the schedule into difficulties, the schedule gets altered. When it is dry again, play on the Centre Court starts at noon instead of two o'clock. But no one turns up to watch apart from the devoted crowds of standing, all-night queuers. The rest are all eating and drinking in their executive marquees. I had a good solid swing at the entire corporate hospitality industry.

It is all rather like Club Class on aeroplanes. The point is not the comfort; it is the sense of privilege. Club Class is good because you know the people in Economy are worse off. Corporate entertainment would lose its point if lesser people did not queue all night and suffer in order to get a far worse place than the one you have for free. The queuers are the cannon-fodder of the corporate hospitality industry. And this is all reckless folly: you need real punters at sporting events, people who care, people who love the stuff, people who yell and get excited. The more executives you get, sitting with their backs to the play, or lingering in the marquees, the more the sense of occasion is lost. Sense of occasion is the point of the event. Sport always seems to go for the short-term gain: it does so at its peril.

Wimbledon continued, in a pleasant rhythm of personality pieces, the occasional column of vituperation, and good companionship when the day's piece had been filed. Filing had assumed a new ease and comfort: I was no longer dictating the words – 'McEnroe cap M cap E' – but using a Tandy. A Tandy is a make of portable computer, a paperless typewriter that remembers the words you hammer into it. You then plug the machine into a telephone socket and by a piece of magic, the words whizz down the line and into the computer at *The Times*. As with all hi-tech, it is absolute bliss when it works.

As the second week progressed, Court Number One came within a toucher of adding itself to my vast collection of Places I Have Been Thrown Out Of When I Had A Perfect Right To Be There. An unpleasant corporal – the military do all the ushering at Wimbledon – with a perfectly enormous ginger moustache that could not possibly be genuine, had decided that his day would not be complete without getting me thrown out. But the prospect of a really good row was ruined by the appearance of the urbane press officer, Richard Behrens. 'Any problems?' he asked the corporal.

This seemed to be the moment the corporal had been waiting for all his life. ''im. 'e 'asn't gotta ticket.'

'I think we'll let *The Times* watch the match, don't you?'

It would have been a lovely row, too.

The end of the fortnight was now in sight, and this was the stage I would normally withdraw from Wimbledon, leaving Rex to flex his muscles and take the entire event to himself. By the semi-finals, Wimbledon is all terribly tennis. But this time, I stayed on for the men's singles final. I watched the rain fall all Sunday and returned on Monday morning for the actual match. The work split easily enough: Rex would take the match and I the winner and the post-match interview. The winner, you may recall, was Stefan Edberg, the leggy, fragile-looking Swede. He beat the mad axeman, Boris Becker, in the final. 'It's like Mike Tyson against Bambi,' someone said in the bar, and that was the second line in a fortnight I nicked. It prompted the subs to write what was easily the most peculiar headline of the year: 'Secret Fires Ignite Deep Inside A Nordic Bambi.'

After I had written and filed my piece I went for a beer, and met Roy Collins of *Today*. 'That was a tough match,' I told him. 'So tough I watched it from under the table.'

Roy laughed. 'Got to be consistent, haven't you?'

'You know that story still pursues me?' I said. 'About how I watched Mike Tyson from under the desk in Atlantic City.'

'Really? Alan Hubbard actually rang me up to ask if it was true, before he did his thing in the *Ob*.'

'I don't believe it.'

'True!'

'God, I'd love to know how that story started.'

Collins had been chuckling, he now commenced roaring with laughter: 'You don't know?'

'Not the least idea.'

'It was me.'

'What?'

'Me!'

'You bugger!'

'I was making a joke after the fight, after you'd gone staggering off to bed with your flu. We all went for a meal, and I said, just as a joke, that

Bambi, with legs a-wobble. Stefan Edberg wins Wimbledon and leaves the press desperately hunting for something to say about him.
(Phil Shephard-Lewis/Professional Sport)

the fight was so tough you hid under the table. I never expected anyone to take me seriously.'

'People should know better than to believe a newspaper man,' I said. 'Especially a lying bastard like you.' Still laughing uncontrollably, I gestured at the barmaid, indicating that further refreshment was required. Much more of this, I thought, and I'd be under the table once again.

14. THE RABBIT-PACK TAKES TO THE SEAS: BIZARRE DEALINGS WITH A MANIAC

I am pretty good at declining invitations, but not *that* good. They were holding the world powerboating championships on Guernsey in the autumn, and they were very anxious to get someone from *The Times* down there for a pre-event publicity shindig. I refused not once, but twice. Then came the follow-up call. 'It'll be awfully interesting.'

This I doubted. Who cares about powerboating?

'And there'll be a lot of Fleet Street people there.'

That was not an added temptation. 'I really am very busy right now.'

'We're going to have a very good lunch at a seafood place . . .' If there is one thing I can turn down without any shadow of regret, it is lunch.

'Sorry, I really am very busy indeed, what with the Olympics coming up, and . . .'

'There'll be a chance to have a ride in a powerboat.'

'Thank you, but I am perfectly capable of throwing up in the privacy of my own home.'

The message, I flattered myself, was beginning to penetrate. I know public relations people have to try, but you just have to be firm with them.

That evening the phone rang again. It was Tony Jardine, he who had fixed the Piquet interview. I like Tony, and this gives him an unfair advantage. The Guernsey thing was his stunt. 'I'm not just saying this,' he said, which is always a dead give-away, 'but you really will get a good story from all this.' It was, at the very least, the right argument. I have long believed that a drink you pay for in the company of your choice tastes far better than a free drink consumed with people who are trying to sell you something.

I don't quite know how Tony managed it. He somehow implied that a refusal would be wimpish, that this was to be a memorable experience. Anyway, he managed to talk me round in about 90 seconds, which says a lot for his ability, and even more for my strength of character. 'All right,' I said. 'On condition we don't have to run for the plane or anything. My nerves aren't up to your firm's cavalier way with aeroplanes.'

So there I was at Heathrow, and the first one there, inevitably. After a while I was joined by Mike Calvin from the *Daily Telegraph*, an old friend and a good journo. I asked him what we were doing here, and he seemed uncharacteristically unsure. However, he was extremely keen on one thing: as each journo arrived, he cross-examined him on the question of whether or not he was to file copy that day. Some papers are like that: the first thing they do is look at all the rival papers, and they get cross if they don't have exactly the same stories as everybody else. They wouldn't dream of running a story on Thursday if any other paper had run the piece on Wednesday. It is an extraordinary business, newspapers. I don't understand it at all. So far as I was concerned, every journo on the trip could write a piece for the following day's paper, and I would be perfectly happy to write a day later.

This is because I am writing for readers, and readers only read one newspaper. If you read more than one paper, it is normally because you are in the business: journos, PR people, ad-men, *meejah* people of various kinds – not what you'd call readers. *Telegraph* readers, I would hazard, neither know nor care what is in *The Times*, and vice versa.

But there is a great conspiracy in the newspaper person: people strive to prepare newspapers in order to impress other people in the newspaper business. This is not the way of rabbit-pack journalism. It is all connected with a swaggering, macho attitude to journalism: hard-nosed men getting hard news stories hard on top of the hard hard deadline. I live in perpetual terror of sharing a phone with half a dozen such journalists when I have covered the same story. They will be yelling such things at the copy-taker as: 'English soccer was rocked to its foundations yesterday evening brackets Tuesday unbracket . . . team supremo . . . paint mogul . . . megabuck dealing . . . sensational development . . . point ends thank you love.' I take my turn: 'Are you filing for today?'

'Absolutely.'

'Well hurry up then.'

'This is my intention . . . hallo, copy? Here we go: I think it was, ah ah, Marcel Proust who said . . .'

This tough no-nonsense theme continued as Calvin and I got onto the plane and started discussing the Olympics and, the crucial factor, the time difference. The time difference is the difference between an easy and a hard time when you are working abroad. So far as I had worked out, the difference would work perfectly: everything that happened would be just too late to get into the following day's paper . . . which meant loads of time to write for the day after. Looked good, yes?

'Nah,' said Calvin. 'A lot of the finals will be in the morning. We'll be filing live to get them into the last edition.'

'Ah, sod it. I never thought we'd have to do live copy.'

Calvin is a nice man, but he does wear a leather jacket and a moustache, which must be said to be something of a give-away. He said, with a tinge of contempt: 'The Olympics isn't just nice features, you know.' And by God, he meant it to sting.

This represents the prevailing chic in Fleet Street. Hard news is the thing. Features are effeminate things, mere decoration, not work for a Real Man. It represents a touching, pre-television notion of what a newspaper is really all about. Calvin is a feature writer himself, and I have known him to quote Yevgeny Yevtushenko. But all the same, his features are never without a tang of hard news. On the rare occasions when I find myself with a hard news story to put over, it always has the tang of the feature, a thing which needs no date for its justification. Different approaches, different pieces, different journos, different papers.

The journey had been, by Jardine's standards, uneventful. True, he had led us all out into what he thought was a plane, but which in fact was a vast stretch of empty tarmac. 'Where the hell have they put the bloody plane?' he asked peevishly – but this was pretty mild stuff, and we found the aeroplane really quite easily. We reached Guernsey in good order, and Calvin was in good cheer. No one was filing that day. The glint of journalists preparing to lunch was in every eye.

We were driven across the island to the Guernsey Yacht Club, and we had a few speeches about the world powerboating championships. Everybody took turns to say how brilliant everybody else was. The journos watched with eyes aglaze. None of this would make a line in any paper in the world. We knew it, and the PR people organising the event knew it. But the PR people also know there is no point in trying to stop people making speeches at events like this. The events are only nominally for the sake of getting copy into newspapers: really they are there to foster the sense of self-esteem among the clients. The clients will later blame people like Tony for failing to get anything into the papers. PR is also a strange business: Tony and his staff were bending over backwards to get us a story, while their clients were trying to bore the journos into rebellion with speeches. Well, at least the speeches were short. Perhaps that was Tony's suggestion.

When the speeches were over, we were all introduced to a man called

Steve Curtis, the world Formula One powerboating champion. Well, here we all were. Why don't we ask a few questions of Steve now, and get that out of the way? I mean, before *lunch*. The client people all trooped off, and we had Curtis to ourselves. He surveyed us with eyes of an unnaturally piercing shade of blue. He was very freckled, with a great mane of fair hair. What on earth does one ask a powerboating man?

One of us, not me, opened the bowling with a fair ball on a goodish length: 'So tell us about your preparations for the world championships, Steve.'

We all set about scribbling in notebooks with dutiful expressions on our faces. Now we had come to the put-to, there was an uneasy feeling in everybody's mind: that this was all the most colossal waste of time. There was going to be nothing *in* this day, nothing to justify those who had taken a day away from the office.

But then a most extraordinary thing happened. Bit by bit, the realisation began to spread – here was the most marvellous story. Ears pricked up around the room, eyes brightened, lips were licked, dulled, routine attentions were suddenly sharpened. The dutiful expressions were replaced by predatory grins. Every face I could see reminded me of a dog that has just heard the world 'walk'. Except that the word here was 'story' and I knew that the same idiotic expression of eagerness was mirrored on my own face.

'Er, Steve, no one had much heard of you, and so do you, er, mind being a low profile champion?'

'Low profile? I don't call ramming a ferry low profile. I did it just the other day, it was ever so funny . . .' Curtis began to laugh rather wildly. 'The passengers were all leaning over the side, waving at me . . . and I got closer and closer, travelling at about 80 miles an hour . . . and there was this moment when they all realised at the same time that I was going to hit them . . .' He laughed some more, not exactly laughing, but more of a demented giggle. There was not a jot of self-consciousness about him, not the least suggestion that he was putting on an act. He was a straightforward, honest, dyed-in-the-wool maniac. 'I mean, it just happened to be in the way, you know? And anyway, it was only a *glancing* blow. Normally a ferry is quite easy to miss . . . I mean, on the whole you'd back yourself to miss a ferry. But you see, my steering had broken and . . . well, that's it, you see, I just like to make things go fast. Right from being a kid, I liked to make things go fast, everything I had, I tried to make it go faster . . . and then I broke it . . .' That giggle again.

It was clear that what we had before us was not the ice-cool, calculating person you find in Formula One motor-racing, Nelson Piquet lurking behind, picking off his opponents one by one and waiting for Mansell to fall by the wayside. With Curtis you had an out-and-out nutcase; a classic case of Spitfire Pilot Mentality. In a war, he would win the VC, or die in some madcap, unauthorised scheme. In real life, he would be a chancer, a misfit, perhaps even a criminal. But in this most dangerous of sports, he was fulfilled. 'Crew abandon me. They think I'm going too fast. They're all very macho on the shore, but out on the water, they back off. I've had three drivers walk out on me. One walked out after just one race . . . mind you, I wouldn't want to be a driver for me. Christ, no, you'd have to be bloody man. Some people go out to race really hard, but others really don't want to. They just don't want to. They want to be there, they want to take part, but they don't want to go hard and win things. Me, I pull out all the stops, without a shadow of a doubt. If you have to scrap a boat after I've taken it to the world championships, I just don't care. In fact, they *did* scrap a boat after I won the world championships in 1985. Half a million quids' worth.'

I was impressed by the distinction between himself and the brave talkers who back off, who want to be a part of it all without being there, without really travelling close to the edge. And powerboating is not a sport in which you risk getting hurt. What you risk is getting dead. It is the most deadly of sports: you have all the power of a Formula One motor car, but the surface on which you run is utterly unpredictable. This is off-shore racing, through real seas: not the natty little pond-skaters that race in harbours and docks. These are bloody great rhinoceroses that smash through the waves at 120 mph, bucking like mad bulls and roaring like a pack of famished wolverines. Two powerboaters had already died that year in America. The previous year, Didier Pironi, a friend of Curtis's, had died in a race off Britain. 'He loved to race, he loved the life,' Curtis said. 'I know it's the way he would have chosen to go.' Curtis didn't say so, but he implied it: it was the way he would choose to go too. It is frightening to think that by the time this book is being read, Curtis may be dead.

'A friend of mine was killed in the world championships in 1985. But I didn't even think of walking out of the championships. No, and he wouldn't have walked out if it had been me. It's just something you accept in this sport. I'm here to race, and the dangers aren't something I think about. I just love the sport – five tons of boat leaping 20 feet in the air – there aren't too many sports like that. It's a neat feeling, running really sweet, it's a different feeling to anything else, oh yes . . .'

The interview was at an end: it was time for our boat ride. We filed out, all the journos nodding to each other and grinning.

'Glad I came now.'

'Great bloke.'

'Great story.'

And onto the water. We each took a turn around the waters of Guernsey in a class two powerboat. Not the 120 mph jobs, just things that will shift at a mellow 80 or so. As luck – or Tony Jardine – would have it, I was the first to go out with Curtis. Crash-helmeted, clad in waterproofs (it said 'Camel' on the back) and looking utterly ludicrous, I scrambled awkwardly into the boat. I plugged myself into the intercom: 'All right?' asked Curtis.

'I suppose so – Christ!'

That was Curtis moving off, and bouncing the back of my helmet on whatever it was behind me. 'Hold onto the rope.'

'What rope? Oh this – Jesus Christ!'

'What?'

'Nothing.'

Every time you hit a corrugation of the surface, the boat jumps out of the water. It is supposed to run more or less on the props at the back, but the rest of the boat slaps and jerks about on the lumps in the water. At 80 mph, water is made out of concrete. When you jump clear, as you do about 30 times a minute, you land, sometimes with a jolt that shatters your spine. These are the easy ones: every now and then you land and dig in with a bang that loosens every filling in your mouth and bounces your head on the dashboard as an afterthought.

'Christ!'

'What's that?'

'Did you do that on purpose?'

'God no, I've no idea what this bloody thing is doing.' Maniacal laughter rattled through the intercom. 'You just can't tell whether you are going to skim when you come down, or whether you're really going to dig in.'

Curtis then decided that we were not really jumping high enough, so he started to make passes through the wake of the mother ship, on which the rest of the party was gathered. Bang-Christ . . . Bang-Christ . . . and you find a treacherous response rise up inside: do it again, Steve, go for it, Steve, won't this crate go any quicker – Christ! In a mad, gritty way, it became rather good fun. Curtis then decided that he

How many long-haired hooligans in this boat? The author tries his Spitfire-pilot smile alongside the then Formula One World Powerboat champion, Steve Curtis.

had got the hang of the boat, and to test this theory, he wanted to see how close he could get to the mother ship. Scraping the paint of a moving boat at 80 mph on a surface he admitted he couldn't predict with any degree of reliability – oh well, there was nothing to do but to put your faith in his abilities, or in his luck. They hollered at us from the mother ship: 'Take your helmets off! Then make another pass for the photographer!'

We did as asked. Curtis took a sidelong glance at me, for I had climbed aboard as an anonymous, crash-helmeted figure dressed in full Martian regalia. 'I see,' he said, 'just a couple of long-haired hooligans in this boat, eh?'

'Only one,' I said, 'only fucking one.'

We all took our turn at being frightened by Curtis, and then made our way off to the serious lunch. I ended up sitting next to Curtis. Not only is he an extremely entertaining man, he had absolutely no desire to make conversation about vegetarianism. He went still higher in my estimation.

We got back to London in good order. Things must have gone badly wrong, because Jardine got us to the airport in plenty of time to catch the plane.

Oh, before the lunch they had staged a little race for the journalists in some rather jolly little motor-boats, like floating dodgems. I declined the invitation myself; mechanical things and I have a relationship of mutual incomprehension and loathing. Everyone else went, so the rabbit-pack was, as usual, represented by me alone. I can't remember who won. But on such occasions as this there is always someone who pushes his luck a mite too far and takes a ducking. It was Calvin. Ha. Powerboating is not all nice features, you know, Mike. And I meant it to sting, by God.

15. FORMULA ONE IS DECADENT AND DEPRAVED

There is a fat book like a bible that lives in the sports editor's office. This is the Diary. In it, on the appropriate date, you find every sporting event of interest to *The Times*: Test Matches in Rawalpindi, golf tournaments in Miami, cycling events in Rouen, swimming in Barnet, football matches in Liverpool and Manchester. In the far right-hand column is the surname of the person covering the event: Woodcock, Miller, Bellamy. Or Agency, which means, of course, no one – we take the report from Reuter or whoever. More exciting still in the left-hand column is the place where the event takes place, a litany of delights to anyone with travel in the blood.

Since meeting Nelson Piquet I had wanted to cover a Grand Prix, and so I went to Wapping and turned the pages of this magician's book. What could I conjure from it? Mexico, I thought, Mexico – but common sense told me not to push my luck. Well, then, the Hungarian Grand Prix; I had never been to Hungary, never been to an Iron Curtain country for that matter. And so I fixed it up: five days in Budapest, going through the Iron Curtain to penetrate the secret world of Formula One motor racing.

Motor racing is one of those closed, self-involved worlds. You either know nothing about the sport, or you know everything. It is rather like horse racing, a secret world with its own smells, its own language, its own intricate, always-taken-for-granted skills. I had spent a year researching *Horsesweat and Tears*, getting to learn the ways of a racing stable. I wanted to spend a weekend trying the same trick with motor racing, meeting the team from stable lads to governor, as it were, and feeling something of their excitements and horrors. I wanted to be given a visa to explore the interior of Formula One Land. The difference was that I know something about horses; I know nothing about motor-cars, not even how to drive them.

Naturally, the first place I tried was Tony Jardine and the Lotus team; and, Tony being Tony, naturally this was the only place I needed to try. Yes, yes, yes, Tony would fix everything, bill the office for the aeroplane. Everything was under control.

'Oh, Tony?'

'Yes, Simon.'

'I will say Camel.'

'Byron will meet you at the check-in desk with the tickets at one o'clock.'

'Isn't that a bit late for a two o'clock flight.'

'You worry too much about aeroplanes.'

'You don't worry enough, and nor do your staff.'

Tony laughed as if I were making a joke, and promised that Byron would be there. And so there I was at Heathrow at ten past one, watching the last passengers check in for my flight and twitching. At half-past one I had the public address system baying out Byron's name. No sign of him. By ten to two, I was calm again. Obviously it had all gone wrong, and I would never make the flight. At five to, Byron arrived – with a Vesuvius of excess baggage and an overwrought expression. 'We'll never get that on,' said the ticket clerk with quiet satisfaction.

'You go!' said Byron, thrusting a ticket into my hand with the gesture of a man doing a far, far better thing. A groundcrew man materialised by my side.

'Grab yer luggage!' he said. 'Foller me.'

In American football, when a running back drives for the line, he will generally have a player to run ahead of him, deflecting opponents from his path – a 'lead blocker' in the jargon. This heroic groundcrew man elected himself my lead blocker. He led me at a flat sprint from one end of the terminal to the other, scattering old women and small children to the right and to the left, skidding along the lino, bouncing unnervingly high along the moving walkways, and I followed, bags bundled to my chest, like Walter Payton hammering into the endzone for the Chicago Bears. At two precisely, we reached the gate, my lead blocker shouting instructions to everybody as I huffed up behind him. We made it. I gasped my thanks to this remarkable man, and he ambled back, conscious of having discharged a duty to the best of his ability. I went to sit down and pant for a while, and the public address burst into life. They regretted the delay of the flight to Budapest, and apologised for the inconvenience to passengers. As it turned out the delay was so long that even Byron was able to make it. He appeared in the departure lounge muttering about taxis and office inefficiency and fate and things like that. At last we got on the plane and flew to Budapest.

My first entry into an Iron Curtain country was singularly uneventful. Certainly, immigration procedures were a lot less vexing than I have known at, say, Minneapolis. I checked into my hotel, and in the evening dined with Tony and Byron. The restaurant featured gypsy violinists, who kept playing *The Blue Danube*, gazing straight into our eyes as they did so. It is hard to eat soup gracefully under such circumstances. In all good restaurants all over the world, they have a no smoking area. I have often wished that they all had no music areas as well, but never quite as fervently.

So much for local colour. At dawn I was off to the track. This was Friday, and the racetrack, the Hungaroring, was to be the centre of the universe for the entire weekend.

Formula One is a global village. It moves from one place to another throughout the season, across the face of the earth, and everywhere it touches ground, it is the same place. There is the pit lane, and there the sausage-beans-an'-chips-twice café, with the same mechanics – a breed predominantly English – slapping the bottoms of the sauce bottles. There is the same row of trailers that transport the cars and the vast array of equipment they require. There are the motor-homes, the wheeled palaces in which the councils of war and the entertainment of sponsors take place. The same people are always there: the drivers, nonchalant and handsome in their Adidas fireproof boots; the journos looking cynical; the PR people looking eager; the sponsors looking disgruntled; the mechanics and engineers looking forever hopeful. The hangers-on are noisier here than elsewhere, the camp-following girls more elaborate. There is always a pair of East German twins, each identically stunning, and whose stereo flirtatiousness is calculated – to the fourteenth decimal place – to make anyone in Formula One go weak at the knees. It's a man's life in Formula One: no question about that.

This is a land of money and prestige, and places that blaze with money are never lonely. This is a world gaudy with logos of companies from across the world: every motor-home is a blaze of company colours. The Lotus team gathered around the most strident motor-home of them all: this was a bright yellow world where everything and every person bore a bright blue dromedary. This was Camel-ville, a major town in Formula One Land: the dromedary smirked at you from umbrellas, from the walls, from the awnings, from the ashtrays, from the bosoms of the waitresses, from the pen they gave me, from the match-boxes, between the shoulder blades of the mechanics, and from the plastic boxes that hold the noisome earplugs that are the one essential item for the well-dressed follower of Formula One. 'Best chat-up line in the world,' said a man from Camel. 'Allo, darlin', want a pair of earplugs? Here, take a couple of boxes, you never know . . .'

The rain was hammering down without mercy, and the Camel umbrellas were up. This was the first official practice, and the cars were out, roaring and squealing past us as we sheltered under the awning of the motor-home. Where was the yellow dromedary-bearing Lotus? No sign of it, but there was the unfathomable Nelson Piquet, not driving but watching, and not watching with scientific, detached interest, either. He was roaring with laughter and as each car came to the tricky hairpin, of which the motor-home had so fine a view, he was shouting: 'Go for eet!' When a car obeyed his unheard instruction and spun off, he gave a great bellow of delight. Occasional dark looks were flung his way. Was this the way a world champion should seek to defend his title? The man was obviously a non-genuine, untrustworthy type. Huh!

The thing about Piquet is that he does not give a toss what anyone thinks – never has, and never will. It makes him a uniquely dangerous sort of person. There was tension in the air – the Lotus people were all crackling with it – but if you have a mind like Piquet's, you are a man in a suit of armour. 'How are you going to go on Sunday, Nelson?'

'Don't know. The car eez not so queek. Fah!' He gave a shrug and a curl of the lip, gypsy features more suitable for a Gitanes ad than one for Camel, and went back to watching the traffic. 'Go for eet – yes!'

The car had not been so queek all year. The confidence of that spring day at Le Castellet was long gone. This was the year, you may remember, when the McLaren team won everything. Just about every race finished Senna–Prost or Prost–Senna. The rest of the world was competing for third place at best. This was embarrassing for everybody, but it was more embarrassing for Lotus than for anyone else. Lotus not only had the world champion, Piquet, they also had the same Honda engine as the McLarens. Therefore, there was only one thing to blame – and that was the rest of the car.

However, if you preferred a more colourful explanation for repeated failure, you could always blame the driver for not trying. This was an option people were taking in increasing numbers.

Thanks to Tony's introductions, I was given freedom to roam about everywhere in Camel-ville. This included the pits, the unbelievably spotless and organised workshops for the mechanics and engineers. There is absolutely no resemblance to anything one might associate with a garage: the smell is different, the noise is different, the sharp urgency with which every task is completed, the edgy keenness with which orders are obeyed – there is nothing to which a mere car-driving person can relate. I spent the morning chatting with the mechanics and engineers, engineers being the officer class in this universe. 'We try all the time,' said Bob Dance, the chief mechanic, trying hard not to overstress that '*we*'. 'Wind tunnel tests, work on the suspension – we try something new every race. But if you do a lot of work and you don't get the results . . . well, you feel you deserve a bit more.'

'What do you think of Nelson's results this season?'

'We have to believe Nelson's doing a good job. We have to believe in his ability. But a lot of people thought he would have gone a lot better this season . . . you're asking rather difficult questions, aren't you?'

Consistent failure is one of the great eternals of sport. Naturally, everyone reads more about the winners, it is the winner of an event that matters, he is the person the journos must go for – 'How did you feel when you scored the winning goal, Bryan?' – but the most important thing a professional athlete must learn is how to cope with failure. In the race on Sunday there would be one winner, and virtually every journo would write about him. There would also be 25 failures; 25 drivers and their teams who need to cope with disappointment. The method for doing so is simple: asinine optimism. It is one of the few sane ways of handling it. Put that one down to experience, next time we'll get it right. Now we've cracked it. This is not an attitude that can be assumed, it has to come right from the soul; unquenchable competitiveness is allied with ludicrous optimism. 'We've certainly got the car going better,' said Chris Dinnage, who is the number one mechanic on Piquet's car. 'We have found something like one-and-a-half seconds a lap, maybe two. We still have a bit to find before we can catch the McLarens . . . but we have a few more things to try.'

I wrote a piece for Saturday's paper, and then telephoned the office from the track. There was a practice for the saloon cars in full swing at the time and the racing noise, the spectacular rising and falling Doppler-effect howl, filled the ears. The press centre had plenty of telephones, though you had to fill in a form before you could use one. At last I had some feeling of being in a communist state. I got through at once: 'Hello, Tom (yeowww!) I'm here at the (yeowww!) racetrack.'

'You don't have to make these noises, Simon, I believe you.'

Which prompted me to tell him one of my more shameful stories. It was when I was working for the *Surrey Mirror*, and was instructed by my chief reporter (who thought I was the worst reporter she had ever seen in her life) to go to a horrible place called Merstham and try to find a story or two. This is a ghastly practice called 'local calls', an exercise from which I never ever found any stories. (No news is good news, right?) With my usual fit of the sulks, I stomped about Merstham for a bit, and then temptation touched me lightly on the shoulder and I turned to embrace it. I hopped aboard a train to London and home at the sinful hour of five o'clock. At Clapham Junction station I left the train and went straight to the phone-box I knew I would find on the platform, congratulating myself on this piece of local knowledge as I did so. I rang the chief reporter: 'Hello, I'm at Merstham station,' I said, train noises in the background providing verisimilitude. 'It's half-five, so it's hardly worth coming back to the office, is it? I'll get a train home from here, if that's all right, yes?'

The chief reporter drew her breath to speak. Then the Tannoy burst into life above my head, and in a voice of singular sweetness, loudness and penetrating quality, it said: 'Clapham Junction. Clapham Junction. This is . . . CLAPHAM JUNCTION.' I must add that it made no difference to my relationship with the chief reporter. She hated me already.

By the afternoon, Piquet had decided to act like a racing driver, and took the car out in the afternoon practice session. The rain had stopped. 'This time, we have thrown our cap at the moon,' said the Camel Lotus team director, Peter Warr – he who had poisoned Byron with shaving foam. 'We have gone into this practice session with a very experimental set-up – that is why we didn't try the car this morning in the rain. We only had one of these experiments, and we didn't want to risk spinning and damaging it.'

Optimism is, as I say, an essential part of the make-up of any sporting person. Certainly these experimental adjustments made a difference to the car – they made it worse. Piquet managed to qualify the car in 22nd place. Fah!

On Saturday morning, I was at the track good and early once again. I had already realised that my hopes of seeing anything of Budapest (other than the bloody gypsy violinists at every meal except, mercifully, breakfast) were minimal. But then, I was not in Budapest at all, I was in Formula One Land. Here nothing matters more than motor-cars; apart from money, that is. The questions of the world are: who is going faster than whom, who is doing what to whom and how often, and is it true about what he did with *both* the East German twins?

Talking of money, it does seem rather strange that this spectacularly capitalistic sport should be taking place in a communist country. But the Camel men, and with them the Marlboro men, and the Gitanes men, and the men from two other cigarette companies involved in Formula One, were not about to complain. Many of the Western countries have complicated, and always different, rules about tobacco advertising. This involves what you can and what you can't do with Piquet's overalls, the mechanics' overalls, and the car itself. In France, you can't have the word Camel on either car or overalls – but Camel Racing Service is acceptable. In Britain there is a voluntary code, but it is strictly adhered to, and under it, neither car nor overalls can say Camel. The yellow livery and dromedary logo are permissible. In West Germany the dromedary is only allowed on the car; mechanics can wear overalls in team colours, but without the team logo. But in communist Hungary, the tobacco merchants can spread their word unchecked, and there it goes by on the television screens across the world. Communists always remember to say Camel.

The car was going better. This was still not saying a great deal. But I noticed something about Piquet, as I hung around the pits. Every time he stepped out of the car, eased off his helmet and shoved the fireproof balaclava back from his head, he would smile: a great lazy, self-satisfied, reflective smile. This was not for the team manager, not for the mechanics – it was just for himself. This small man, with his gypsy's face, just happens to like driving, and that moment of stepping from a high-powered motor-car gives him a second on which to reflect on his intense joy in going fast.

These machines are unbelievable things. Most people would accept that there is an interstellar gap between the experience of driving a Deux-chevaux and driving a Porsche. Well, there is a far, far greater gap between a Porsche and a Formula One motor-car. When you stand in the pit lane you can feel the earth shake as the cars go past: no figure of speech from the globe-trotting journalist here, I am being tediously literal. You feel your toes buzz inside your shoes. When there is a massed start you can feel the tremors right through your body. This is raw power: is this what makes the sport so addictive to some people?

And the noise is phenomenal. When they race the engine in the pits, and you are standing alongside the car, it just blows your head off. There is no thought of speaking: the team all wear headsets, through which they can communicate with each other on a radio link. Peter Warr, being the number one, orchestrates and motivates, jokes and banters in the ears of his teams at all times when the business is serious. The team talk back. Very occasionally, Piquet also talks back. Mostly to say something bad about the car.

'If I have a criticism of Nelson, it is communication,' Warr said. 'He will say, I want the car two millimetres lower, I want this changed, or that changed. He never says *why*. I wish he would tell us more.'

Tension, tension. The previous season, Lotus had had Ayrton Senna, an indefatigable keenie, and who had then never won the world championship. He talked incessantly to the mechanics, never left them alone, and the mechanics loved it. They were fulfilled and appreciated. But Piquet just gets into the car, drives it, gets out, smiles to himself in that opaque manner of his, and then starts whinging. The mechanics were working *with* Senna; now they were working *for* Piquet.

Piquet is cool. He has done it all. He doesn't need the money; he doesn't need to enhance his reputation. He doesn't care what he says to anybody, or about anyone. 'It takes more than six months to find out how a team works,' he said, when I asked him about the tensions within the Lotus team. He just shrugged, and gave that characteristic curl of his lip. He really is the most arrogant sod. 'To learn what is right, what is wrong, what to do. It takes time to know who are the liars, who are the good guys, who are the idiots.'

'So what about the race this weekend?'

Shrug. 'A bad car,' he said, showing his unique diplomatic skills. 'We can improve it, yes. We cannot transform it.' Piquet is an odd man, there is no question about that. He would be odd anywhere, and, as at the Paul Ricard circuit in early spring, I felt an odd liking for him.

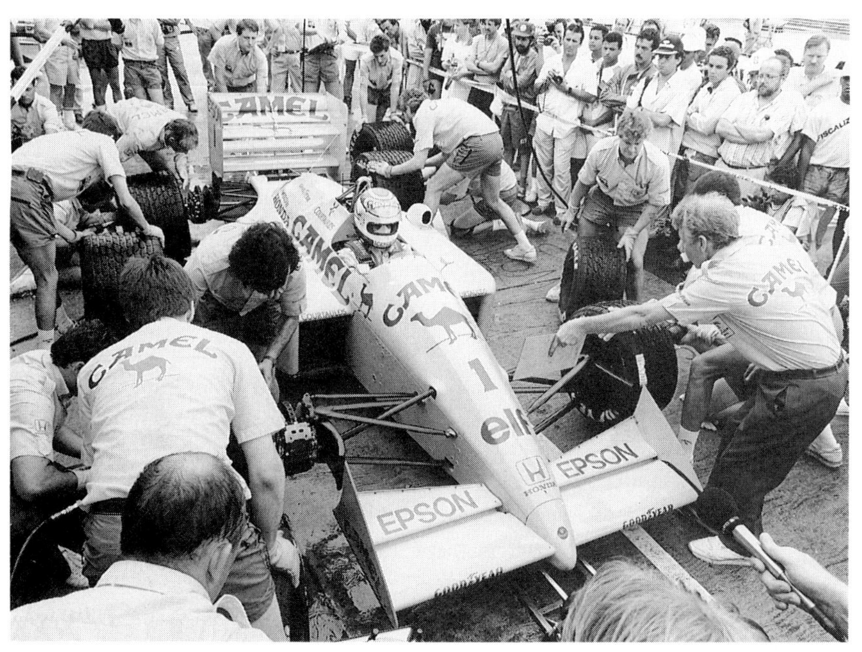

The Lotus pits team change Nelson Piquet . . . ah, but in Formula One, there are wheels within wheels within wheels . . .

'All we can do now,' said Warr on Saturday night, 'is to say, we're sorry, Nelson, but this heap of shit happens to be the best we can do. You are one of the best, and one of the best-paid drivers in the world. Please do the best you can with it.' On that thought, on into Sunday.

Racing Sundays see Formula One Land *en fête*. The Camel motor home was packed out with sponsors and others who wear their VIP-badges as if it were their birthright. In the pits, tasks were performed and everything that could be checked was checked again. The teams rehearsed their high-speed wheel changes: get it down to seven seconds for all four wheels, lads. The car engines howled and roared as adjustments and checks continued. This is the time at which tension reaches its apex, and the moment when the 26 drivers feel it the sharpest: the teams risk their reputations every racing Sunday, but the drivers also have their lives on the line. So what does Piquet do? He sleeps. He goes into the motor-home, closes the door behind him, curls up on a bench and sleeps. It is the most extraordinary facility. The only athlete I have heard of with the same gift is Sebastian Coe. An athlete once told me: 'Before a big race, he just curled up like a little dormouse and kipped.'

Lotus fixed me up with a team headset, so I was able to eavesdrop and to share the emotions of the team throughout the build-up to the race, and the race itself. I was, for a few hours, an insider. You can get to some extraordinary places in sports reporting; before the race, I hopped onto the track with the team, and walked along the starting grid, all 26 cars lined up and ready to start, the drivers staring ahead with the impassivity of robots in their helmets, eyes eagling down the track. The air was crackling with ambition and desire. These men are not like Steve Curtis, the powerboating lunatic. They meet danger in a manner that is circumspect and shrewd: they are more icy, more calculating men than Curtis. They are governed neither by fear, nor by the desire to spit on fear. Recklessness is frowned on here. They are not Spitfire pilots, they are more like astronauts.

I left the track, climbed over the pit wall, and crossed the pit lane. The traffic lights turned green, and the earth shook itself like a wet dog and the sky was torn apart with the howl of the massed start. The race was beginning, and – would you believe it? – the McLarens were in the lead. And after a few minutes Piquet's voice crackled in my headset: 'I am coming een. New weeng, new tyres.'

He had tangled with another car, been dinged in one of those eternal yes-I-did-no-you-didn't shunts of motor racing. He had damaged a wing, spoiled a tyre with the sudden braking. He roared into the pits, the change was made at spectacular speed . . . but then the clutch started giving trouble. Piquet finally rejoined the race in 22nd place. It was embarrassing.

Piquet went out and drove a roaring, virtuoso race. Through the headset, I could hear Warr chanting the gap in front of him, how much Piquet was gaining. He picked his way through the field, bit by bit, and it was a perfectly marvellous drive. And totally useless, too. Piquet finished eighth; his team-mate, Satoru Nakajima, was seventh. World championship points start at sixth place. Fah!

Later in the press room while I was writing my piece, I was given a cynical earful by a very serious motor racing journalist. The message was, if I thought Piquet was trying then I was a naïve fool. OK, then, I am a naïve fool. I also know David Gower, and Piquet seems to me to suffer from the same affliction. Both look as if they don't care. But to believe that would be hopelessly unsubtle. You don't get to win things at sport just by being good at them. Gower has one of the finest batting records in history; Piquet has a triple world championship and is up there with the greats. You cannot achieve such things without a colossal mental strength: dedication, determination, and a ruthless delight in doing the opponent down. Gower dominates bowlers, Piquet dominates lesser drivers. Neither punch the air when they win; neither will fall on his sword at failure. That doesn't mean that either is indifferent to victory – or to failure. It certainly does not mean that either of them will be doing anything other than giving of his best.

I happen to like both of them. Gower is the most amiable of men, and Piquet makes me laugh. Both are men of style, and both are champions. No wonder people resent them: they prefer their athletes to have more humdrum qualities. It is small wonder that when things go wrong for either Piquet or Gower, people line up to criticise. But it was ever thus, in sport, or in anything else for that matter.

I had enjoyed my weekend immensely, a weekend of privileged peering through the keyhole into a secret world: into Formula One Land. I still had not managed to find Budapest, but on Monday, Byron and I had lunch in the old section of town. There were no gypsy violinists. It was not much of an insight into a great city, but at least we managed to catch the plane.

16. OUT OF MY DEPTH IN BARBADOS: COCAINE AND STREET VIOLENCE IN NEW YORK

I wasn't feeling smug. I was feeling quite revoltingly and appallingly smug. In fact, I was feeling like James Bond – not an uncommon experience for me, as it happens, but this time there was some justification. There is a line in one of the books in which Bond reflects on his current assignment, and muses that there are times of great luxury in an agent's life when he is required to play the part of an extremely rich man. This was me to the life on this trip.

I was settled comfortably in the humpty part of the plane, the cosy Club Class bubble. I was sipping a cold beer – not a James Bond drink, but never mind, certainly a Simon Barnes drink (I see myself as the thinking person's lager lout) and I even had a James Bond book in my bag. It was called *Birds of the West Indies*. James Bond was the author. When Ian Fleming was looking for a name for his superhero, he ran his eye along the bookshelf, as many an author has. He read the name on the spine of the bird book he kept, so that he could put a name to the birds of his beloved Jamaica: James Bond. That will do. This is still the standard field guide to West Indian Birds. My bag also contained mask, fins and snorkel. Oh, and there was a notebook and pen in there somewhere too, because this was a working trip. Oh yes.

I was flying to Barbados, as a guest of the Barbados Board of Tourism. They were keen to promote Barbados as a destination for the sporting person: Barbados as more than mere sun 'n' sand. They wanted me to cover a small cricket tournament.

I had made the same trip the previous year, and, being self-employed, had naturally tried to get as many stories from the place as possible. I did a piece with Sir Garfield Sobers, who was probably the greatest cricketer of all time, I wrote my Diary from Barbados, I wrote about the cricket tournament, and then about the mad, delightful Barbados races. I also did an interview with the Minister for Sport and Tourism: this was Wesley Hall, the former tearaway fast bowler. He had the longest run-up in cricket, charging in from about half-a-mile away with his shirt unbuttoned to the navel, and a gold crucifix bouncing between soup-plate-sized pectorals. He is a delightful man, and he it was that took me to the races, where we met his son, who is a jockey, backed a lot of losers and then went to the bar and put a few away. He remains the only Minister of State with whom I have ever seriously knocked it back.

So I was going back to Barbados in good spirits. I would be put up at a nice hotel. I had been offered a car, but I refused it, on the grounds that I wouldn't be able to drive it. So they gave me a chauffeur as well. God, life can be tough at times.

My main aim was to get an interview with Malcolm Marshall, and I had about a dozen half-promises on this. Marshall is probably the finest fast bowler there has ever been (I hope this is not impertinent, Minister), and certainly the most fearsome. He is not a man much interviewed; he is rather a suspicious man. But I was confident that the combined clout of Wes Hall and the Board of Tourism would sway the balance.

The main event, from the Board of Tourism's point of view, was a schoolboy cricket tournament that pitted teams from schools in Trinidad and Barbados against English schools. This was a better story than it sounds because at that age the cricketers were pretty well matched. The West Indian fast bowlers were not much faster than the English quicks. That summer, West Indies had beaten England 4–0 in the Test Matches: what happens to cricketers between the ages of 17 and 22? Answers on a postcard to Lord's.

I went to the final, and after it was over had a couple of beers with Wes Hall, and various other prominent Bajans. I was introduced to Marshall, who glowered at me unsmilingly behind his smoke-grey sunglasses. I proposed an interview: he agreed, though warily. We would fix a time later. I was more than pleased. I would come away with three stories: the schoolboys, the Diary, and an absolute whopper on Malcolm Marshall, England's destroyer, a piece on Where The Summer Went Wrong.

I managed to find time for a few treats for myself. I went down in a submarine, down to 120 feet and looked at fish, a spectacular trip. And I made a couple of journeys out to a decent spot of coral where I could cruise about with my snorkel. There was a great shoal of squid one time. It was tough, but I was up to it. That will be all for now, chauffeur, come back in 90 minutes and don't be late or I'll tear you ears off.

One of the nicest things about Barbados is the notion of times. In most places when you arrive you must set your watch to local time: in

Barbados you must reset your brain. Time here is an elastic concept, and to hurry is to commit a solecism. The Bajan driving style requires you to place one hand on the roof and another on the volume knob. Emerson, he who had the unlikely task of driving me around, was un-Bajan enough to hold the steering wheel and was possessed with a curiously non-Bajan respect for objective time. He had lived for a while in America, which had probably caused this affliction: 'But after a while I come back home again. It is more important to be happy.'

I fixed time and place with Marshall on the telephone, and we arranged to meet on the morning of my last day in Barbados. I prepared all my questions. I really was extremely happy with all this. We would meet at ten in the morning at my hotel. I went to wait for him, my tape recorder in my pocket.

I waited half an hour. No show. Was he just Bajan and late? I rang him. 'Sorry, I just don't feel too well today.'

My brain was not as fully adjusted to Bajan time as I had thought. I replaced the phone with white knuckles, and cursed him with both fervour and volume. Then I recollected myself. I grabbed my snorkel, and went out to have a final check-up on the squid. Emerson drove me there and back. When I was 20 feet below the surface in the company of a shimmering parrot-fish, I felt I had adjusted to my disappointment. Smugness, never more than 20 feet below my own personal surface, reasserted itself.

Indeed, how could it not? For I had been incredibly smart. I was going from Barbados to New York, to spend ten days in the city. There was the US Open tennis, and anything else I might come up with. True, the firm was paying for the next leg of the journey, so I was back in Economy where I belong. But New York was waiting, and my room in the Mayflower was booked.

I sound a pretty cool traveller, do I not? All this talk about different sorts of aeroplane tickets and the grooviest hotels. I can, if you wish, bore you to death with comparisons of departure lounges of the world, and add the priceless information that Barbados is the only departure lounge I know where you can buy fresh fish. You can buy dead flying fish in a box, to take home with you. 'That's it, laugh,' said the man behind the counter. 'You know something? Only the English laugh at these fish. Every other nation in the world thinks it's a *wonderful* idea.'

I laughed and laughed at the folly of the fish stall, and as I did so, I did something quite mind-snappingly stupid myself. I did nothing. I got on the plane, which was fearfully late, and arrived in New York. It was only then I remembered I didn't have any dollars in cash. Only travellers' cheques: it was two in the morning and there were not a lot of banks open.

I took a taxi from the airport, still financially stark naked, and not explaining the extent of my folly to the driver. I thought that would come better when we were actually at the Mayflower. So off we went, and soon the magic fairy fortress of Manhattan loomed up ahead – it gets me every time, it gets everybody every time. Except perhaps a taxi driver wailing for his forty dollars. Around Central Park we went and cruised to a halt. 'I'll, ah, just change a traveller's cheque and then give you some, ah, money.'

'No prablum.'

But there was. The Mayflower night desk has a policy: no cash. This is, after all, New York. The taxi driver came into the lobby, and we all set about discussing this interesting prablum. I had been lucky in my taxi driver: luckier still when after 15 minutes or so, someone discovered 100 bucks that someone had forgotten to put in the safe. The prablum was solved: have a nice night. You too, have a nice tip. I went to bed resolving never to be as foolish again. No suite this time, but on the other hand, no flu. I felt rather good. It's a wonderful town, don't you know?

I slept late, rose, had eggs Benedict for breakfast in the Conservatory restaurant. It was a Saturday, so I had nothing to write, and no need even to feel guilty. I didn't feel any urge to buy a pair of boots, either, but there was no denying that there was something in me that yearned to make a fairly serious book collection. The bookshops of New York are legendary and cheap. Well, I reasoned, if I didn't spend $150 on boots, then I was $150 in profit, right? So I had $150 to spend on books. It was like finding money in the street. Right? Right.

I spent Saturday with friends, and the following day made two pilgrimages. One was to the *Tyrannosaurus rex* in the Museum of Natural History, a thing I had always longed to see; the other was to the planetarium to which Woody Allen and Diane Keaton repaired in that torrential rainstorm in *Manhattan*. I walked past the starry night against which their heads, so close together, had been silhouetted, and across the lunar landscape where their acquaintanceship had begun to defy gravity.

I closed my Sunday by going to meet Jerry Lisker of Fox TV. I watched the transmission of his sports programme, and was unable to believe my eyes. There was a black man with shoulder-length gelled hair in ringlets, a pair of shades of the science fiction variety, a pair of shoulders of the barn door variety. In his hands he held a doll that was wearing a nappy. The red light on the camera turned on: the black man clearly already was. 'Tyson, Mike Tyson, he's a sissy, Cicely Tyson, he's a homo, he's a faggot – see this, this my doll and I call it Tyson, an' I call it Tyson 'cos it's a faggot homo sissy.' And he started slapping the doll about with great gusto. As a bravura performance of the stoned-out ghetto idiot, this was unmatchable. The man in question was Mitch 'Blood' Green. That week, he had been involved in a bout of street fisticuffs with the world heavyweight boxing champion, Mike Tyson. Green, a former contender himself, lost. 'That faggot, he sucker-punched me. I want to get him in the ring, he says he'll fight me for charity. Well, man I *am* charity. I'm poor and I want to whip his ass for *money*.'

New York was deeply into one of its periodic fits of self-congratulation. The punch-up had taken place outside a tailor's called Dapper Dan. It was four in the morning. The tailor's was open. Tyson was calling in to collect a white leather jacket, one that on the back carried the legend 'Don't believe the hype'. In what other town could you find such a thing, New York gloated. It was Damon Runyon to the life: a romantic, picturesque lowlife comedy, and every single character involved seemed to know exactly what was expected of him. Tyson appeared on television to give his side, and was tough and monosyllabic, and wearing his arm in a monstrous plaster cast, for he had apparently damaged a bone in his hand after punching Green. Green was loquacious and idiotic, and on every television station in the country: clearly he had not had so much fun in years. Jerry Lisker told me he had persuaded Green not to remove the doll's nappy before the cameras: he had wanted to show the world what lay beneath, for he had cut the doll's cock off. He compromised by saying: 'He ain't no man, he ain't got what it takes – ain't you seen him with his trainer before a fight? Man, they kiss, they kiss *on the lips*, man.' I quoted much of this, and *The Times*, in an uncharacteristic fit of nice-mindedness – or a characteristic fit of legal-mindedness – cut out all the faggot and homo bits.

I also reported that I had a great feeling of unease about the story. Of course it was an over-the-top delight . . . but that was to miss the point. There was something weird about the way the violence in the story was made picturesque, was dressed up and made acceptable. The dandification of criminal lowlife in fancy nicknames, stylish behaviour, flashy jackets and sunglasses and recondite patois made the story all the more amusing, but I was not happy about it.

It all seemed part of the great schizophrenic myth of the boxer: the man whose trade is violence, but who is all gentleness and gentlemanliness outside the ring. 'It's my work, he said, and I do it for pay, but when my work is done I'd just as soon be on my way,' says Hurricane Carter in the Bob Dylan song. This is the myth of the boxing man: his fists are fearsome things, but they are kept for the noble purpose of the Holy Sport in the sacred confines of the Squared Circle. He hates violence in every form but this. He is the savage civilised: he is man's atavistic nature symbolically tamed. He is the tame black man with fists of thunder: he is Violence Bound – yet so thrillingly unchained in the ring, where all is at last legitimate.

These impossible contradictions destroy boxer after boxer. This street brawl was the second sign of Tyson's tendency to self-destruct (more were to follow in the coming months). People were talking about Tyson as a time-bomb: he was a ghetto criminal and he would revert to type, they said, and did so with something close to relish. A New York adman, a breed notoriously sensitive to such things, said: 'If it was just an isolated incident, it wouldn't matter. But a pattern is emerging. It makes advertisers very nervous. Their question is, what will be next? If you're an advertising agency that has to appeal to the whole country, you can't afford to take that risk.'

Tyson's retort had something of the directness that is his most remarkable quality. 'What if I got shot or stabbed? What if I became paralysed? They don't put no paraplegics in Pepsi commercials.'

He added, 'Sometimes it ain't that easy being Mike Tyson,' and I believed him. His job is to fight duels in public, his profession is violence, and he is praised across the world for his savagery. And yet he has to act nice every time he shows his face in public. With his mad marriage, the death of one of his mentors, and the rush of the entire world trying to make a buck out of Tyson while the going is good, it is hardly surprising that life goes funny on him every now and then. And he is only 22.

On Monday I went to the tennis, awarding myself high marks for street cred by travelling to Flushing Meadow by subway. The marks were unmerited, because the subway is not the last circle of hell, as its PR seems to insist. It was an easy rattle into Queens: not a lot like Wimbledon, save in the weather. It poured down. I met up with Rex Bellamy, resplendent in his C & A 'Jazz' shirt, and, there being no tennis, I went back to Manhattan to write a piece about the television scheduling of the event. This, like the schoolboy cricketers, was a better story than it sounds. At the US Open the telly people control the playing schedule – well, they should, I suppose, considering the dizzy amount they pay, which is reckoned to be $15 million. Naturally they want American heroes on the box at prime time – they want to sell Wheaties, after all. The previous year, the all-time nonsense record had been set by Gabriela Sabatini, who, thanks to the absurd scheduling, was forced to play a match so late in the evening that it did not finish until 1.19 a.m. One of the best matches of the women's singles matched two Americans, Lori McNeil and Zina Garrison. They were sent to an outside court, with no television, and they played a belter. Could the fact that they are both black have anything to do with it?

'Let's face it, we're selling a product here. This is an American tournament.' Oh yes, it made a nice little piece.

The following day brought us some tennis, and I was able to start enjoying the atmosphere of this very special tournament. 'What are *you* doing here?' people kept asking me in the press box.

'I wanted to come here. I *asked* to come here.'

'You must be mad.'

Perhaps. But it's different for a non-specialist. A proper tennis reporter has to cover everything, daren't risk missing anything. But I, with a very different assignment, could cruise about, and enjoy whatever was there to enjoy, and keep an eye open for any other story that might pop up. For the tennis writers, the low-flying jets – Flushing Meadow is practically on the main runway at La Guardia airport – are a headache, the noisy, partisan crowds a perpetual irritation, the packed walkways a hideous nuisance, and the ludicrous site of the press box, about 300 feet up in the air above the main court, a professional horror. But for a columnist all these things were a hoot, the Coney Island hot dogs a piquant detail, and all the while the Manhattan skyline lifted my heart every time I looked that way. 'You should have been here last year, then,' someone told me. 'When the press box got hit by a tornado.'

There are four Grand Slam tournaments, and of these, Rex likes Paris best, Wimbledon second, Australia a fairly distant third. The US Open is not even mentioned. Most tennis writers would heartily agree. But I found the tournament awful-yet-irresistible – just like New York; just like John McEnroe, who is the symbol of New York's self-regarding soul.

However, marketing men, looking as ever to the future, were crowing with glee about the emergence of the youthful prodigy, André Agassi. Tennis needs a strong America – at least, it does if it wants to make lots of money. And until Agassi, America had nobody that was real box office, other than that pair of fading old rascals, Connors and McEnroe.

Agassi is a treat for us all. With his long hair, denim shorts and his fresh face, he looks just like a rich kid playing for the heck of it: loser buys the sodas. And as he plays, he shines with niceness, playing to the crowd with his clever fancy tricks or 'showboating' as Americans call it, cracking jokes, applauding his opponent's shots. 'It's wonderful that he is so nice,' the tennis marketing men say, but the truth is that his niceness is just a bonus. What matters is the fact that he is so American, and a winner to boot. He is a born-again Christian, but he wears that as lightly as it is possible to wear such a thing. Naturally, everyone is looking for flaws in his act, but they can't find any. This is because his act is for real. (It was when he started losing the following year that he began to get criticism.) 'Don't you find it kinda tough, playing to the crowds all the time, Ahn-dray?'

'Oh no. It's just the way I am. I like to make jokes, entertain people. It makes a better environment for everyone. It isn't a strain at all. It just happens. But I guess I'll have moments when I get upset. A few years down the road, we'll see.' The talent is glaringly obvious; he really does fetch the ball the most awful swipe. All players, even the best, seem slightly knocked back when hitting a big forehand. But Agassi *advances* into the ball. 'Strength is important, and I guess I'm kinda waiting on that,' he said. His strength is in his phenomenal timing. Pressure, his every smile asks, what pressure? He really is a rather remarkable fellow. Pretty girls in the crowd give him flowers when he steps on court.

Back in the mean ol' city, Tyson had been knocked off the back pages, and both front and back had been taken over by Lawrence Taylor, linebacker of the New York Giants: a superstar and another New York love-object. Cocaine had been found in his blood – the second time that had happened. A few months ago he had claimed to be cured of cocaine addiction; claimed, in fact, to have cured himself by playing golf. As a player, the man is a defensive genius, and a superb athlete. That is all anybody has ever cared about. So long as he was able to maintain his superb form, no one was ever likely to give him a moment's worry. 'I live life in the fast lane – and always have. I drink too much, I party too much, I drive too fast and I'm hell on quarterbacks. It's always been that way. When someone says I'm crazy, I take it as a compliment.' Thus Taylor begin his ghosted autobiography *LT – Living On The Edge*.

Taylor, his addiction, his denial of his addiction, and his ability to maintain his brilliant form despite his addiction, reminded me at once of an old friend from Hong Kong. I will call him Jamie, since that is nothing like his name.

'When people say I'm crazy I take it as a compliment.' Lawrence Taylor of the New York Giants: superb athlete, defensive genius and drug fiend.
(*Steve Dykes/AllSport*)

Jamie and I worked together briefly, and after that we used to meet every now and then for a few beers. This, for some reason, always happened early in the evening. A very nice man, good company, very funny, and a good, competent journalist – the sort you can rely on utterly, a rock on the subs' desk. No newspaper would ever come out without people like Jamie.

A year or two back, when I was back in Hong Kong for a brief period, Jamie and I arranged to meet. Naturally we met in a bar. 'Beer?' I asked as he came in.

'A tonic water, please.'

'What's this? Losing weight?'

'Not exactly no. I'm off it.'

'Oh yeah? Antibiotics or something? How long for?'

'For ever.'

'But . . . I mean, how long have you, been off it, how long has this fit been on you?'

'A year. Just over.'

'Bloody hell – why?'

'Because I'm an alcoholic, Simon.'

This was something I simply did not wish to deal with. I knew Jamie. A man like me, who happens to like a beer or three, right? Like us all, right? This is what a good journo, and a good companion, always does. So how come he had given it all up? He said he had been on a bottle of spirits a day (or better still, two) for years. For about as long as he could remember, not that his memory was all that much practical help. He had never been to work without a few stiff ones under his belt: it just was not possible to start the day without them. Day after day, getting through was a matter of keeping topped up.

'But Jamie, I never saw you pissed. I mean, you were subbing copy, making the bloody computer work. You need to be at least three parts sober to do that.'

'No, that's not true. I should know – and it's very common.' Jamie had suddenly adopted the manner of a lecturer in social studies. 'Alcoholics need to stay in touch with the bottle. Need to know where the next bottle is coming from. And for me, that meant staying in work. Because of that, it was essential to do the job competently, so I did – even though I was pissed every minute of every day.'

I saw then that I and everyone who knew Jamie or who worked with him had been part of the conspiracy to keep him drinking. Oh, *he's* all right. Does his job, doesn't he? He has a few in the evenings, but who doesn't? He must be all right if he can sub copy and make the computer go. He never misses a deadline, does he? So he must be all right. So long as your addiction doesn't make you inconvenient, no one is interested. Everything is fine: thus the addict is able to maintain his addiction. People help him maintain, almost encourage him to maintain. He becomes almost a justification for one's own more moderate intake: blimey, if he can keep going on the amount he puts away, I must be all right, mustn't I? That the addict may be putting away a great deal more in secret is not even considered: no one wants to know. Jamie was an example and an encouragement to us all.

Jamie sipped his tonic water and told me more stories I didn't want to hear: waking in the morning and discovering that his jacket pockets were full of vomit – that sort of thing. Secrecy and guilt, self-deception and deception, desperation and its conquest by self-justification, by denial of the problem. The support of the world in his deceptions and his self-deceptions: oh, *he's* all right. Does his job, doesn't he?

He went on to tell me of his decision to take the cure, making the decision in the knowledge that he could not face the thought of the cure when sober. This sounds paradoxical, mainly because it is, but it made perfect sense to Jamie at the time. He got himself thoroughly tanked up, and took a taxi to the hospital. He made his request to be admitted to the hospital for the purpose of taking the cure by leaning out of the taxi window, waving his arms about, and yelling: 'Let me in! I'm fucking pissed!'

They did let him in. He went through the DTs, during which he believed he was constantly under attack by flying parrots. Jamie, always a good story-teller, made much of this sound funny. It obviously wasn't. But he came out sober. This is how he refers to it: 'Since I was sober.' He had been more or less unbrokenly drunk, he estimates, from his teens to his middle 30s. Somehow he had picked up a family of three children in that time. Relearning them was one of the great rewards of sobriety.

I have seen Jamie a couple of times since that meeting, when I have returned to Hong Kong for the rugby Sevens. He is still sober. 'Being sober is better,' he said once, 'but it doesn't make life easier.'

'What's difficult?'

'Oh, you know . . . getting out of bed. Putting my clothes on. That sort of thing.'

People try to jollify journos and their drinking habits, just as they try to jollify the lowlife of violence and crime. Both are pieces of vicious dishonesty. Lawrence Taylor was caught up in the dishonesty side of it himself, with his belief that he cured himself by playing golf – 'the denial stage' is what Americans call it. 'My therapy, not recommended for anybody else, was to enjoy myself as much as I could, to live, not like a sick or confined person, which the books and the theories tell you you should when you're addicted – but like a healthy person, able to make choices in relative peace and freedom.'

It sounds good, and people will help you to deny, to maintain that illusion as long as you can maintain your performance of your role, your job. Jamie stands for me as a there-but-for-the-grace-of-God figure. I think of him often, and hope he can keep off the stuff. For he knows that now he is sober, nothing will ever be easy again.

I wrote a long piece on Lawrence Taylor and the 'denial stage'. With Jamie very much at the back of my mind, I tried to make it an important piece. Sportswriting is not always about sport, thank God.

But there was one other sports story I had to get hold of: that was a piece with the American television network, NBC. The world was paying a total of $409 million for the rights to cover the Olympic games on television. Of this, NBC were paying $300 million. And they would make a profit on this. Sport is about many things, but it is very much about money as well.

The Olympics were looming ever closer. I left the Mayflower and got a taxi to the airport, knowing that in eight days I would be flying out to Seoul for the Olympic Games. It seemed a fearsome and preposterous thought. I had a horrifying wait before getting on the plane, because I was put on standby, but ten minutes before it was about to leave without me, I was given seat 1A, the best seat on the aeroplane. Upgrade to first class. I was James Bond once again: beer, please, and if it's not cold enough, I'll tear your ears off. And 16 hours after take-off, I was playing cricket for the mighty Tewin Irregulars.

17. WHEN *THE TIMES* GAINED A WRITER BRITAIN LOST THE FINEST ALL-ROUND SPORTSMAN IN THE HISTORY OF THE WORLD

There is one more question that I get asked a lot. 'What sports do you actually do?' Or if I am at some loathsome cocktail-type function: 'Are you frightfully sporty?' The last question really means, when interpreted, 'Oh my God, how on earth did I get landed with you, and how long will it be before I can join the fascinating conversation I can half-hear behind me?' This enquiry into my sporting prowess is never made with awe, or even respect. A raised and derisive eyebrow, more like.

There are many sports reporters who are, or who have been, most frightfully sporty. Srikumar Sen, as I said, is a boxing blue, Ken Jones of the *Independent* played professional soccer, Pat Butcher, our athletics man, was a respectable athlete, at least in terms of athletic performance. Chris Brasher of the *Observer* has a gold medal. But it is at the cricket that you find the greatest concentration of lapsed players. Sometimes it seems that half the press box played for England, and naturally, they look down on any pro-turned-journo who never got beyond county cricket. But whatever you do, never ask Mike Selvey of Middlesex, Glamorgan and the *Guardian* if he regrets never having played for England. It is a fascinating but little known fact that he played two or three Test Matches. Certainly he is Test class as a writer.

You might expect the cricketers to look down on the non-cricketers in the press box, and so they do, to an extent. But the trouble is John Woodcock, former cricket correspondent of *The Times*. He still writes for us, though a little less often than before, since he is no longer a slip of a youth. He is one of the best cricket writers of all time, yet was never much of a player – at any rate, his playing days are shrouded in mystery. But his fulminations, his knowledge and his Olympian judgements have had a profound influence on cricket writing and on cricket itself.

For ability at sport is no guarantee of being able to write about sport. A good playing record is only really an advantage when it comes to one-upmanship. I sometimes yearn to write: 'It is always a hard thing to judge a ball coming out of the Oval gasholder, as I well remember . . .' Or perhaps: 'Once you have reached your double century, the entire game of cricket becomes a simple matter.' There are some cricket writers who stoutly maintain that only former internationals can write about international cricket, but this is manifest nonsense, on a par with the argument that only actors who are also murderers are capable of playing Macbeth. The former player has certain advantages, but these can readily be lost in clouded judgements and self-deceiving memories and, worse still, in an inability to know what's going off out there.

In most press boxes, the commonest species is the sportsman manqué. These are people who love sport above all things, have always played sport and always will, but who were never quite good enough to play the game for a living. For them, writing about it, being involved with it, is a good second best. Me, I am just a writer, and I say that with the most airy insouciance you could imagine. Though I do play a bit of sport here and there.

I have already said enough about my heady days as goalkeeper for Gwai-Loong FC. These Gwai-Loong stories show an activist spirit, but they don't really compete with Brasher's gold medal in terms of sporting achievement.

I also play cricket, though it was not a game I played with any regularity until I returned from Hong Kong in 1982, aged 31. I play for the mighty Tewin Irregulars, that team which seems to get a mention in my Diary column just about every other week. It was founded by me and my two brothers-in-law. It happened at a family gathering in the Christmas of 1983. We agreed it would be nice to play cricket the following season: that we must join a team. Then an ugly silence developed. What team in creation would want me for a wicket-keeper, Salty for an opening bat and Roob for a bowler? And all at the same time?

Then we remembered the fat kid: the fat kid who always plays at centre forward in the playground, although he is absolutely useless. The reason for this is simple: it is his ball. Well, if it was Our Ball, or rather Our Team, we could pick who we liked. Agreed? Agreed. We struck a deal for use of the sacred turf of Tewin Green, a village in Hertfordshire, and thus the Tewin Irregulars were born.

And though the Tewin Irregulars is the source of a thousand jokes, please do not think that the cricket is ever anything less than serious. We play as hard as we can, and to win, if we can. We have some good players – a good few club cricketers actually like to play for us – and we have other players of abilities closer to my own who would die rather than miss a game.

I am not being modest when I say I am not much good. I am being accurate. I keep wicket, and the strongest side of my game is certainly the appeal. And sometimes, when batting, and finding that I have missed that *infuriating* legside flick once again, I wish I had been coached at school, wish I had played for my school team, wish I was the hero of Tewin and the toast of the Plume of Feathers. But on games afternoon at school, I was never there.

I hated games. I skived off; I went down the pub with my friend Ralph, and we would drink halves of Watneys Starlight Bitter and talk big about *Finnegans Wake* and *The Rainbow*. 'Two more halves of Starlight, please . . . but look, Ralph, the whole point of literature is words –'

'Cheers, no, balls, Simon, the point of literature is ideas and . . .'

'. . . Lawrence's phallic never-never land . . .'

'. . . Joyce's masturbatory obsession with words . . .'

'. . . the whole point of life . . .'

'. . . but if a Martian was to come down . . .'

'. . . I thought it was a Martian that *wrote* . . .'

And, tipsy on a pint and a half and drunk with our own pretensions, we would weave our way home, while the cricketers cricketed on, learning to keep the bat *absolutely straight* when playing the legside flick, and the head *absolutely still*. And so, as I bat on for the Irregulars – 'Hard luck, Simon, that was a brute of a ball' – I do sometimes regret never having been coached. But not if it would have meant missing those hours of talk. Sport is a pleasure but books, words are my life.

I am not much of a sportsman at these ball games, but I do ride horses passably well. For some reason that never seems to impress people, and believe me, I have tried. But of all the sports in which I have been an activist, it is horses I love the best.

Which is not to complain about the match that pitted the Tewin Irregulars against the *Daily Mirror* Badgers, 18 hours after I had left Kennedy airport. It was a beauty, a crackingly competitive game in golden autumn sunlight. We scored a lot, they chased 'em and lost wickets, we tempted and they lost a few more, they shut up shop and blocked for the draw, and in the end, we blasted them all out but the last pair. Paul 'The Fish' Fisher gave them a horrible last over, but they stood firm. A lovely game, and afterwards, we drank beer and talked. Summer was over.

'So I suppose you're off to the Olympics, Simon?'

'Oh . . . ah, yes.'

'Are you worried about all these threats of terrorism? And all the riots you see on television?'

'No, I'm not worried. Just scared shitless.'

'When do you leave?'

'Week today.'

'Best of luck. You'll need all you can get.'

'Absolutely.

That night I had a dream that I had lost my accreditation to the entire Olympic Games.

I was reminded of an occasion when I had ridden a horse I owned in his first three day event. He was a former racehorse, had raced for eight years, and when he came to me, he had two speeds, walk and piss off. I had done all his schooling myself, not necessarily a fact that inspired confidence. I was not sure quite how deep my lessons had gone. The horse, a lovely beast whom I called 'Trevor', was, I knew, just a little too inexperienced to be wholly reliable when it came to charging round the country over fences . . . and some of the fences had me speaking fluent French of the Ginny Leng variety. It was going to be awfully tough trying to get round, never mind about winning. It was to be a learning experience for the horse: what it was to be for me was in the lap of the gods.

As I warmed my horse up before setting out, I could feel that my old friend peritonitis was back. The old knife in the guts. The voice in my ear was saying: 'It would be stupid to go on. You know it would. You're too ill. It would be too dangerous, it would be dangerous for the horse. The only sane option is to get off, go on, do it right now, tell the starter you are terribly terribly sorry, but you have peritonitis and you are forced to withdraw.' And all the while you know that whatever the voice says, you are going to go for it. And that makes the waiting even more horrible.

'Thirty seconds Simon Barnes.'

Jesus, this is the last chance, explain now, withdraw at once, tell him . . .

'Ten seconds Simon Barnes, nine, eight, seven . . .' and the horse takes a great bite of air and bunches himself up underneath you, bouncing up and down with over-eagerness, you check-check-check, and, as you get to the first fence, you aim him like an arrow; you lean forward, nudge him with your legs, and tell him GO! And you are over it, off and rolling, and you are standing in the stirrups, arse in the air, teeth in the mane and the great champagne-fizz of excitement in your veins; there are 29 more fences, to go and you love them all – Christ, you'll jump a house if they put one in the way, just let them try and stop you now.

Ah yes, good times. But as I check-check-checked for the 32nd time that day, to see if I still had my traveller's cheques, passport, credit cards, plane tickets and, yes, my Olympic accreditation, I felt the familiar knife in the gut. Was it really wise to attempt to cover the Olympics when I had peritonitis?

18. THE OLYMPICS: SILENCED MACHINE-GUNS GUARD THE SOLDIERS OF THE PHONY WAR

'Velly solly, mister – no lecord of your accleditation.'

'I, ah ah ah, beg your pardon?'

'Glo black to Rondon. Glet your arse out of Kolea, mister. We no wantee lighter like you.'

Surely it wouldn't be like this, would it? This ludicrous (not to mention racist) cartoon figure had become my waking nightmare. The velly-solly man haunted me as I sat there at Amsterdam airport, waiting for my connection to Seoul and the Olympic Games. It wasn't Asia I was worried about, for I knew that side of things pretty well. It was the Olympics. Passport? Don't be an idiot, how would you have got as far as Amsterdam without it? Money? Traveller's cheques? Credit cards? Olympic accreditation? Yes, and it was dog-eared from the number of times I had checked it. The beer was cold, but Barnes was utterly uncool.

I checked my Olympic accreditation once more for luck and ordered another beer. There was no disguising facts: I was extremely nervous. I was nervous of the riots, and of the threats of international terrorism: students were throwing Molotov cocktails every night on the news, and the bizarre statements from Pyongyang, capital of North Korea, did not imply that the matter of the Olympic Games could be concluded in any rational way. The eyes of the mavericks and the opportunists were raking across Korea. But that was not all. I was also worried about the sheer immensity of the Olympic Games. This was, after all, to be the first time I had been to the Games. Well, of course, when you analysed that side of things, there was nothing to worry about. I knew I could write sports stories, and the Olympic Games is, whatever else it is as well, a load of sports stories. Another day, another story: surely there would be no problem with that? But I did not know the ropes, did not know how to reach people for interviews or what an Olympic Village would be like, or how you get into the events. Well, that would be made plain very soon: it was stupid to get worried. So I sipped my beer and worried a little more. Wouldn't it be awful if I missed my flight?

Well, I didn't miss it. I even managed not to be first on board, a fine example of self-restraint. And joining the flight was like joining the Olympics – the plane was full of Poles in tracksuits, plus a team from some sport or other who looked so remarkably clean and fresh that they could only be Dutch, and, all dressed in wickerwork hats like lampshades, the Lesotho Olympic team, gabbling excitedly, a genuine Olympic exoticism. I wondered if any of this planeload was a tracksuited terrorist: I repressed this thought with a stern effort of the will.

It was time I started looking cool. Perhaps I was overdoing it – indeed, when I got to Seoul, one of the Korean greeters told me: 'You look just *like* a writer,' a clear indication that I had overdressed the part once again. I was wearing a Rohan safari jacket, with a Greenpeace badge pinned to one of the enormous number of Useful Pockets. Frightfully intrepid-looking. On the plane, I sat next to the Polish physio, and after we had chatted for a while, I began to write my first Olympic piece. The Saturday *Times* now had a colour section, and needed copy a long way in advance. I had to write 1500 words on women at the Games. I try not to work on planes, because planes make my writing go peculiar. The atmosphere on a plane is weird, so remote, it is hard to have any connection with the real world, and this seems to affect what I write. The piece I wrote was mad: the first 400 words were all about Mary Decker's teeth, and contained a searching analysis of American orthodontistry. After that, however, it began to get *seriously* weird.

The excitement of all the athletes on board bubbled through the plane, and had me in great good cheer. The jumpiness was wearing off: I felt not only frightfully intrepid but wildly glamorous as well, off to the Olympics in my safari jacket. These props to my self-esteem were brutally chopped away by the stewardess. She glanced at my Greenpeace badge as she served me my vegetarian meal (rabbit-pack journalism still rules OK) and she asked me, with awe in her voice, if I was going 'on the ice'. The ice? Like bourbon on the rocks? Oh, the *ice*. We were making a stopover at Anchorage, Alaska. 'I mean, you work for Greenpeace, don't you? Isn't that why you are going to Alaska?' she said. All my glamour fell from me at once.

'No. I'm just going to the Olympics.'

'Oh.' I have never seen anyone's face fall as far and as fast. Well, it is important to keep a sense of perspective – but it is a lot more fun to be puffed up with self-congratulation. With me thoroughly put in my place, we flew to Anchorage. We left the plane. I took a brief stroll up and down to rev up the circulation, inspected the stuffed polar bear (another James Bond character; it appears in *You Only Live Twice*) and then I saw one of the most beautiful sights in the world. It was a neat and cosy little all-American bar. I walked in.

'Hi!'

'Hi,' I replied, cool and streetwise, placing a ten on the bar. Yes, I had actually learnt something; I had dollars this time. 'Wild, ah, Turkey on the rocks, please.' Greenpeace man on the ice. I had two, returned to the plane in good heart and slept all the rest of the way to Seoul. The finest way to travel is unconscious.

One of the most marvellous things about long-distance air travel (this was a 26-hour journey) is that it leaves you so shattered and disorientated that on arrival, you simply cannot summon up the enthusiasm to be neurotic. The launch into the unfamiliar should be the worst part of the journey, but exhaustion and disorientation make you capable of accepting everything that happens with the same dislocated grin. Bureaucracy? International terrorism? Rapacious taxi drivers? I cared nothing for any of these. I felt like Stringham in Anthony Powell: 'I am now in a perfect condition to be received into one of those oriental religions whose only tenet is complete submission to Fate.'

I queued in several queues, and some of the queues were the right queue. I wated for an eon or two by the baggage carousel, was greeted by a blazered greeter, and was given a 'pin' or enamel badge that said 'Welcome to Kimpo Airport'. I declared several million items to Korean customs, and had my baggage X-rayed about 42 times. X-ray machines damage computers, and I had my Tandy with me. Ah well, if Fate wishes to destroy the Tandy, Fate will destroy it. Just is the wheel. On I went into the maw of the Olympic Games. Everything was either brilliantly organised or utter chaos: the two can look very similar and I was in no position to make fine distinctions. At intervals a different charming Korean in a yellow blazer would smile and bow and bid me Welcome to Korea, and ask me where I was from. It spoiled things if you asked them a question in return, it was heart-breaking to see their faces fall as they wrestled with the ridiculous English language. And my Korean was not up to much, either.

To my surprise, I found myself entering a coach that would take me to the Village. 'Do you mind travelling with the Iranian journalists?' Terrorism? Here we went, I thought. An invitation to bloodshed and horror? I smiled weakly and climbed aboard the bus. Just is the wheel. Off we went, timing it nicely to hit the rush hour. I looked out of the window and favoured Seoul with my rabbit-in-a-car-headlights look. I had been there twice before in my Asian Period, but I never managed to get the hang of the place. In fact, it was the one place in Asia I ended up thoroughly disliking: I found it impenetrable and obstreperous at the same time, a bewildering combination. I could remember nothing of the city as I looked out of the window: all I could see was a vast number of suitable places for the concealment of snipers or of suicide bombers. I felt that my brain had been accidentally unloaded at Anchorage, and would be sent on to me, perhaps tomorrow. This seemed a city of broad streets and endless jams. After an eternity or two of travelling, the last thing you really feel like is another eternity of travelling. But after sitting in the coach for a timespan roughly equivalent to the entire Pleistocene era, we pulled up. A vast sign said: 'PRESS VILLAGE'. This looked very like the right place. The moment of truth was upon me. I squared my shoulders and marched in, prepared to face the velly-solly man.

My bags were X-rayed a couple of times more to send the Tandy into a neurotic fit if it wasn't in one already. I waited calmly, having already submitted to Fate. I went from queue to queue, desk to desk.

'Your name please.'

'Bar-nezz.'

'Welcome to Korea.'

I kept signing things, and moving to another queue and signing a few things more. Impassive men carrying machine-guns broke up the pattern of busy, smiling people in yellow blazers. At one stage I handed over a perfectly enormous sum in dollars. The only credit card acceptable in the Village was Visa, by virtue of some sponsorship deal; more or less the only card I did not possess was Visa. I made a vow never to carry Visa as a small piece of revenge, and handed over the poor man's credit card, the American dollar. At one stage I had my photograph taken for my Olympic ID card. I was aware that I would have to wear this picture for the next three-and-a-half weeks, so I drew my safari jacket about me and assumed an expression of streetwise cool. 'The neurotic Iranian terrorist look,' said Matthew Engel later.

And then, with bewildering suddenness, it was all over. I was fully accredited to the Olympic Games. I had a room in the Village, paid for. I had a telephone in that room, paid for. I had my ID card that would get me into every event. What more could any journalist want? Well, sleep, and before that, a perfectly enormous glass of The Famous Grouse. Neither would be hard to find.

I was driven across the Village in a small van. I peered out: a series of tower blocks, destined when the Games were over to become rather expensive flats. The Press were to be the first occupants; one's heart went out to the subsequent buyers. The place looked rather like a barracks. Bleak squares, perhaps for the drilling of defaulters, broke up the pattern of the towers. Occasional half-hearted efforts at children's playgrounds interrupted the acres of concrete.

The van took me to my block. At the ground floor, a team of young Koreans took over. They were charming, energetic and T-shirted, and looked about 16; naturally they were all Army regulars of long experience. The Asian face seems not to age between the years of 16 and 45; Americans had thought the Vietnamese were sending armies of teenagers against them, but they were all grizzled veterans of jungle warfare. One of these soldiers showed me to my room. It was in a flat, one of four based around a common-room.

It was an experience which, to quote Powell once again, drove a relatively deep fissure through the variegated seams of time. I had the illusion that I was walking straight into a student hall of residence. There was no one there but John Goodbody, the *Times* sports news reporter and our official linkman or *chef de mission* as he preferrd to describe it. He was looking immensely dashing in his *déshabillé*, an authentic Japanese kimono. Well, I would wow him later with my Balinese sarong. Goodbody looks like Clark Kent: the same prodigious muscular development, the same black glasses. A little more hair on the top of the head would have completed the illusion. Goodbody weight-lifts, judo-plays, and ultra-distance swims; he has a Blue for shot putting, and tells me he is a member of the Hawks Club, which is apparently a very difficult and splendid thing to be. He has a number of academic distinctions as well; well, he would, wouldn't he? He reads as easily in French as he does in English, and claims to be at least as well read as I am.

Not that I was quite up to literary one-upmanship when I arrived. I made a heroic decision to eat some food, knowing how much happier this would make me in the morning. Goodbody directed me to the dining room but did not prepare me for the shock.

I approached the door. Three pretty women in enormous pink dresses like pregnancy smocks (this is Korean national dress), plus two smart men in dinner suits, formed an aisle through which I had to pass. Each separately bowed, smiled, and said: 'Bing-bong seyo!' (Or something like that; I never did quite unscramble the consonants of this charming greeting; after all, I only heard it 24 times a day for the next 25 days.)

Bing-bong seyo! Everywhere you went in Seoul, thousands of ladies in pregnancy smocks – the national dress of Korea – greeted you with an avalanche of charm.
(Gray Mortimore/AllSport)

I grinned back feebly and bowed. I entered the room: well, not really a room, more an aircraft hangar, in which about two thousand people could dine at once. At this hour, I had it almost to myself. I ate a plate full of something, and returned. I poured myself the aforementioned octuple Grouse from my duty-free, and Goodbody gave me a great deal of sensible advice about Seoul and the Olympic Games, not one word of which I remembered. I went to bed. Sleep came with the swiftness of a blow from a rubber truncheon.

I still felt as if I were in a dream when Goodbody awoke me the next morning. The first thing he did was to inspect my book-pile: 'Hm, Dante . . . how good *is* your Italian? You know, of all the translations of Dante I think the Sayers is the least . . .' Chattering on, he acted as my Virgil and led me to breakfast. I felt, and rightly, that at the Olympics, a good breakfast would be a vital pre-emptive strike against the vicissitudes of the day. Load up on the cholesterol and then attack the Games: such was my resolution. I descended to the aircraft hangar with Goodbody.

'Bing-bong seyo!'

'Bing-bong seyo!'

But a yet more awesome prospect was in store. Inside the hangar, there were about a million sports journalists, all loading up on cholesterol, and, in a cacophonous babel of languages, sport was being discussed. Sport is the Esperanto of the world.

It seemed that every sportswriter I had ever known was there. For a moment I thought I had died and gone to the place where bad sportswriters go. I helped myself to scrambled eggs and hash browns (a kind of American thing they do with potatoes) and thought vaguely: but we are supposed to be *good* sportswriters, are we not? Good enough to be at the Olympics, anyway. Even me?

Goodbody chattered on gaily over his enormous plateful. He was in his element: this was, he told me, his sixth Olympics. He was rubbing his hands with glee over the three-and-a-half weeks of writing stories – literally, no exaggeration, he was rubbing his hands like a character in a Victorian melodrama. Goodbody is a well-read man with his mind in the gutter. We are all of us in the gutter, but some of us are looking at the stars, said Oscar Wilde, a writer Goodbody is fond of. Goodbody is in the gutter with the rest of us, but he is looking at *The Star*. He loves scandals; he loves exposé journalism; he loves drug stories; there is not a journalist in the world that knows as much about drugs in sport as he does. He was expressing his hopes of some enormous story breaking: 'There's always something, my lad, there's always something. Drugs, dirt, sex, violence. Always something.' His favourite writer is Henry James.

Breakfast done, we passed back through the aircraft hangar, greeting one British sportswriter after another. There was Hugh McIlvanney, Ken Jones, Dudley Doust. There was Ian Wooldridge, there Matthew Engel.

'How was your journey?'

'Know anyone who's got his Tandy working?'

There was Alan Hubbard, my old pal from Atlantic City, he who wrote that little gem in the *Observer*. I gave him my best Paddington Bear stare. That would teach him to call me a somewhat sensitive soul. There was an entire table of people from the *Telegraph*, with Mike Calvin preparing not to write nice features. Goodbody moved from table to table, giving messages to everyone. This is his way; he cannot bear to pass any journalist from any paper without passing on a message of some kind. I went with him. He approached the table with Hubbard, and I prepared a dose of cosmic radiation. Then, unusually, good sense stepped in. I could hardly keep on radiating cosmic radiation for three-and-a-half weeks, now could I?

'Hello, Alan.'

'Hello, Simon. All right?'

'Not so bad, thanks. Got your Tandy working?'

'No.'

The Camp David Accord had been reached. What big-hearted people we journos are, eh?

Tom had told me to get to Seoul early, and not to feel any pressure to write until I had got my eye in. Good not to feel pressure, but no batsman feels he has his eye in until he has a single on the board. I wanted to feel like a Working Journalist at the Olympics. I wanted to write.

This was the Phony War period, the half-dozen days before the opening ceremony. Nothing was happening save that people were arriving and getting tense and trying not to show it. There were no *stories*. So the British Olympics Association organised a few press conferences, mostly intended to shove the minor sports into centre stage. On my first day, we had judo and shooting. Goodbody, naturally, took the judo, and I got the shooting and, if I had but known it, a run of the most perfect Olympic luck began to roll, and I found myself all at once with the story of the day.

Malcolm Cooper was the shooter we all wanted to talk to. He had won the three-position event in Los Angeles, and was favourite to win the gold again, despite the hotter competition from the Soviets, who boycotted in 1984. But when the British press got to the rifle range on the other side of town, Cooper was not talking to a soul. Now, we journos hate it when people from minor sports start chucking their weight around and acting like prima donnas. There is just a whiff of a feeling that it is us doing them the favour by writing about them. But I felt Cooper had a point. Someone in the media had broken his rifle.

It was an accident, of course, but that didn't make the gun any less broken. A woman from the BBC had knocked it off a table. The Beeb then asked if they could make a film of Cooper mending it: nice one. If there was a request demanding a two word answer, this was it. And they got it, too.

It was Sarah Cooper, Malcolm's wife and another Olympic shooter, who made the day for the British journos. She fielded all the questions we might have wanted to put to her husband. We formed a group around her and asked her about the nature of shooting and guns, and what happens when they break. 'Like Jack Nicklaus breaking his putter before the Open?' said my friend Jim Lawton of the *Express* hopefully.

'Yes, exactly.'

Get that down, lads. Sometimes a training set-back, or some imagined injustice, can be a great motivating force for the hot-blooded athlete, but shooting is a sport that works backwards: a sprinter seeks to explode from the blocks, but a rifleman seeks stillness. Scores improve all the time in shooting: it seems that riflemen are capable of reaching a stiller stillness than the riflemen of the past. 'Adrenalin helps a runner,' Sarah Cooper said. 'It is detrimental to us. A surge of adrenalin sends the heart-rate up; we strive to keep our heart-rate down.'

With the help of Sarah Cooper and the lady from the BBC, my own adrenalin was beginning to flow nicely. I returned to the village, and wrote. I then rewrote my piece on Mary Decker's teeth: thanks to great self-discipline I managed to make it touch ground in one or two places. It was for use in nearly to weeks' time: such is the nature of colour deadliness.

I dictated the pieces through the telephone word by word. The blasted bloody Tandy would not work. This was not the fault of the X-rays but of the instructions I had been given. There is nothing quite as irritating as technology that works, but which you are not capable of operating, especially when you can blame some absent person for this failure.

The following day we had two more press conferences. Goodbody took the modern pentathlon, I did the gymnastics. This was stuff to keep the Olympic pot boiling, no more. The conferences were held in the Athletes' Village. Getting there involved a half-mile march between two 15-foot wire fences, under the eyes of soldiers with silenced sub-machine-guns. Why were they silenced, I wondered every day of the Games as I passed yet another uniformed pseudo-teenager. Every time you went into the Press Village you were greeted –

'Bing-bong seyo!'

– and your bag was searched and you went through a metal detector. I was required to remove my hat every time –

'Kamsa hamida!'

– or thank you. Smiles and bows and every time you went from one place to another, it was Checkpoint Charlie. Under normal circumstances, I and anyone else would hate such a routine. I loathe the calm, self-righteous insolence of the gateman. I hate the man with the false ginger moustache at Wimbledon, the waiter at the Café Royal, the weighing-room man at Aintree. But the Koreans were all charming, whether they wore pink pregnancy smocks or carried silenced machine-guns. They were security, and, at the threatened Olympics, they succeeded in making you feel secure.

I talked to the gymnasts, who explained why they were not going to win any medals, and how the Soviets and the Romanians had a different system which meant that no British gymnast could ever compete against them on equal terms.

'Would you *want* to train six hours a day from the age of four onwards?' I asked Karen Hargate.

She thought about that one. 'No . . . though I wish I *had* done.' A piercingly honest answer. She trains, she told us, in a deconsecrated church. Get that down, lads. Me, I would sooner be an amateur training in a silly place like a dead church and hoping against hope to finish in the top one hundred, than a cosseted item of national prestige trained from a tiny child until I reached my peak at 16, and my useful life was over.

The British Olympic Association then told us that Ian Taylor, the hockey goalie, was to carry the flag at the opening ceremony. This was a good choice. Taylor is part of the army of gym teachers and sports goods reps that plays such a part in the sporting life of Britain. He is an extremely nice, extremely ordinary man: a nobody in East Grinstead, a superstar in hockey-mad places like India and Pakistan. He was his usual charming and modest self when he gave his press conference. Many of the big-deal British athletes would miss the opening ceremony, partly because it would interrupt their sacred preparations, and partly because it looks so cool to be an absentee. 'I feel very sorry for them,' Taylor said. 'I have had a long and distinguished career, and this is the pinnacle. It is the greatest honour that can be bestowed on any athlete.' Get that down, lads. I can get depressed about all the flag waving that goes on at the Olympics, but not about Taylor. He is a truly good sort.

The only thing that left a bad taste about the interview was an eccentric and rude man accompanying Taylor. This was apparently Roger Self, the team manager. Oh well, I told myself, ignore him.

The next day, I wrote my first Olympic Diary: no shortage of copy for that, either. More and more journos had arrived. So had Florence Griffith Joyner, the American sprinter, she who was clearly destined – indeed, determined – to be the one great star of the Seoul Olympics. She was holding a press conference the following day, and I would be there; so indeed would anyone else in the world who fancied himself or herself as a sporting journo. I was beginning to see that at the Olympic Games, it is not only the athletes who are competing. This is also the number one event for the writers. To succeed or to fail here would be the most dreadfully public event. Over the next fortnight or so, the eyes of the world would turn to the sports pages. Newspapers would work back-to-front and the sports pages would be read first. The Olympic Games are also the Great World Sportswriting Championships.

Flo-Jo tomorrow. My blood was up. The phony war was over: let the Olympics begin.

19. THE MAN WITH THE BROKEN GUN AND THE SLOE-EYED SIREN OF THE OLYMPIC GAMES

Round and round they went, following their banners as the music played endlessly on: 160 nations, following 160 flags. Some marched with strutting feet and swinging arms; others shambled and waved to show how little of the military they possessed. The French wore boaters. The United States contingent was so large and so sloppily arrogant that it overwhelmed the nations on either side, a very unsubtle piece of symbolism. The Lesotho athletes wore their wickerwork lampshade-hats; Ian Taylor carried his flag with duty and obvious pleasure. The Mongolians, three of them, marched in nothing but boots, loincloths and cloaks, and looked like superheroes from a Marvel comic. They were easily my favourites.

I was, as I say, reading Dante at the time (not the Sayers translation, John), and, if you will forgive me, could not fail to relate this to the opening ceremony of the Olympic Games.

> *And so I looked and saw a kind of banner*
> *rushing ahead, whirling with aimless speed*
> *as though it would not ever take a stand . . .*

These lines are about those who cannot get into heaven or into hell, who are wanted neither by God nor by the Devil: this is the kingdom of the half-baked, 'neither faithful nor unfaithful to their God, who, undecided, stood but for themselves.'

This last line, at least, has something of the sporting life about it, and, for that matter, the sportswriting life. Athletes and sportswriters all seem to spend much of their lives whirling about the place with aimless speed, acting but for themselves. It was a sobering thought with which to move into the Games.

At last, the parade was over. This would be the perfect theatrical moment for a terrorist attack on the Games: a bomb; a troupe of mad students with blazing beer bottles; a suicide squad of Iranians falling out of the sky with unsilenced machine-guns. I looked up uneasily for a moment as the teams lined up behind their national flags, and then I had a sudden vision of what the opening ceremony should be. The torch should be lit and, one by one, the flags of the nations should be cast into it. Under the banner of sport, nationhood and with it enmity would be declared dead, ritually banished for the duration of the Olympic fortnight, a special period of grace in which the normal rules of hatred and suspicion would be set aside. Similarities, not divisions would be emphasised; the athletes would regroup not under their national flag but under the banner of their own sports, and the Games would become a festival not of jingoism and differences, but of friendship and things in common. Fat chance.

For it is jingoism that makes the Games box office: it was jingoism for which the United States television company NBC paid $300 million when they bought the rights. The company was praying for American winners, because Americans get neurotic when they see Americans lose. It makes them think that maybe America does not have the monopoly on greatness, and that makes them feel very insecure indeed; so insecure that they grab the remote controller and zap to another channel. A profitable Olympics needs American winners. Well, had there ever been in history a more surefire American winner than Flo-Jo?

You only had to look at the cover of *Newsweek* to see that. There she was, Florence Griffith Joyner, the sloe-eyed siren of the Games, clad in one of her preposterous one-legged siren suits, a pose designed to emphasise that muscled thigh bared to the waist, and with it, just the subtlest hint of brown cleavage. I don't know much about athletics, but I know what America likes. And what America likes, the world wants to look at: to share it, or to gaze with baffled curiosity, or to mock. Or all three, I thought, as I entered the Main Press Centre for the Flo-Jo press conference and braced myself for the chaos I knew I would find within.

The writers pushed their way to the best places in a manner that was almost decorous, and the still photographers fought their way to the front with elbow and shoulder. The newsreel crews, using their heavy cameras as weapons – it is a characteristic of the television cameraman that he spends his life in perpetual amazement that the world does not open up before his every step like the Red Sea – kicked, fought and bit their way to advantageous positions. In a day of Dante-esque visions, this was a relatively deep circle of Hell I found myself in: 'Siddown!' yelled the journos at the back.

'Siddown yourself!'

When she was ready, she came. Flo-Jo: the one calm person in the place; – 'Siddown! I said will the cameramen siddown!' – the dead-eyed star at the eye of the storm. She adjusted the microphone with unruffled serenity, an elaborately made-up vision in a United States tracksuit, a faint, self-gratified smile on her face.

'I'm just focused on winning the gold,' she husked into the microphone. She was so self-contained, it was frightening. 'I'm not really a mystery. Sometimes I'm just by myself. I spend a lot of time thinking, maybe praying. Sometimes I'm dreaming. Or maybe I don't want to share something.'

Or maybe sharing isn't her long suit anyway. That inner stillness really got to me. She just sat there like Lao-Tzu, smiling with some kind of inner certainty, undisturbed by the fact that the world had gone demented all around her.

'Flo –'

'Use the microphone! Questions through the microphone.' And a microphone was passed among the writers like a relay baton.

'Flo –'

'One at a time!'

'Could you tell me –'

'Will the bastards at the front sit fuckin' down!'

'Who do you see as your main rivals, Flo?'

'The main competition is myself. I'm just going to concentrate on myself.' This was not something I had any difficulty in believing whatsoever. I have never seen anyone so focused. She was so accurately, so finely focused on that final goal that her eyes had gone opaque, had gone completely dead. There was nothing behind them at all except the sheer certainty of her victory, of her self.

'Can you tell me where you stand on drugs, Miss Griffith Joyner?' This was Chris Brasher of the *Observer* asking the Big One.

'My recent improvement is all down to hard work,' she said with a smile, knowing that any athlete who puts up a spectacular improvement will be suspected of drugging. Her smile reminded me of Margaret Thatcher; in fact, the longer I sat there, the more Flo-Jo and the Prime Minister seemed to have in common. There was the same inner certainty, the same triumphant smugness, the same inner peace. And Flo-Jo even talks like Thatcher; both use the technique of the closely miked, voiced whisper, which is a showbiz device to soften the voice. Unkind souls suggest that the reason Flo-Jo does this is because she has taken so many drugs that she has been carried to the boundaries of masculinity, and that her voice has more or less broken. The whisper trick is used to disguise the fact that her real voice would make her a

Passez-moi le sick-bag. Florence Griffith Joyner does her stuff for the camera one more time.
(Tony Duffy/AllSport)

natural for the singing of *Ol' Man River*. But Flo-Jo just denied everything. 'I am training three or four times harder than ever before,' she said. 'I am just focused on winning the gold.'

I sat at this press conference in delight. A fascinating monster like Flo-Jo is a writer's dream. You simply could not find it possible to write a boring piece about her. This was her moment. She was a walking, running, whispering, over-made-up story, and there was I, right on the spot. That I had had a fit of the vapours in Amsterdam airport seemed impossible. There was nowhere in the world I would rather be than this stuffy hall full of yelling people and that dead-eyed weirdo at the front. 'The Olympics is not all nice features, you know.' Calvin's words came back to me. Well, this was going to be an *awfully* nice feature – with Flo-Jo in such good form I couldn't lose. 'Follow your dreams,' she said. 'Follow your dreams and stay cool.'

The Games were off and running, and the days fell into shape. The rhythm of life and the patterns of work established themselves effortlessly. *The Times* had a team of seven. Goodbody was liaison man, and David Miller was doing his chief sportswriter bit. He didn't stay in the Village, but in a downtown hotel for easier access to the men of power that so fascinate his journalistic instincts. We also had a riots and politics man, Gavin Bell, who had been based in Seoul for the previous year. As the Games moved into the first week, to my surprise his work-load decreased rather than grew. There were no disruptions of the Games by international terrorists, and the conflicts between Korean students and the police were not riots, but formalised expressions of dissent, as spontaneous as Japanese Noh drama, in which the Molotov cocktails were a kind of symbol of protest rather than weapons thrown with intent to put Seoul in flames. The demonstrations were organised, and they opened and closed to a previously arranged time-table. 'Riot at ten o'clock,' said Matthew Engel. 'If wet in church hall.'

The Times lined up with three specialists, Pat Butcher, the athletics correspondent, Barry Pickthall, the yachting man, and Jenny MacArthur the horse person. We also had two freelance pay-your-own-way people, the veteran hockey writer, Sydney Friskin, a delightful man and a great enthusiast; and Steven Downes, young and ready to do absolutely anything that would help him recoup his fare. As a bonus, he actually knew something about swimming. This was a relief to us all, especially to John Goodbody, who also actually knows about swimming and but for Steve, would have had to do it all himself, when his time might have been better spent chasing horror and scandal.

There were plenty of specialists at the Games, but so far as I could see, it was the non-specialists who had the better deal. For as the Games started, I found myself increasingly amazed and entranced by the massiveness of it all. I have been to plenty of famous places here and there, and sometimes I have found myself sniffing in a superior way and wondering what all the fuss was about. But there are a few places, like the Taj Mahal, or the Manhattan skyline, or the Burmese ruined city of Pagan, that have you gasping, unable to believe that such things exist and that you are there amongst them. That was how the Games looked to me. If you watch the Olympics on television in Britain, you are looking through a keyhole, a British keyhole, and practically all you see are the Brits. The Brits are one one-hundred-and-sixtieth of the Games. I was amazed, and more amazed with every day.

And so, in my position as non-specialist, I went down on the second day to cover the modern pentathlon. Once again, I got lucky: this was a better story than it had seemed when I set out. There was a monstrous cock-up, and I was there for it.

The modern pentathlon is a ridiculously poetic event and only Baron de Coubertin could have invented it. Each competitor is a heroic messenger: he leaps on his horse and when the horse is shot from under him, he fights his enemies off with a sword. He flings himself into a river and swims across it, and on the far side shoots still more enemies to death with his pistol. Then he runs across country and triumphantly lays the message at the feet of his king. This pretty tale is expressed competitively as a show-jumping event, followed by a fencing competition, a swimming race, a pistol shoot and a cross-country run.

I went for the first stage, the horsy bit, and it was obvious that if anyone shot the horse from beneath these competitors, they would fall on their knees with gratitude. I have never seen such a dodgy set of beasts in my life.

I have seen plenty of bad horses and ridden not a few of them, but most of these were worse. They were awful. In the modern pentathlon, your horse is allocated by lot, and you ride it round a show-jumping course. Riding an unfamiliar horse in competition would not be an easy task for a show-jumping specialist; for these sporting polymaths it is hard enough at the best of times. But on this load of dogs it was impossible. Some had been so sloppily schooled they left a leg at every fence, sending pole after pole a-clatter. Some were so pig-natured they stood on their hind legs and refused to take any part whatsoever, sending their unlucky riders away sorrowing with zero points to their names. To make things worse, there were a few decent animals in there as well. After the first day, the Egyptians were improbably in first place, and the Soviets unthinkably buried in the pack. It was disaster. I spoke to Ron Bright, the British team manager, got a load of stuff from him on the nature of the cock-up, and disappeared to write it.

It was not a bad story, and to make life better, I did not need to dictate it. Pat Butcher, the athletics man, had turned up, and he had all the right kinds of cables to connect the Tandy. It worked like magic – well, it probably is magic – and it was pleasant to have Butcher join our student commune. With his penchant for sweaty running shorts, he did not add to the high standard of *déshabillé*, but his little bit of cable for the Tandy was a life-saver.

The Village never failed to remind me of The Village in Patrick McGoohan's demented Kafka fantasy, *The Prisoner*. 'We only sell *local* maps, sir. Be seeing you.' No one can get out, every one is watched: this was a world apart, governed by strange rules of its own, and characterised by bizarre patterns of behaviour.

The Village was as grey and drab as a village could be, but the sport provided all the colour you could wish for. The day began with the ritual telephone call from Tom, talking through what the day held for all of us, and what events he wanted us to cover. Tom being Tom, we all had a say in this ourselves, though Tom naturally made the final decisions. After that, I had breakfast in the hangar. I spent the day watching sport. I came back and wrote about it, and then I had supper in the hangar. There was little serious drinking: there was always a big story to do the following day, though there were three bars in the Village, so you could be sociable at will. And also you could choose to be unsociable, to lock yourself in your room with the pile of books and perhaps a slug of the jealously conserved Famous Grouse.

On the first Monday, I went to cover the rowing, and to get a piece on Andy Holmes and Steve Redgrave, or Holmes and Redgrave as they rapidly became, like Bourne and Hollingsworth or Burgess and Maclean. I had to cover their expected victory in the heats of the pairs event on the first day – no story in their winning, though, the thing to do was to get a word with one or other: to 'get the nannies', in short. This was not as easy as it sounds: there was a barrier between competitors and the rest of the world, and neither side was allowed to cross it. The press contingent sent messages that a word would be appreciated; we stood there by the barrier, under heavily armed guard, a forlorn bunch only wanting to talk about rowing and prospects for gold. It is not like this at Stamford Bridge, I thought. Stamford Bridge is much more forbidding.

In the end, Redgrave turned up and said fine, so long as we smuggled him back the other way, because he wanted to see people among the spectators.

We worked a piece of ingenious shuffling, and managed the swap. Redgrave did his stuff. He reminded me an awful lot of Flo-Jo. He had exactly the same deadness behind the eyes, the same focus on the distant gold. You did not need to be Sherlock Holmes, or even Andy Holmes, to work out that Redgrave was going to be in a gold medal winning crew, or would die in the attempt.

How strange, I thought, for this fierce and focused man (quite affable, but you could see the potential for ferocity in there) had made such a hash of his attempt to be a single sculler. He had won gold in the four in Los Angeles, had tried single sculling but had discovered that his wits flew out of the window when he was on his own. So he went into a pair with Holmes: surely this must be the worst of both worlds. You get neither the pleasures of team spirit, nor the fierce joys of individual sport. You live a life in which three is company and two is none.

I was hungry to get to events, eager to write on anything. Some journos claimed they were out for a quiet life, writing as little as they decently could. Only the biggest of the biggies was good enough for them. For me, everything was a biggie. Every event was something people had worked all their lives for, and I wanted to go to every event I could, so long as I could write about it.

It was this mood of insufferable keenness that got me to the weight-lifting to watch the admirably named Mitko Grablev win his gold. He clean-and-jerked three times his bodyweight to do so. Fancy being a weight-lifter, I thought, spending all your time locked up in some horrible sweaty gym, emerging into the light once every four years to try and lift the entire world above your head with a single great theatrical roar. You gamble all your life for that moment of fulfilment, that one half-second in which everything is perfect, and you alone have the gold medal. For that moment of utter, utter perfection, you must give everything: hours of work, until you ache with the boredom of it; hours of pain locked in that stinking gym, lifting stupid lumps of iron and grunting. I find it hard to imagine a young man at the peak of his prowess taking a drug that he knows will affect his sexual life – but I find it still more incomprehensible that anyone would be willing to spend all those intolerable sweaty hours of mind-crunching boredom in pursuit of mere glory.

I wrote some of this, mentioning the drugs quite heavily, and was glad I had not succumbed to an attack of nice-mindedness and left the drugs out of it. Because a couple of days later, Grablev was disqualified after failing a dope test. Goodbody was rubbing his hands again and explaining about diuretics that can illegally bring you down within the limits of your weight category, and also help you piss the steroids out of your system. The first scandal was on us: the Olympics were gathering pace. But as everyone agreed in the bar, it is always the stupid weight-lifters that get caught, isn't it? Never anyone really important.

The drugs rumours multiplied. Look for the prognathous jaw in female athletes, someone said. It is a dead give-away that they have been taking human growth hormone. What about him, who is always claiming everybody is on drugs? Is he so squeaky-clean himself? Surely the lady doth protest too much. And her? Blimey, I saw her caught in a cross-light when she was doing a television interview, and, clear as anything, you could see her five o'clock shadow.

My greed for events continued unsated. I went to the men's gymnastics, to see one of the most incredible sights of the Games: a Russian called Vladimir Gogoladze performing a triple somersault as part of his floor exercise. It was not that long ago that the double was considered a daring move, and the triple simply beyond man's capabilities. It still looks beyond man's capabilities: this was the first time it had been done at the Olympics, and I just didn't believe it was happening. One, two – bloody hell, were there really three in there? I found a television monitor, and I counted them out and I counted them back. Three. But a few minutes later, I found that doubt had overtaken me again. I went to an American gymnastics specialist, and asked him. Yes, he said, it really was three. And I hurried back to the student commune to write still more words.

How thankful I was not to be writing for a Sunday paper. All the time I was writing, they were worrying. They each had one big piece in which to get to the essence of all that had been happening in the week. Not that they, butch chaps as they are, would call it worrying. They would call it thinking, or maybe drinking. Two of them had a spat about which of them could walk the faster, a fairly clear indication of the pressures they were under.

This happened at the cross-country day of the three day event. The horses always looked like being the best midweek story for the Sundays; it looked like being one of the best stories of the week, with a solid chance of a British gold medal. I went down on cross-country day looking forward to a pleasant day with a splendid story at the end.

I suppose I was no more than half right on both counts. Normally the first thing I do when covering a cross-country event is walk the course. After about an hour and a half, I was forced to give up: the security was so widespread and so tense that any walking about at all made the guards eye you up suspiciously, and generally brought some kind of rebuke or order. This was interesting sociologically, but it palled fairly quickly. With its rambling, spread-about nature, this was probably the easiest event in the Olympics for any terrorist. But the awareness of this did not make it much fun to report.

The story was of a Great British Cock-up. Mark Phillips was selected, amid mild controversy, into the team, and chosen as the first one to go in the cross-country: the 'pathfinder' in the jargon. This left Lorna Clarke, one of the finest riders over fences in the world, as reserve. It was whispered that Phillips's reputation and relations were the strong point in his game: that his horse was not good enough.

There was a near sensation at the vet's inspection before the event. Vets have draconian powers in three day eventing, and can throw out any horse that looks to have the merest hint of lameness. The vet took a long, hard look at Cartier, Phillips's mount, and set him aside for a second look. After long consideration, the horse was passed fit. Phillips had a poor dressage test, and the following day he set off to find the path for the rest of the team.

The one thing Phillips wanted was to post a score that counted. In the scoring system for the team competition in a three day event, it is the scores of the first three riders of the team of four that actually count. Phillips has never posted a score that has counted at the Olympics. In 1972 he was fourth man home; in 1976 he was the reserve; in 1980 his was one of the few sports that went along with the American-led boycott; and in 1984 he didn't have a horse good enough.

He didn't have a horse good enough this time. He took the horse through the 'roads and tracks' section and, shortly before the start of the cross-country, he was forced to pull up and abandon the event. The horse had gone 'lame as a crow', as Phillips bizarrely expressed it. Lorna Clarke, a brilliant rider with a fit horse, was reserve and not riding; and the inexperienced Karen Straker had to lead the team over the fences. She took a rather predictable ducking at the water. It was, in short, a quite monstrous cock-up or, as we journalists would say, a good story.

It was almost an even better one. Ginny Leng took a head-first plunge at one fence, and a fall there would certainly have pushed the Brits out of the medals. But she performed one of the finest pieces of in-saddle acrobatics I have ever seen, throwing the reins away, and flinging both arms over her head in an instinctive attempt to get some weight behind her, instead of in front. It worked: she stayed on board and completed the course clear. I wish I knew what kind of glue she uses; I'd buy a box-full.

The gold had gone, but the team managed a classy regrouping effort to take the team silver the following day, with Ian Stark pounding in to take the individual silver. I had missed my British gold story, but I had an idea I would make up for that. This was the shooting, and the day when Malcolm Cooper, The Man With The Broken Gun, had his chance to shoot for a gold medal.

They were using a new format for the event in an attempt to make it a bit more box-office. Under the old system, the contestants blaze away in their three positions – standing, kneeling and prone – and at the end, all the scores are added up and you work out who has got the gold medal and who has not. Under the new system, the competition would not stop there: each of the leading contestants would have ten more shots to be added onto the score and taken standing. This is the most difficult position. Under the old system, Alister Allan, another Brit, would have won the gold; Malcolm Cooper the bronze. But this time we had the shoot-out, and splendidly nerve-racking occasion it was.

This is not a spectator sport, and there was little provision for spectators. But it seemed that half Korea was there, everyone equipped with a press pass and a single-lens reflex camera. Everything was razor-sharp elbows and roaring motor-drives: how the shooters were to concentrate I could not imagine.

There was Cooper, fierce and squat, bearded and absorbed, a headband low on his brow and a little monocle over his eye. Allan, big and bluff, bald with a grey fringe of hair, stood fidgeting expertly with his rifle. Over each competitor there was a television monitor, giving the crush of spectators and amateur cameramen a view of the target. And it began: in half an hour of sustained tension the medals were won and lost.

Each time the command 'Fire!' was given, a ragged volley of shots rang out. All fired but one. There was Cooper, the Squat Man, the Man With The Broken Gun, still with his shoulders hunched about his rifle, waiting, waiting and waiting. Fire you stupid sod, and get it over: telepathic messages were flashed to him from everyone, but he seemed immune, displaying the kind of cool that would seem far-fetched in a Clint Eastwood movie. In his own time, when he was ready, and not an instant before, and – Bang! Ten points, thank you very much.

'There's a fine edge between holding still and another wobble,' he said afterwards. 'That's why I take so long. If I'm not still, I aim again.

That's much better than trying to hit on the move.' Easier for him, but not as easy on the nerves for the rest of us. It was not simple-minded patriotism that affected you: it was the finely-honed drama of the situation.

Cooper was relentlessly and remorselessly cool. He shot his way through to the gold medal, and Allan had to be content with the silver. 'Did you enjoy that?' we asked Cooper afterwards.

'Enjoy? Not exactly enjoy. You're tanked right up on adrenalin. It's a question of trying to control yourself.' The Great Britain rifle coach had put it slightly differently when I spoke to him earlier: 'It's a question of trying to control your arousal level,' he said.

Cooper is uniquely capable of controlling his arousal level. And Allan was quite delighted with his silver: 'Malcolm is the best shooter in the world and it's an honour to come second to him.' This was a very pleasant story to write. Well, if you can't write a decent story about Brits winning a gold medal, you might as well give up.

The Games rolled on, the days continued their bizarre rhythm, and the journos continued to live their hothouse existence of one good story after another. Every day was about watching sport, and writing about sport, and refuelling at the aircraft hangar, gossiping at the bar, and going on the occasional reading binge. It seemed that I had spent all my life surrounded by pseudo-teenage soldiers carrying silenced machine-guns, that to have one's bag searched a dozen times a day was part of the right and proper pattern of life. We lived our days in a whirl of courtesy:

'Bing-bong seyo!'

'Kamsa hamida!'

Search, search. Smile and bow. The toughest journalists in Britain found themselves undermined by the Korean charm: you saw them bowing and smiling back, walking away from their searchers with a smile still lingering on their lips.

On Friday, I went to cover the women's hockey. This was to go in the paper on the same day as my piece on women at the Olympics – yes, the stuff I had written on the aeroplane, all about Mary Decker's teeth, was at last to see the light of day. Colour-page deadlines are very throwing to a daily paper journo.

And so to the hockey. I claim to be an opponent of boring things like sexism, and am a great supporter of women's sport. I had cursed 'bimbos' tennis' at Wimbledon, when I write I use 'athlete' in preference to 'sportsman' as a non-sexist term, and on occasions I twist my prose like a pretzel to avoid generalising with 'him' and 'his'. I am most adamantly of the opinion that female sport should be judged on the basis of sporting achievement, not on the relative comeliness of the athletes. It was in such a frame of determined goodness that I went to watch the women's hockey, and to do a few interviews afterwards.

The Brits lost. They were a bunch of nice sporty ladies, and it was a pleasure talking to them. I was in the middle of an interview with one of the goalies, a lady called Wendy Banks, when I totally lost my grip. What happened was that Alison Ramsay walked past. My eyes peeled away from Miss Banks, and adhered to this person: tall, slim, fair, still wet from the shower, clad in a white singlet. I dare say my jaw fell idiotically agape. 'Go and talk to her,' said Wendy Banks. 'She's much more interesting than me.'

I wish I could say that I gave a hearty laugh and a gallant 'No, no.' But I did not. With a silly smile on my face I approached the lady in the singlet.

'Hello. That was a . . . was a . . . difficult game.'

'Yes. It was. We lost.'

She was, in fact, charming and helpful, and would have been quite good copy if I had possessed enough control over my brain to ask any sensible questions. I am non-sexist, but there is no accounting for the caprices of male nature. It all made for a most peculiar piece. The crucial point in non-sexist journalism is to control your arousal level.

The track and field was to start the following day, and I was to go to the stadium. I must admit, I was slightly disappointed. I had wanted to go down to the river to see Holmes and Redgrave win their gold medal. I did not know at the time that my Olympic luck was still running hot and strong. As it was, I accepted that David Miller should go to the river, while I went to the athletics. Well, I was sure there would be something for me there, the hundred metres, for example. Carl Lewis against Ben Johnson . . . well, I consoled myself. This would not be a *bad* story.

20. DRUGS, HORROR AND DISASTER: A SAVAGE JOURNEY TO THE HEART OF THE OLYMPIC DREAM

A sportswriter can sometimes suffer from a weird feeling of alienation when he is covering a sporting event. You can feel remote, uninvolved, and as if you were not really *there* at all. You sit, with your desk in the press box all cluttered with notebooks and pens and team-lists and statistics sheets, and your mind all cluttered with thoughts of how you will write the story and how you will try and get the nannies, and you can find involvement, let alone pleasure, almost impossible to come by. The paying punter leaps to his feet and cheers, totally caught up in the spectacle, determined to get his money's worth. But the writer, with his free seat, has lost that sense of privilege.

His profession can give him immunity from the atmosphere, immunity from the excitement, immunity from the sense of wonder that fine sporting performances can inspire. He can sit in the Olympic stadium, and wonder if those little people in running vests are real people after all: are they not puppets, or cartoon characters? Surely this is not the real thing. In some ways, the act of being present at a sporting occasion demeans it. Television can bring the mighty to your living room and make them seem still mightier than they are. But sometimes when you see the mighty in the flesh, they seem diminished.

It is quite possible to watch great sport and feel weirdly untouched by it all. It is something of an occupational disease among sportswriters, just as front-line news reporters can get immune to disaster and they suffer a kind of compassion fatigue. This wave of so-what-ness can strike at the highest moments of a writer's privilege: for a sportswriter at Cup Finals, at Test Matches, at the Olympic Games.

I claim to be more immune to that than many, mainly because I do not have to walk the treadmill of a specialist beat. I frequently commit the ultimate solecism of cheering in the pressbox. But sitting in the press box at the Olympic Stadium watching the races of the early morning had seen me go vague and restless. I was looking for something to inspire and excite me, and found nothing . . . but then I fell upon what was, at least for a while, the greatest moment in the history of sport.

The hundred metres final was something I will never forget. Easy words, and I see a lot of sport, and can, as I say, get vague and jaded in any press box you care to mention. But you can be sure that I will not forget the name of Ben Johnson.

Carl Lewis was the man for me. I was certain he would win: he had been posting better times than Johnson throughout the year. He was clearly in better nick, the form horse. 'Nah,' said my neighbour, Pete Nichols, the athletics writer now with the *Observer*. 'Johnson. He'll win, or pull up injured. Nothing less.'

The athletes appeared and went through all the usual self-conscious walking about before the start. The future lay a little over one hundred yards, a little less than ten seconds of action away. Then came the fidgety settling into the starting blocks, the ducking down and rising again, the competition to be the last one down. Then followed the eternity-long pause. And then the bang of the gun.

It was probably the greatest feat of athletics the world has ever seen. Johnson, the red-eyed, the shaven-skulled, the human bullet: Johnson for victory and a world record, Johnson the king, the man destined to be a hero of athletics for all time.

It was a moment of head-shaking wonder. It was beyond belief, and certainly beyond words. Peter and I sat side-by-side, conversation restricted to the occasional incredulous obscenity. We had seen the laws of physics and of biology defied before our eyes in a triumph of the human spirit. Those two final, floating strides, as Johnson raised his finger to the sky: Ben Johnson – Numero Uno – no question.

A brick wall might have slowed him down, but not by much. He would have lost maybe a couple of hundredths blasting through it. Ah, those centred, focused, dead man's eyes, those red eyes focused on a point one hundred metres ahead: the head-on camera caught it all to perfection. The eyes pointed straight ahead and there was nothing in the world that would stop the man or slow him down. And Lewis: the head-on caught his own doubts and insecurities for all time. Three times during that race, his eyes slithered out sideways to Johnson, a look of fear, a look of awestruck helplessness. Lewis – the entire world – was awestruck.

I wanted to do nothing else, nor see anything else for days. To see another event would be a kind of blasphemy, would blunt the sense of wonder and disbelief. How *could* any man be so strong, so fast, so mentally powerful?

This man is perhaps the greatest athlete in history: hero, villain and victim of the 1988 Olympic Games.
(ASP/George Herringshaw)

But I was there to write, to cover the story, and so it was off to the medal-winners' press conference. This was held underneath the stadium, in a concrete bunker like one of the car-parks at Heathrow. Here, the awestruck press of the world was gathering. I caught Goodbody's eye across the crowd, and made a gesture to him: how about that? He replied also in gesture, grinning, and miming the use of a hypodermic needle. What an old cynic Goodbody is.

Johnson did not come. The buzz came through that he was having difficulty giving a sample to the dope control. Was this a story, someone near me wondered. It was not. It is often quite difficult for a competitor to provide a sample. After you have given your all and fulfilled your life for ever more, you are a bundle of elations and tensions, and the last thing in the world you feel like doing is peeing copiously into a glass receptacle in front of witnesses. Before a big event, a competitor wants to do nothing except pee: afterwards it is next to impossible. They drink and drink until they are at last able to give what it takes, and in sufficient quantity. Then they can be freed, but not yet to taste their victory. They must talk to the world's press. Not everyone sees this as a treat, either.

The wait stretched into an hour and went on. A new rumour went the rounds of the crowd: that it was not the waterworks that were the problem. Johnson was trying to get out of the press conference. Heavyweight people were allegedly even now being called in to persuade him. My sympathies were with Johnson, for all that I wanted to hear what the man had to say. Eventually he appeared. He came in hunched, defensive and sullen. Johnson has a stutter, and lacks the professional American sense of comfort before an audience; he is a Jamaican-born Canadian. He sat there, a stuttering black man in front of a sea of white faces, with lowered eyes and monosyllabic answers.

Carl Lewis, who had the silver, and Linford Christie of Britain, who won the bronze, were much the same. Black athletes get criticised for their arrogance: there is not a British sportswriter who does not have his Daley-acting-like-a-pig story; there is not an American sportswriter who cannot tell you of the occasions when Carl Lewis acted like a prima donna. This 'arrogance' is obviously a simple defensive mechanism, a device to combat the natural one-downness of the black man in such places as Britain and the States, a one-downness most apparent when the athletes confront that sea of white faces at a press conference. Black athletes are revered, but only up to a point. One step out of line and the world will cave in on him. Carl Lewis is 'arrogant' and nicknamed 'The Flying Faggot' because of a whisper campaign that alleges he is homosexual. The world loves that kind of smear, and loves it with a special glee, it seems, when the man in question is black. Let the black hero do something wrong and the world will trample itself to death in the rush to condemn him.

'Ben, what means most to you: winning the gold medal or setting a new world record?'

'The medal. You set a world record, people can beat it. But a gold medal – that's something no one can take away from you.'

The black heroes have the odds stacked against them, but all the world loves the gymnasts, the little tumbling pixies, and on Sunday I went along to the gym to write about them. Gymnastics is one of those sports that looks better in reality: on television it is hard to believe that they are real people performing their feats above the real, unforgiving ground. It is nice to get yourself near one of the press box televisions to see the slo-mo and count the somersaults. But when you watch gymnastics in the flesh, you are always acutely conscious of the sense of gravity.

It is an amazing sight, but I find myself acutely uneasy with women's gymnastics. I mean, where are the bloody women, for a start? There must be something wrong with a sport at which only tiny little girls can excel. And surely there is something not quite right about pre-pubescent girls, over-made-up, rolling their hips and their eyes at the judges and interspersing breathtaking tumbles with coy gestures and sexy little pouts.

Aurelia Dobre was world champion in 1987. She has a pretty face, is neither woman nor child, and has a great scar on her knee after 'reconstructive surgery'. There is an American girl who, as the Olympics continued, was lying in a coma back in the States, after hitting her head in an attempt at a vault. Now I have no objection to danger in sport, but there needs to be an element of choice. Just how much choice do these tumbling pixies really have, trained by fierce-faced teachers and cosseted by sponsors or sponsoring states? How many rejected and damaged children does it take to make one ratings-boosting, prestige-winning pixie?

Yet who could deny that the skills are wonderful to watch? This is a truly ambiguous sport, and I enjoyed it with great uneasiness in my heart.

In the Village, life got more hectic by the day, the rumours about sport, and about fellow-journos, flew about with ever-increasing preposterousness. The Sunday men pondered their yawning deadlines, the daily men churned out their prose a yard at a time, and among all this the best remained the calmest and the most affable. Prominent among this élite company was John Jackson of the *Daily Mirror*, the rotter, the rotter's rotter, the thinking man's rotter. A 'rotter' is a journalist who covers a sporting event looking for news stories. He finds naughty vicars at Wimbledon, hotel-smashing and tumbling in the hay on cricket tours and goes to football matches for the hooliganism. John is urbane, charming, a fine operator in his weird field, an intelligent, widely travelled man with a mind caught halfway between a seaside postcard and the main sewer of London. He was fine and cheering company as the Olympics rolled on, though if you ask him about Naughty Vicar Stories he has known, you are letting yourself in for a long evening. I wish I could write the best of these down here; I reject it not on the grounds of prudishness, but because it requires as part of the punchline a sweeping gesture along with an expression of preposterous innocence that only Jackson can command. 'And the Archdeacon said it is my bad arm and I've *got* to move it like this *all* the time . . .'

One of the lesser rotters had filed a story which said that a journalist had been seen in possession of a bottle of vodka. On the face of it, this does not seem such a brilliant story: Journalist Has Drink Shock is hardly hold-the-front-page material. But the journalist in question is called Carol Thatcher, and she is the daughter of the well-known Prime Minister and Flo-Jo impersonator Margaret. To my considerable surprise, I found Carol immensely cheering. She turned out to be most excellent company, a compulsive and vivid talker, and fully capable, should she wish to do so, of drinking any of the rotters under the table (with the honourable exception, perhaps, of John Jackson). She and I had covered the women's hockey together, and had enjoyed much banter during the game.

'Simon, what's that short corner for?'

'No idea.'

'What shall we do about it then?'

'Carol, if I was you, I'd fudge it.'

'Simon, I shall take your advice.'

'Carol, this is the first time anyone in your family has ever taken the advice of a card-carrying Green Party member.'

You would have thought that bearing such a surname as Thatcher was a handicap in a rough-and-ready society like that of sports journos, but she is a lady capable of holding her own anywhere. It was generally agreed that the Carol Thatcher Drinks A Vodka story was pretty low behaviour, and the hapless rotter who filed it got told so by several rather tough journos over the next few days, until he wished he had never filed the piece.

Carol was writing for the *Daily Mail*. Their chief sportswriter is, of course, Ian Wooldridge, the aforementioned brilliant, globe-trotting, award-winning etcetera, and also, joint holder of The Curse of Trinidad title, as already recounted. He and I turned up for the men's hockey, and we forged an alliance for the rest of the hockey competition. He is one of the few people besides me capable of forgetting himself to the extent of cheering in the press box.

The first match we saw was the one that took the British team through to the semi-final. India, so long the lords of Olympic hockey, the undisputed global masters of the game, were scientifically and comprehensively stuffed. Britain won 3–0, and David Whitaker, their coach and a tactician of considerable perspicuity, explained: 'They can play the up-and-down game brilliantly, much better than us, but why let them? Even in the first half, when they had most of the ball, we still dictated play, pushed them wide, refused to let them build up, let them feel the frustration.' These players were all amateur, but they played their game with an unambiguously professional attitude. Their destruction of India was as professional as a City take-over.

I also managed a word with the team manager, Roger Self, and for the second time in two conversations which lasted a total of maybe 30 seconds, he was gratuitously offensive. What had I done? 'Nothing personal,' a hockey journo told me. 'He's like that with everyone.' I thought about writing about this, but then changed my mind. One of the great pleasures of being a sportswriter is that if anybody gives you a hard time, your opportunities for shafting him are prodigious. If ever a man deserved shafting, it was Self . . . but then if ever a bunch of athletes deserved good things, it was the hockey team. I felt so good about the hockey team, I let Self go.

This was an easy and a pleasant day. I wrote my piece, ate my supper in the aircraft hangar, had a beer, read, and went to bed. And then all hell broke loose.

At four in the morning the telephones of the entire Village leapt into life as one telephone. Newspaper offices across the world read the report on the news agency wires that Ben Johnson had tested positive for anabolic steroids, and had been stripped of his gold medal. The papers wanted an instant response.

I must say without any pride whatsoever that I slept straight through most of this emergency. I woke, and then went back to sleep again. The *Times* nightwatch was handled entirely by Goodbody and Miller, the obvious and inevitable choices to write the story. Goodbody had been waiting for a doping scandal of this magnitude for all his professional life. 'Did the earth move for you, John?' he was asked the following morning. He rang a million drug contacts in the middle of the night, and David Miller followed with some heavyweight stuff of his own.

The Night the Johnson Story Broke is something that all journos dream of, and all journos dread. It is the sharp end of the profession: the middle of the night, the biggest story in the world and ten minutes to get a piece in the paper. Pick up the phone and start ad libbing: this is the ultimate test of professionalism. I am not sanguine that I would pass such a test myself. David Miller, like myself a columnist, opinion-monger and theoriser, can at will turn himself into Scoop Miller, ace reporter, the man with a dime for the phone and a redhot story to tell. His performance at the Heysel disaster (the football match at which 37 people were killed) was quite remarkable: he ad libbed the front and the back page leads as the world collapsed all around him. I could not have done that.

The day after the Johnson story the Village was full of hollow-eyed journos boasting about what time their office had called. It made a nice change from conversations about why the Tandy didn't work. The place felt even more like a student campus than before: everyone staying up all night and meeting in odd corners to talk about drugs. Me, I was buzzing with a million thoughts on Johnson, and was asked to write them up for the following day's paper. With my mind full of drugs, or at least, the thought of drugs, I went off to the diving pool. And on the Day of Disgrace, I found honour and glory; I found graciousness in victory and graciousness in defeat. I also found one of the heroes of the Games.

Or to put it another way, I got lucky once again, and I had the pleasure of writing one piece about the hero and one piece about the villain of the Games, on the day when it all mattered most vividly.

I went to see Greg Louganis, the all-American hero. This was the perfect counterpoint to the Johnson story. I left Goodbody in the student commune, busy compiling a minute-by-minute breakdown of the disaster. ('11.15. Johnson drinks three beers in the doping unit before giving sample.') 'What are you calling it, John? The Time-Table of Shame?'

'Ooh, yes, lovely, I like that,' said Goodbody, rubbing his hands and grinning. The Henry James enthusiast seemed temporarily in eclipse behind the scandalmonger. I went to the pool and savoured all the Olympian courage and grace you could wish for.

Louganis (you must call him Lou-gay-nis, he is an American, after all) had already won one gold medal, and in dramatic circumstances.

One of the requirements in diving is to descend as close to the board as possible. Louganis had overdone this a trifle in the springboard event, and clouted his head on the board on the way down. He refused to drop out, he refused to take pain-killers, for fear they would affect his balance, and he refused to watch the disaster on television in case it affected his confidence. He had three stitches in the wound, and then, serene and untroubled as you please, he won his gold.

I went along to the final of the highboard event, at which Louganis was attempting to win his second gold medal. A couple of years ago, a Soviet diver had hit his head during a highboard event. He was dead before he hit the water. Louganis came out and let rip. He never looked like a winner. He was dogged at every turn and often outdived by a Chinese competitor called Xiong Ni. They traded tumbles, they traded cool, they traded rip entries. There was Louganis, fearfully handsome in a slightly smarmy way, an all-American superstar. He was already preparing for his future as a film star, reading scripts in his room in the Athletes' Village, and wondering whether to accept a part as a gigolo, or another as Tarzan. Beside him was Xiong, aged 14, weighing about six stone, and looking like a horrid little urchin throwing dives as a dare in some ghastly corporation swimming-pool.

Xiong was three points ahead going into the last dive, and the dive he threw was a real beauty. Silver and anticlimax for Louganis: that was how it all looked to me. Louganis took his stance, and held himself for that long motionless moment in the diver's crucifix position. 'I knew then that whatever happened my mother would still love me,' he told us afterwards, in his charming, smarmy way. He plans to go to Hollywood, but he will never have a scriptwriter as recklessly adroit in the use of the cliché as the one who guided his tumbles that day. The dive was an ace: daring and grace perfected. He won the gold by 1.4 points, or the breadth of a hair.

This was followed by a press conference of remarkable modesty and grace. 'It is an honour to compete with Greg Louganis,' said Xiong. 'I am proud to stand beside him, he has always been my idol.'

'He is so talented, so tough to beat,' said Louganis of Xiong. 'I'm really looking forward to watching his growth and development.' All in all, I thought, this was just what the Olympic Games is supposed to be like.

I went back to the Village and told the tale, walked about a bit, had a cup of coffee, and then gathered my thoughts for the Johnson piece. It is the kind of piece you want to make a good 'un. I had a huge advantage over the instant response people, of having had the day to think things over. Thinking about it made it more complicated: a simple piece of outright condemnation of Johnson really would not do. Sure, he cheated, but a lot of people cheat, and some of them get caught, but they do not get vilified like Johnson: sent home in disgrace with politicians across the world queueing up to condemn him. Goodbody, the Time-Table of Shame completed, was working out how much money the disgrace would cost Johnson: it worked out at at least five million quid.

I tried to catch something of the mood of sudden flatness that came over the Games. Johnson's victory had been a triumph of human endeavour: for those less-than-ten-seconds there seemed to be something superhuman about him. Now we were told there was something inhuman about him.

There is something about the idea of drugs that inspires a bizarre, out-of-proportion horror. Some cultures feel the same horror of alcohol as the West does of, say, opium. There is a terrible atavistic fear of what a strange drug might do to you: this has been a staple of myth and fiction throughout eternity: read the *Odyssey*, read *Alice*, read *Doctor Jekyll and Mr Hyde*. Or read the newspapers of the 60s and their hysterical stuff about LSD turning people into raving beasts. For that matter, read the Acid House journalism that greeted us all on our return home from the Olympics: it was the 60s revisited, with all the monsters and the people leaping off the roof with their heads full of mind-destroying drugs. What is there about drugs that so fascinates and appalls? Why are drugs always, in no matter what form, a *story*?

The Olympics are supposed to be about human endeavour. We identify with the successes and failures of people. It is human vulnerability and human strengths that we thrill to. The emotional reaction to learning that these glorious people were not human beings at all, but the creatures of pharmaceutical companies, is very strong indeed: the world felt let down, felt utterly cheated by the Johnson Affair. How can we rejoice and commiserate when the people before us are chemical monsters stuffed full of human growth hormone, when bearded ladies compete for mastery and the fastest man in the world is hardly a man at all?

A British international pole-vaulter called Jeff Gutteridge was caught with drugs that same summer, and he is about as low as you can go in international athletics. Johnson was about the top. The Johnson Affair spelled out with pedantic clarity that track and field was riddled with drugs from the top to the bottom. Johnson was certainly not the only offender: he was just the big one who got caught. I felt quite desperately sorry for him. In 48 hours he had changed from the hero of the Games and the fastest man in the world into a stuttering black man condemned to live the rest of his life in disgrace.

The Johnson Affair was easily the saddest story of the year. But hard on its heels came one of the happiest, a tale of jollity and frothiness: the Hockey Story. The day after Louganis and Johnson had separately engaged me, I was back at the Songnam Stadium for the semi-finals, in which the Brits were matched against the Australians. I am not, as I say, one of the great jingoists of all time, but I was saying that when I was not talking about matches against Australia. In 1986 Australia beat England in the final of the World Cup on the sacred astroturf of Willesden: I was there. I went to Songnam for the replay, and for Wooldridge and me, it was a day of hard and bitter agony.

The more sport you see, the more accustomed you get to disappointment. This is especially true if you have a yen for the underdog. It is the sensational wins, the miraculous escapes that you remember in sport, but every time as you take your place in the press box, you are mentally prepared for this routine of disappointment: John Elway at the Super Bowl, Fiji in Hong Kong, Ginny Leng at Badminton, Clive Cox at the Grand National. Disappointment is infinitely more frequent than anything else in sport. You get to think you are unlucky, that the amazing matches always pass you by, but this is just the law of averages in operation. You have to see your necessary quantity of disappointing events and, every now and then, merely maintaining the average yet coming into your life with the drama of a comet, comes the Perfect Match.

I arrived at Songnam feeling less than optimistic. I had watched Australia before, and they looked certs. Their record in Seoul was five wins and no defeats; Britain had three wins, a draw and a loss. The game began, Sean Kerly, the man with the nose like a falcon's beak, trotted to the front, and so began one of the most agonising matches I have ever seen in my life.

Britain went two-up, both goals scored by Kerly, and I could see that this was a tactical error of the first magnitude. I could smell disaster the second that goal number two hit the backboard, I could feel that the time-honoured British tradition of snatching defeat from the jaws of victory was about to be invoked. Within 15 seconds I was proved right: Australia pulled one back from the kick-off.

'God, this is awful!' said Wooldridge. 'Bloody awful. How much time is there left?'

'Far too much,' I said. 'I think we've blown it.' We?

We sat there, eyes flickering from pitch to game-clock and back again, willing the time to hasten. Instead it lengthened and lengthened again: nothing in the world makes time more elastic than watching Our Boys defend a narrow lead. What, partisan? We?

'Oh God!'

'Christ, it must be!'

'Oh, *bloody* hell!'

Australia were level. Disappointment had made its masterpiece. Extra time looked a certainty: already I could read the headline about Our Brave Boys Go Down Fighting. There were just three minutes of play left, and I was mentally absorbing the disappointment, preparing to laugh it off and make a cynical joke or so in the bar.

But it was then that Kerly was taken over by a fit of insane stubbornness, the same kind of dementia that overtook Alan Ball in the extra time of the World Cup Final in 1966. He had been hammering through the middle all through the match, and he did so again, this time in pursuit of a lost cause, making the token last ditch effort. Except that stubbornness gave him wings: he reached a ball it seemed physically impossible to touch, let alone control. He swapped passes with eye-cheating speed, and went for the return – but alas, the ball was too far ahead of him. No one in the world would have been able to touch the ball, no one save Kerly when this fit was on him. He lunged for the ball like a fencer, and with a great clonk of ball against backboard a miracle was achieved, the Brits were in the final, and Wooldridge and I were both on our feet belabouring the long-suffering air with our fists. A splendid day, and a quite splendid story to write. Who could ask for more?

On the same day, I paid a visit to the tennis, and I wrote a piece about how silly it was to have a second-rate tournament of any kind at the Olympics. David Miller disagreed with me, shock-horror: he argued that the tennis players were the only true amateurs of the Games, the only athletes competing for the simple fun of it. He was all for Olympic tennis.

'Tell me, David, is there any subject we have ever agreed on?'

'Oh I am sure there must have been, Simon. It's just that I can't at the moment recall one.'

Someone told me they saw a sight at the Games that looked exactly like a wise, experienced Minister of Sport giving his sage counsel to a keen little cub reporter. David was the man who looked like a minister; Colin Moynihan looked like the cub reporter.

I also paid a visit to the table tennis, which was great fun. Ping-pong is a lovely game, both to play and to watch. I wrote an absolutely batty piece. I occasionally take pleasure in writing a piece that has only tangential relevance to the actual event. This piece spun off into outer space. I shall not restate it here, it would take far too long, but I wrote mostly about a character in Oliver Sacks's book *The Man Who Mistook His Wife For A Hat*, which is a kind of cornucopia of neurological disorders. The character in question was Witty Ticcy Ray, who suffered from Tourette's Syndrome.

'Is this piece *terribly* mad?' I asked Paul Newman, the assistant sports editor back in Wapping.

'Yes.' His voice came without hesitation down the line. 'Tell me, have you got the book out there with you?'

'No.'

'Then how come you remember all this?'

This is a question I cannot answer. I cannot give you England's back four, or name the three best spin bowlers in county cricket, but if you need to know of Tourette's Syndrome and why it has a connection with table tennis, then I am the sportswriter for you. This really was a batty piece, but *The Times* ran it in full, as ever, and God bless them for it.

We had now reached the last Friday of the Games, and I allowed myself an unmitigated treat. Synchronised swimming: how could anyone resist? I remembered that it was funny on telly at the LA Olympics, but I had forgotten quite *how* funny the whole thing is. I sat there, rocking with laughter as one nose-clipped virtuoso followed another. I thought I was the only Brit at the event, but then I saw Matthew Engel a few rows in front. We each greeted the other with the words: 'Might have known *you'd* be here.'

Now it is all too easy to mock synchronised swimming. So we did. There is something irresistibly comic about the sight of a sequinned crotch emerging from an Olympic swimming-pool, rocketing ceiling-wards and then abruptly disappearing again. I sat there laughing and wondering if I would be able to get the word 'crotch' in the paper. How terribly adolescent: Matthew and I sat there giggling and making smartarse remarks like a couple of sixth-formers. (I succeeded with 'crotch' when I sent my copy that evening, to make a good day perfect.)

Matthew was of the opinion that the event was rendered doubly absurd by the pool. An Olympic pool is as brutally functional as Sizewell Nuclear Power Station. 'This event should be held in a heart-shaped pool lined with pink tiles,' he said.

'What a nice line. I shall steal it.'

And I did. Competitor succeeded competitor, each more ludicrous than the last, and not for an instant did the joke pall. Synchro is not even sexy: no woman looks beautiful in a noseclip. What is more, I have never found the thrusting of the crotch at the ceiling while holding the breath an attractive trait in a woman. And, quite helpless with laughter, Matthew and I saw the event right through to the medal ceremony.

The gold was won by a Canadian called Carolyn Waldo. It was Canada's first gold: they had won another, but that didn't work out too well. Carolyn Waldo in her noseclip had brought back the honour that Johnson lost. Matthew and I went on to the press conference. We were not going to miss a single treat that day.

'How did you stand the pressures of the competition, Carolyn?'

'Well, I'm kind of a numb-brain, I guess you could say.'

Wiping our eyes with mirth, Matthew and I wrote this down. Synchro is absurd, absurd beyond belief. Yet what is so frightfully sensible about kicking a bladder about a field, or running fearfully long distances? Or as Sherlock Holmes so peevishly asked, what is so interesting about the fact that one horse can run faster than another? The point is not that some sports are sensible and some are silly: rather that all sports are silly. Sport is pointless; sport is the ultimate trivial pursuit. The thing is that it looks so important that people get suckered into believing it really is. Synchro is perfect: synchro destroys every last illusion of sport as a serious matter. So long as there is synchro at the Olympic Games, there is less chance of treating sport as war, or as religion. Long live synchro, say I.

It was Saturday. After Drug Nightwatch One, we had Son of Drug Nightwatch. The phones had shattered the night once again, and this time there were two Brits involved. Linford Christie, the sprinter, and Kerrith Brown, the judo player, were both involved in positive dope tests. Brown lost his bronze medal, Christie, who had inadvertently obtained his drugs from ginseng tea, was let off. Goodbody worked himself into a state of exhaustion, and retired to his bed for half a day, looking like Clark Kent after a dose of green kryptonite. He had worked like a demon, like Boxer in *Animal Farm*. ('I will work harder. Tom Clarke is always right.')

Saturday was the day of the hockey final, with the Brits taking on the Germans for the gold. It was a grand occasion, but one which lacked the agony and the dementia of the semi-final against the Australians. The Germans played it canny, with 11 men behind the ball; David Whitaker played it cannier, with his team playing possession and counter-punching. The Germans were chessed out of it: out-gambited: there was something calm, anticlimactic and almost inevitable about the match. It was a relaxing and pleasant afternoon, with Wooldridge and I not feeling called on to cheer: simply enjoying the victory of this, the most pleasant of teams. You came close to feeling that the gold medal was deserved on moral grounds.

This was the last good story of the Games, and, for a British sportswriter, a little beauty. I wrote it up with great delight, and this time I actually got stuck into ghastly Roger Self. The phrase 'reckless insolence' appeared on the screen of my Tandy. But then I reread the piece, and reached for the delete button. This was not the moment to act mean-spirited. The Olympics had been shattered and devalued by the epidemic of positive drugs tests, and in particular by the Johnson Affair: the destruction of one of the finest moments in sport that anybody had ever seen. Now we had a reassertion of positive values: a rediscovery not exactly of innocence, or of amateurism, but of simple, straightforward joy, and even more than that, straightforward niceness. For a Brit, the hockey boys brought pleasure back to the Olympic Games.

The final day was the marathon and the show-jumping, but that was no great problem. The Games were over, and this was, in the nicest possible way, a wonderful feeling. It was the sense of standing on a mountain-top, looking down at the time that had passed, the three-and-a-half weeks that I had spent in Seoul: a feeling that was airy, relaxing and slightly smug. It was the feeling of getting off your horse after a cross-country event, absolutely knackered but glowing with the pleasure of finishing, the pleasure of the doing. I had written 29 pieces, more than 20,000 words and covered 14 different sports. It was great.

21. AND SO WE SAY FAREWELL . . .

One of the great literary virtues is knowing when to stop. I have a special technique, myself: I come to a resounding conclusion and then carry on. But as I sit here, staring at the green screen of the word processor with a cup of black tea beside me, I begin to feel irrefragable signs that my Year is coming to an end.

After the Olympics, there is little left to add, and nothing that can compete. My ever-restless colleague David Miller was soon off to Switzerland to cover a high-ranking sporto-political event, and then to Sweden to write about the State of Swedish Sport. For me, the rest of 1988 was fairly quiet. Quite apart from anything else. I had a book or three to write. A Book-Writer's Year is not interesting, at least not in terms of external events. I suppose Marcel Proust managed it pretty well, but he was an unusual man.

I took the week after the Games off; I went for walks in my Timberland boots, and looked at the odd bird through my binoculars, and made arrangements to buy a horse the following spring. I got my filthy Barbour out and rode a few horses. In short, I got on with being in England.

A few weeks later, I was writing and following lines for *The Times*: 'There is a web that links the life of the most bizarrely named bird – say, the lompobottang flycatcher – to the very future of the planet.' Yes, I was writing a green piece, the second *The Times* had published. I found it enormously cheering to be writing on something so different from sport, so important to us all. I had made a resolution the previous January: to have achieved it before the year was quite out was wonderful. In some ways I was happier about this change of direction than I was about anything else I had done that year.

It was because of this that as 1988 drew to a close and I found myself facing another year of sport, I did so with nothing less than enthusiasm. The challenge of writing on a different topic had sharpened my appetite for sportswriting: had given me a new perspective on the nature of sportswriting: new ways of approaching old problems, new feelings about the relevance of the task. Writers are like sharks, they must keep moving forward or they die, and so are all other human beings.

The year moved gently to its close. My restless journeying spirit took me as far as Exeter, and Cheshire. I saw Australia beaten by England at rugby at Twickenham, and I saw Frank Bruno in court. A figure from his past was trying to sue his manager, and Frank was his usual charming self. I interviewed Naim Suleymanoglu, the Turkish weight-lifter and defector. But mostly, I wrote books and drank a lot of black tea.

My final piece of the year appeared, sensibly enough, on 31 December. David Miller and I were asked to write a piece on our favourite

We shall never get sport in a false perspective while synchronised swimming is part of the Olympic Games. Long live sport, and long live synchro, say I.
(Pascal Rondeau/AllSport)

moment of the sporting year. Yet again, we were poles apart, and perhaps bizarrely complementary. He chose to write about Sandy Lyle, the golfer, winning the Masters at Augusta, with that perfect bunker shot that turned disaster into triumph. I found myself writing about Ben Johnson, and how triumph turned into disaster. Ben Johnson, I wrote, was the hero and the victim of the year: a victim of the world's lust for heroes.

I was pleased with this piece, an awkward one, and open to much misinterpretation. Indeed, a few people wrote to me believing this was a hymn of praise to drugs, which was, I trust, a wilful misunderstanding. But writing on such an issue in what I hoped was a challenging way was very satisfying. And where else in journalism, I thought, can you tackle such questions of morality?

In most areas of journalism you are dealing with the material of the historian. You are painting a picture that will never be completed. There are always too many qualifications. Nothing in real life is ever clear-cut. There are the trivial posturings and soap opera of political life; there is the weary treadmill of disaster and death. With such things, it is not the richness of material that confronts you, but its desperate poverty. And art? The arts pages of a newspaper are not full of art, but of criticism, a different matter altogether. And, speaking as a lapsed business writer, I do not understand the business pages.

But sport is not real life; it is more like fiction, and because of this, it is far more real than any incomplete catalogue of facts. Only in sport can you relax. Only in sport are you writing about people. Politicians cover up: athletes expose themselves. An athlete in competition is emotionally stark naked. A sportswriter does not *need* to write of petty advances and setbacks, of grubby scandals, of the gloomy, dreary details of body counts. We can write about triumph and despair. We need not write about facts: we can write about people. We can break free from the tyranny of 'news' and write about our characters with something that approaches the novelist's freedom. If sportswriting is always trivial, then so is humanity, for that is our subject.

It is now 1 January. I have a plane ticket in my pocket. My God – I haven't done my expenses since July.